SOLDIERING

Also by Henry G. Gole

*The Road to Rainbow: Army Planning
for Global War, 1934–1940*

An AUSA Book

SOLDIERING

Observations from Korea, Vietnam, and Safe Places

HENRY G. GOLE

Potomac Books, Inc.
Dulles, Virginia

Library of Congress Cataloging-in-Publication Data

Gole, Henry G., 1933–
    Soldiering : observations from Korea, Vietnam, and safe places / Henry G. Gole.—1st ed.
      p. cm.
    Includes bibliographical references and index.
    ISBN 1-57488-852-8 (hardcover : alk. paper)
    1. Gole, Henry G., 1933–   2. Soldiers—United States—Biography.   3. United States. Army—Officers—Biography.   I. Title.
    U53.G59A3   2005
    355′.0092—dc22
                                           2004010451

Hardcover ISBN 1-57488-852-8
(alk. paper)

Potomac Books, Inc.
22841 Quicksilver Drive
Dulles, Virginia 20166

First Edition

10 9 8 7 6 5 4 3 2 1

I dedicate this book to the memory of my sister Joan Robertson, to my brothers Jerry Gole, Bill Gole, John Gole, Andrew Gole, and Chris Gole, to my "other brothers" of the 1953 Charlie Company, 27th Infantry (Wolfhound) Regiment, and to my other brothers of Vietnam War 5th Special Forces Group, especially to the skilled and brave soldiers of BLACKJACK 21 and MACVSOG.

Contents

Part III: Interludes and Reflections While Safe

Part IV: Vietnam: The Men

List of Maps

Foreword

By Russell F. Weigley

HENRY G. GOLE is admired by those of us who have the privilege of his association—his military friends, especially his colleagues on the faculty of the U.S. Army War College, and his academic colleagues, like this writer—for his acute eye for the good and the bad in the literary depiction of military life and combat. Few of us have read so widely in the fictional as well as historical literature of war as he; few can match his ability to separate in that literature the phony and the overinflated from the genuine recording on paper of what armies and battles are like. So we have all looked forward to his writing about his own experience of armies and war, and this book of vignettes fulfills our high expectations.

From working-class, recent-immigrant family life in New York City, to a young combat infantryman's fears when confronting war directly for the first time with the famous 27th Wolfhound Regiment in Korea, through two subsequent and very different combat tours as an officer with the 5th Special Forces in Vietnam, to the halls of the United States Embassy to the Federal Republic of Germany in Bonn and of military and civilian varieties of academe, Henry Gole depicts places, sights, sounds, and ambiance with all the precision and candor his friends would expect. A career in the United States Army in the second half of the twentieth century could well be a passageway to almost every conceivable sort of locale, hospitable and decidedly otherwise, and the vignettes herein lead us through most of the geography of such a career.

More even than places, however, Henry Gole vividly brings us people: old acquaintances of his family in parts of southeastern Europe where the Empire of Franz Josef still lives in memory, tough Montagnards in Vietnam who in spite of their toughness were almost pathetically attached to their American comrades, and above all a collection of American soldiers of diverse skills, ranks, and national backgrounds, most of them united in unpretentious courage. Inevitably in a book about war and warriors, in Gole's pages many of these men have to die. Inherent in the subject matter here, there is almost too much sadness.

But there are also numerous vignettes of the camaraderie of Army life, and there is in addition a satisfaction with his career that lends a pervasive, positive tone to Gole's memories. He frankly questions whether he chose the right career, one that he can justify to himself, and albeit with the doubts that must persist in any human being of conscience, he concludes that on the whole he did right. Particularly, he feels the gratification of having served the United States in its military forces during an era when, personal doubts and much political controversy notwithstanding, the world really did depend on that country and those armed forces for the preservation of freedom. Perhaps the most moving of these vignettes are the repeated ones in which, even at the height of domestic and worldwide protests against the American war in Vietnam, but throughout his whole career as well, Gole found himself in many countries treated with gratitude and respect simply because he wore the uniform of the United States, or simply because he was an American.

So here are an honest, forthright, even curmudgeonly soldier's memories of his life in that uniform across a turbulent, stirring near-half-century. Henry, you have made your own distinctive contribution to that literature of soldiers and war you love so well.

Preface

BIG GUYS, like Patton, Monty, Rommel, and Ike, are entitled to their full-blown memoirs, biographies, reflections, and various forms of self-justification. Even lesser lights, mere civilians and comedians like Harpo, Chico, and Groucho, or Bob Hope and Bing Crosby, or Agnew and Nixon, are entitled to their books and royalties. Recognizing these basic facts of life, I chose to write little stories about soldiers I've known and admired and about the peculiar subculture we called home in the second half of the twentieth century, the Army.

These vignettes are snapshots from the career of a soldier whose service began as a conscript on 17 September 1952. I asked to be drafted. I didn't want to miss the war in Korea, but I thought two years in the Army was sufficient time for me to win the war and earn a bunch of medals before going on to a life of wondrous, if indeterminate, accomplishments that would somehow give meaning to my life.

Instead, I retired from the U.S. Army War College as a Special Forces colonel on 30 June 1988. My love affair with soldiers continues through my teaching at the Army War College in Carlisle Barracks on an adjunct basis and through the network of reunions and personal contacts with the old soldiers I respect. So, the period from the early 1950s to the late 1980s, plus distinct memories of the 1940s and meditations into the 21st century comprise the backdrop for my stories.

One turns away for just a moment and a half-century slips by! It was a period of accelerating change with most of us hanging onto a wildly spinning universe, trying to understand it, sometimes getting it right, more often failing to register important events, and even more often actually living events without comprehending their significance, without being able to fold events or trends into the wholeness of it all. It's hard to get it right. I certainly didn't get the 1960s right as I lived them, and probably haven't yet. Getting it right requires distance from the events and the perspective to see how events connect after the cooling of passions.

In sharp contrast to the lack of consensus in the 1960s, most Americans from 1941 to 1945 saw their war as a crusade of good versus evil. It was easy to dislike those who bombed Pearl Harbor and overran Europe, so I

joined my little friends in singing improvised lyrics to the tune sung by the
Seven Dwarfs in Walt Disney's *Snow White*:

> Whistle while you work,
> Hitler is a jerk.
> Mussolini is a meanie
> And the Japs are worse.

Future political and military analysts would present a more nuanced
appreciation of political circumstances than life as a morality play pitting
America against jerks, meanies, and worse, but I didn't know that then. I
sang lustily and cheered the good guys. We were the good guys.

We still are.

A compulsion to get it right and tell it right underlies my stories, even
knowing that the task is impossible. One is tempted to present a recitation
of the events that comprise a life as a logical flow, a procession from here to
there by map and compass. That's neat. It is also a lie. My vignettes lack
continuity and cohesion for a good reason: life is neither smooth nor logical.
Forcing continuity and removing the bumps makes fiction of memoirs, rec-
ollections, and biographies. Gaps in memory demand to be filled, and plausibility satisfies the craving for wholeness. But plausibility is an enemy of
truth. It makes sense of human activities—many of which do not make
sense; they just are. It takes lies to connect unconnected events.

My vignettes attempt to get at the essential truth by means of snapshots
of good men with a clear sense of purpose, men who put it all on the line
for a comrade or for something called duty. And then went back to do it
again. They knew what they were doing and why. Few of us do. The nobility
of their acts rarely took into account conscious considerations of national
interests, political objectives, or military strategy. They simply cared more
for one another than anything else in the world and died for one another.
They assumed their cause to be just. Missions and tasks were to be executed.
How does one weave simple facts and complex feelings? Knowing they can
only crudely transmit the feel and understanding of the writer to the reader,
we rely on words. Thank God for the writer's imagination, memory, and
need to tell the story, the reader's interest and patience, and our richly
expressive English language!

I called them "good men," and they were that. Many of the best I knew
in Korea and Vietnam were also coarse, profane, agnostic, sometimes "all
of the above." In fact, the most skilled soldiers I know were the reconnaissance men in Kontum who repeatedly nipped across the borders into Laos
and Cambodia to play a deadly game of tag with the enemy's first team.
Losers died. Intimately familiar with death, they were irreligious.

We were some one hundred Americans and one thousand mercenaries, mostly Chinese, Montagnard, and Vietnamese, in that remote place, and a circuit-riding military chaplain visited us irregularly. Spontaneous memorial services for fallen comrades were attended by all Americans in camp out of respect for our KIA, but I knew that the Catholic priest who showed up one day to conduct a routine and generic religious service would be disappointed. Two of us attended. I don't recall who the other man was or why he attended, but I was there so that the priest would not be embarrassingly alone. The poor man had almost certainly been warned that he was entering the jaws of death. Our daily routine struck some headquarters types in Saigon as flirtation with danger.

At the end of the service, I invited the priest to join me for dinner in the mess hall. As we walked together his downcast look punctuated his observation. He said, "Too bad. I guess the word didn't get out." I responded sympathetically, "Worse, padre. The word got out."

Our soldiers did not attend religious services. They did lay down their lives for their friends. Routinely. Many chose death to deserting a Montagnard, Vietnamese, or a Chinese team member wounded or in distress. It was a "doing" thing, not a "saying" thing. So much for folk wisdom saying there are no atheists in foxholes.

My cohort, born in 1933—a big year, bringing Hitler and Roosevelt to power and me into the world—lived in accordance with the values of our elders, alternating feelings of contempt and envy for the crop of libertines, yuppies, and spoiled brats born a dozen years later. We didn't always do the right thing, but we felt shame when we failed to measure up to norms, expectations, and something called duty. Remember shame? It seems to have gone the way of Joe DiMaggio, the buggy whip, and a broadly accepted sense of propriety.

My crowd is a no-name lot, though in the 1950s there was fleeting reference to The Silent Generation, the one characterized by the ticky-tacky houses of suburbia and personified by World War II veterans who became *The Man in the Gray Flannel Suit*. We were part of the catch-up frenzy of materialism that followed World War II and the Great Depression. Presumably it was to this materialism that the kids of the 1960s reacted, picking up where the Beat Generation left off.

In any event, my mob was sandwiched between the heroes of the 40s and the liberating, if not libertine, generation of the 60s, the first praised as the century and millennium wound down, and the other maligned by people like me. Our fathers, uncles, and older brothers are lionized for surviving the Great Depression, winning The War, and building America into a superpower. Our younger brothers, born after World War II, grew up with TV, and came to what passed for maturity in the 1960s. Wallowing in opulence, they congratulated themselves for their sensitivity. Best to put that on the table now. Despite generous dollops of levity, contempt seeps through my stories.

My remarks regarding generational differences are certainly too neat. (Again, I *got* it *almost* right and *tell* it *almost* right.) They are also smug, for they fail to account for those of the 1960s who risked their lives registering black voters, responded to a young president by volunteering for discomfort and sacrifice in the Peace Corps, and extended themselves to qualify for Special Forces and the opportunity to die with little strangers in a lonely patch of jungle. How infinitely complex God's children are!

The stories reflect my idiosyncratic take on specific events that involved me or took place around me. Some reflect what is grandly—and accurately—called the universal human condition. But even the constant human condition has a look to it that is shaped by the observer's point of entry and early conditioning. My point of entry leaves fingerprints: urban, ethnic, blue collar, Roman Catholic, oldest of seven siblings, romantic, burdened with intellectual pretensions, and supremely lucky. My fingerprints are all over my tales. But there is a general *Zeitgeist*, a spirit of the time, that shaped me in ways I may fail to recognize, and it shapes my stories. I'm glad that I wasn't born into a homogeneous corner of America. In New York City I knew diversity from the beginning. It did not take the terrorist acts of 11 September 2001 for me to discover that cops, firefighters, and construction workers, like the soldiers I have known, measure human worth in acts, "doing the right thing," not words.

I plead guilty to being an unabashed admirer of the American soldier. The professionals I knew willingly and repeatedly risked their lives for their friends, and some of them paid in full or were permanently damaged in body or soul. The one-time volunteers did their duty, even when it meant swimming against the tide of public opinion while following national leaders unsure about the ends desired and the ways and means to be used. I particularly admire the conscripts who didn't have "nuthin against them Viet Cong" and went anyway, because their trusted leaders asked them to go. They and the Vietnamese were the literal victims of confused American leaders posing as savants. With each passing year we learn more about muddled presidents, a secretary of defense who was (and is) an arrogant twit, and top military leaders lacking the guts to confront civilian leadership, or even to ask just what the hell they expected to accomplish. Shame on the leaders.

Civilians don't know what they don't know about their professional military people. Even those civilians who served, including those with experience in the military doing dangerous deeds associated with killing people and breaking things, have only the sketchiest notion of the American military subculture. Because of the life I've had so far, I feel emotionally tied to American soldiers, particularly those who serve in teams, squads, and crews at the cutting edge. I want my fellow citizens to meet some noble men who protect them.

Though I dug ditches, drove trucks, and faked it as a salesman, my life has been spent as a soldier and teacher with America's youth. I've been a teacher in a high school, at West Point, at the U.S. Army War College, and as an adjunct professor at several colleges and universities. When not teaching, I was soldiering or learning. The U.S. Army invests heavily in schools. Basic training, infantry officer training, jump school, ranger school, intelligence school, career course (for captains), staff college (for majors), attaché course, war college (for lieutenant colonels and colonels), and language training add up to over four years. In addition, I studied history for a year at Stanford University, and spent a year running around Germany learning to be a foreign area officer.

I was a Special Forces soldier and an attaché in Germany, a staff officer in the Pentagon and in Germany, and a strategic analyst later in my career. Over the years I've worked with Germans, Belgians, Brits, the Dutch, Luxembourgers, Italians, Norwegians, Swedes, Danes, Turks, Koreans, Vietnamese, and with Cambodian, Montagnard, and Chinese mercenaries. And I've been a transporter, a military intelligence officer, an infantryman, and a medic. That's general background so that readers of these little stories know their source.

This book is organized into five parts in rough chronological order, sometimes peeking back or looking ahead through the eyes of: a blue-collar kid from New York City, a nineteen-year-old BAR man in a rifle squad in the Korean War, a teacher and professional soldier between wars, a Special Forces officer in his 30s on two tours in Vietnam, and, finally, a graybeard musing about an eventful fifty years.

It has been observed that combat is 99% boredom and 1% terror. The part about terror is about right—we can handle only so much of that—but the 99% was not boring.

Much of the 99% is hard work. The innocent don't think about all the digging, carrying, loading, and walking. There was a lot of that. There was also constant fatigue and filth, the rubbing of the winter wool shirt on the neck, the chafing of the hips by belts burdened with heavy stuff—ammunition, grenades, food, water, wire—feet soggy in Mickey Mouse boots, blistered in combat boots, and lower legs shaped like milk bottles from wearing tight combat boots. Combat troops are filthy with blackheads, constant low-grade fever, and defecating in the woods in a hurry if the unit was on the move.

Much of the 99% is also the positive feeling that comes from intimate association with good men, a feeling variously called bonding, camaraderie, or brotherhood. The verbally challenged soldier, concealing the depth of his feeling, says "my buddy." He means "brother."

The affection among men who shared risk and discomfort is a felt phenomenon that cannot be gleaned from reading. It's one of those "doing" things of great intensity and duration. Even to discuss it may seem condescending to those who have not routinely risked their lives with trusted friends, but there it is. One day my life is in the hands of others; the next day their lives are in my hands. Interestingly, if one does that often enough, one discovers that it is easier to be in the tight spot than to be responsible for directing friends in a life-or-death tight spot. In a high-morale outfit, it is often necessary to exercise professional judgment, to say "no" and to control those who would throw caution to the winds out of loyalty to friends in a hopeless situation. Self-sacrifice is routine. Who can forget the American sergeant last seen with the wounded Montagnard on his back who died with the Yard rather than leave his brother? Sometimes one must order soldiers not to die now, to save the gift of his life for later.

And, finally, the 99% discounted as boredom includes joy. The coming of dawn after a tense night is a joyful experience. Taking off one's boots and flopping in a tent in a safe place is pure luxury after weeks in holes and bunkers, afraid to take off boots. Horsing around like kids at the shower point in Korea; forming a defensive perimeter around a swimming hole in a rocky stream in Vietnam to take turns bathing; these are unspeakable joys and indelible memories.

So, hard work, bonding, and joy fill much of the 99% the wag calls boredom. Further, about the 1% of terror, it needs to be said that this old soldier spent three years of a thirty-year career in combat. That's 10%. One percent of the 10% is a small part of a long career.

The Special Operations Association motto, which appears on almost every page of its publications, has it about right. It says: "You have never lived until you have almost died. For those who have fought for it, life has a special flavor the protected will never know."

I dedicate these vignettes about soldiering to Americans in squads, crews, and teams on watch, on strip alert, on outposts, and on patrol, especially when the situation is uncertain, the map sheets overlap at your location, the usually reliable commo breaks down, and you are in the dark. Alone, except for your weapon. And your buddy.

Great writers have come close to capturing the essence of soldiering, but hearing Taps—anytime, day or night—penetrates my sophisticated defense mechanisms every time I hear it played. It does so in ways that words cannot. Forgive this foolish romantic for beginning your reading with a description of a German military ceremony whose combination of sounds, sights, and soldiers in ranks is incomparable in getting to the heart of the matter.

Acknowledgments

JOHN PEPPER AND CHARLIE ROMANO, my Korean War buddies with whom contact is maintained, allowed me to use photos from their personal collections. Jo Kremer and my uncle George Finn gave me the photos of the WW II sailor and one of the original "Screaming Eagles." Unless indicated otherwise, photos are from Gole's private collection. Jim McNally took me by my hand to Jim Kistler, who transformed vintage 1953 and 1966 paper maps into electrons that pop up again in this paper book. Jim Fenlon, Bill Roderick, and Billy Boggs read and confirmed my recollection of BLACK-JACK 21. Edward M. Coffman, "Mac" to his friends, read a very early version of *Soldiering* and provided encouragement and expert advice. Reg Shrader listened attentively to my telling of these tales over the years. Greg Todd, Managing Editor of *Parameters*, suggested that I write a book about my military adventures. Finally, I want to acknowledge and thank my teacher, friend, and distinguished historian Russell F. Weigley, who died on March 3, 2004. He wrote the inspired Foreword for this book, one of his many generous acts in support of colleagues, students, and the history profession.

Kamerad

SOCIAL SCIENTISTS have refined the concept of bonding in a simple way. The relationship of soldiers to the army is "organizational bonding," to officers and NCOs is "vertical bonding," and to one another is "horizontal bonding." The latter, loyalty of soldiers to one another, goes by many names, "buddy" suggesting that attachment to American soldiers, "Kamerad" to German soldiers. There seems to be a consensus among academics and veteran professional soldiers that in extreme situations it is horizontal loyalty to buddies—squad, crew, and team—that causes individual soldiers to put others before self, even unto death. To be clear, soldiers risk death most often for one another.

A traditional German military ceremony gets to the essence of this feeling of soldiers for one another. The ceremony has its origins in the Thirty Years War (1618–1648). A sergeant with an armed group was sent around the campfires with drums to signal "party over," time for quiet so that people might sleep. Its modern derivation is called Zapfenstreich, crudely expressed as "shut down the [beer] taps."

For very special occasions, a Grosse Zapfenstreich—replete with torches, mounted drummers, martial music, and marching troops—is conducted just after dark falls. The total effect of the atmospherics and symbolism moves the objective observer. It reduces a certain kind of old soldier to choking to stem the tears.

At an emotional peak, making it the heart of the ceremony, a command is given to soldiers under arms to remove helmets. Then a simple tune is played and simple words are sung by soldiers at attention in ranks. The removal of military headgear under arms is very unusual. That's the point.

Your scribe was rendered helpless by the ceremony. That was certainly the case one night in the middle 1970s at the ruins of the Heidelberg castle as the Germans honored the departing Commanding General of the United States Army, Europe. The song is "Ich Hatt' Einen Kameraden." Here is the German and my free translation:

Ich Hatt' Einen Kameraden

Ich hatt' einen Kameraden,
Einen bessern findst du nit.
Die Trommel schlug zum Streite,
Er ging an meiner Seite,
Im gleichen Schritt und Tritt.

Eine Kugel kam geflogen,
Gilt's mir oder gilt es dir?
Ihn hat es weggerissen,
Er liegt mir vor den Füßen,
Als wär's ein Stück von mir.

Will mir die Hand noch reichen,
Derweil ich eben lad'.
"Kann dir die Hand nicht geben,
Bleib du im ew'gen Leben,
Mein guter Kamerad."

I had a comrade,
A better one you'll never find.
The drum summoned us to battle,
He marching at my side,
Matching my steps.

A bullet flew toward us,
Meant for me or you?
It ripped him away,
He lay at my feet,
As if a part of me.

He wanted to reach his hand to me,
Even as he lay.
"I cannot give you my hand,
Remain in eternal life,
My good comrade."

Part I

Blue Collar in New York

. . . in which our narrator is born in the Great Depression, watches the big guys go off to World War II, decides to win his war in Korea, and cuts his apron strings.

The Zeitgeist and My Little World

The world celebrated my 3 August 1933 birth in Saint Vincent's Hospital, New York City, relegating the rise of Roosevelt and Hitler to power in the same year to the footnotes of history. The period from my birth to 1952, when I began soldiering, was the backdrop to profound changes in American well-being, power, and psychology.

The Great Depression and the Second World War conditioned our people first to unemployment and deprivation and then to individual sacrifice, both grand events emphasizing the value of cohesion and community. The post–World War II period, including the 1950–53 Korean War years, saw a celebratory binge of consumerism, a kind of self-reward for a decade and a half of hard knocks. Symbols of American prosperity were visible in big cars with big fins and the exodus from rented city apartments to owned houses in the suburbs.

The USA possessed half of the world's wealth, weapons, and delivery systems capable of reaching and destroying cities with a single stroke, farmers able to feed the world, and a film industry that projected abroad images of paradise on earth. Blue-collar kids— thanks to the GI Bill of Rights—went to college, bought houses, entered the professions, and joined the middle class in great numbers. Individual rights and personal gratification reigned. America had paid its dues. Let the good times roll.

My little world reflected the old and new values and realities. Stories of hard times told around the kitchen table contrasted sharply with luxury manifest in the objects in the house and parked in front of it. We had lived in a dozen cold-water flats with shared bathrooms in Greenwich Village, moved to Chelsea, and then trekked east over the 59th Street Bridge to Woodside, Queens. By 1944 we lived in a private house in Queens Village that cost a princely $4,750 and no cents. In 1946 my father drove a 1946 Dodge delivered with 2x8-inch wooden bumpers. The chrome bumpers came later as the war production industry converted to toys and as citizens and voters became buyers and consumers. Television entered the Gole house circa 1950, and Uncle Miltie held the world at bay. But the world was still out there, waiting.

The Red Army was the most powerful force between the White Cliffs of Dover and the white snows of the Urals. It blockaded Berlin, and America led the Berlin Airlift as the Cold War took shape. But my concerns were the discovery of girls, wearing preppie white buck shoes, playing football, and watching the Ed Sullivan Show on Sunday nights, Sid Caesar on Saturday, and Uncle Miltie during the week. Superpower competition was off and running, but life was good to me at Chaminade High School from 1948 to 1952, except for the unpleasantness of math and science. The big world had troubles. My little world was idyllic. That would change.

The Village, Chelsea, and Over the 59th Street Bridge

Should we believe those who say, "My earliest memory is . . ."?
Much "memory" of childhood comes from stories heard and over-
heard so often around the kitchen table and at family gatherings that
truth becomes the embellishment of how precocious we were as kids before
joining the legion of dull-witted adults. That is, we remember the oft-
repeated stories rather than the events themselves. Further blurring of truth
with strands of hope, legend, and myth is the handiwork of notorious liars,
writers. They pronounce on the subject, usually themselves. Memories,
despite one's best efforts, are almost certainly neither in strict chronological
order nor unembellished. Nor are they complete. Let us stipulate that the
ordinary makes dull copy. But I do remember at least the places of my childhood.

Greenwich Village of the late 1930s was greener than the rest of New
York City, maybe because it was Italian. I clearly remember 114 Perry Street
because my recently widowed maternal grandmother, Helen Finn, lived at
117 with my uncles Bill and George Finn. The Hudson River was close, a
seaplane was moored there, and on Sunday mornings, while Mom was at
Mass, my father and I walked on West Street as the police packed bums into
paddy wagons. Their crime was sleeping off a drunk in sheds and on loading
platforms. The hot dog with sauerkraut and mustard from a pushcart with
an umbrella cost a nickel. While on Perry Street, my grandmother remar-
ried. I started school and got scarlet fever.

The health department put a sign on our door: QUARANTINED! My
isolation protected the rest of the human race from me. It worked then, but
since then the human race has had to take its chances with me along with
the rest of God's creatures. I haven't worn a bell nor been quarantined since,
unless long and faithful military service counts. Various great-uncles and
other benefactors risked the wrath of New York City by ignoring the sign
and visiting "the lad," me. They brought fruit and talked of the "Troubles"
(pronounced troobels with a roll of the R) and "the goddamned Black and

Tans" in the kitchen as they commiserated with my mother while sipping beer. I remember scratchy whiskers, beery breath, and a big window in the front room converted to my sickroom. (The current occupant of 114 Perry could tell us if the front window on the second floor is really big.) There were pears, oranges, grapes, and bananas. Apparently the crazies to whom I was born believed that scarlet fever and beriberi are best remedied with the ingestion of fruit by sick kids and sailors.

Uncle Pete visited. I had seen his main act while hand in hand with my mother. He rode on a horse carrying a red flag. All traffic in the vicinity of the docks stopped when Uncle Pete unfurled that flag. God, what power. In those days, a train crossed West Street and rolled onto a barge that had tracks. The barge crossed the river to New Jersey, proving both that Jersey had tracks, and that there was life out west, on the other side of the Hudson. I found my calling. I wanted to ride a horse, controlling traffic, trains, and the known world with the wave of my red flag, but, alas, that calling went the way of my other careers as a cowboy or firefighter. I failed to make the cut. Hitler, Mussolini, and Hirohito got to carry the red flags. I attended grade school.

Uncle Bill Finn, an 8th grader when I started school, was charged with getting me to Saint Veronica's parochial school alive and in one piece, but he preferred sneaking smokes with his buddies. One day early in my academic career I got lost, cried, and was rescued and delivered to Perry Street. I was pleased to blow the whistle on Bill and more pleased when my father clouted him.

Bill later taught me to sing to the tune of "A Tisket, A Tasket, A Green and Yellow Basket," but the lyrics he taught were "a bastard, a bastard, a green and yellow bastard." I was pleased to sing my new song to my father, who asked where I learned it, and I was more pleased when my father clouted poor Bill, who took many a lump as a failed babysitter. I may have been the original whistle-blower.

Uncle George was a year younger than my mother and, like her, had red hair. He was called Red or Buster, because he was a middle-weight boxer. When I stayed with my grandmother at 117 Perry Street, it was a special treat to spy on the serious and purposeful Buster, then in his middle twenties. He jumped out of bed in the morning, did his sit-ups and push-ups and departed to do his roadwork. Upon his return he boiled a potato and ate it. That was part of his "training." (I saw linoleum as I spied. Lots of it. That's probably because small children spend a great deal of time close to the floor studying the world from the ground up.) In 1933, George went away for a year with the first contingent of CCC (Civilian Conservation Corps), a program of physical improvements designed to do the country some good while making unemployed young men feel useful. The work was constructive; city slickers discovered the out of doors and far away places "out west" beyond

New Jersey, and $25 of the monthly $30 dollars earned went to needy parents at home. Uncle George recalls the experience in glowing terms seventy years after the adventure. Sleeping outside on the ground, he saw countless stars, including falling stars.

George and his pals attempted to enlist in the armed forces on 8 December 1941, but they were sent home until late December, by which time the bureaucratic wheels were greased and ready to prepare civilians for war. The names of George Finn, Bill and Bob Willis, Jean Kremer, Lou Fugazy, and the other young men from the Village can be found on a plaque at Saint Joseph Church.

Ironies abound. George was accepted by the U.S. Navy and spent the war in Puerto Rico and New Jersey, while his best pal, Jean Kremer, was rejected by the Navy. Jean's eyes were not good enough for Navy work, but they served him well enough as a proud member of the Screaming Eagles, the 101st Airborne Division, in whose service he was wounded three times while making all of the Division's combat parachute jumps in World War II.

When I wasn't being lost by Bill or spying on George, I made frequent visits to Saint Vincent's Hospital, where I was born once and repaired several times. After a couple of stitches in my eyebrow I got a Meloroll ice cream cone and a comic book for being brave. When my tonsils were removed I got another ice cream cone and a comic book. Saint Vincent's was OK. A visit to the emergency ward combined pain and pleasure. It was like life.

We moved a lot. Much later, when I asked why, I learned that landlords seeking a high rate of apartment occupancy were prepared to give rentless days as an incentive to attract poor tenants. Rent was paid by the week, so enlisting friends to move the few sticks of hand-me-down furniture a couple of blocks to another part of the Village saved a few bucks. This was no small matter, since my father was either unemployed, forced to go to sea, or, in due course, the proud earner of $18 per week. A few days of no rent was sufficiently attractive to my parents in the middle 1930s that we lived on Perry, Henry, Christopher, Barrow, Bank, Charles, Jane, and 11th Streets. Then we moved to 29th Street between 9th and 10th Avenues, directly opposite the big Post Office that much later swallowed up our dwelling place. I attended Saint Colombo's parochial school that was on 25th Street between 8th and 9th Avenues.

The Chelsea, a movie theater known as "the itch" (unlike the elegant "RKO 23rd Street" that had mirrors, fountains, and very high ceilings) was on 8th Avenue near my school. It cost ten cents to see a double feature, news, a cartoon, and "a serial," whose episodes ended with the hero hanging from a cliff by his fingernails or in a tunnel flooded or in flames. These serials and comic books featured the adventures of what we later called superheroes.

On Saturdays I was accompanied to the movies by Roger, a big kid in the 3rd or 4th grade who lived in our building. Mom gave me a quarter that was invested in a hot dog and big mug of Hire's root beer, five cents each, a big O Henry bar for movie snack, also a nickel, and the dime for the Chelsea. That got rid of me on a Saturday afternoon from noon until suppertime for two bits. I reckon that as five cents an hour for babysitting.

I walked under the 9th Avenue elevated tracks, called "the El," to get to school. That El was the one torn down just before the Second World War and, according to local folk wisdom, sold to Japan as scrap iron to be dropped on Pearl Harbor as bombs.

Looking in the back of my 1st grade reader and sounding out the syllables of the word REP-RE-SEN-TA-TIVE, I was puffed up with my erudition and the sheer joy of discovery and progress from "See Spot run." I told my smiling nun what I discovered. To this day I believe in phonics—and nuns.

In a geography lesson I learned that the United States had a population of 135 million people, including a boy in my class from Finland. He became a hero to me because my dad cheered at the radio news accounts of Finns initially beating up on Russians in the Winter War. The Finns were good guys, scooting around on skis and raising hell with the Russian bullies. Later the Belgian family in our building earned our admiration when the Germans invaded Belgium and the rest of Western Europe. I regretted pushing the Belgian kid into an auto bumper, putting a big scratch mark on his back, but I was defending my little sister. Belgians were also good guys, except for the one who picked on my sister.

My father made unkind references to Italian flags that were flown on some occasion, perhaps Columbus Day, and to the German Bund meetings, one of which was held in Madison Square Garden, to which we walked to see ice shows, rodeos, and the circus. Many of my friends were Italian and German kids. They seemed OK to me, but life was complicated. The Russians went from good to bad to good very quickly from 1939 to 1941. The Chinese were good before turning bad in 1949. The Japanese were bad Japs before becoming good Japanese. Same with the Germans who were Nazis and Krauts before becoming Germans again. The English were transformed from oppressors of the Irish to noble defenders of democracy as bombs fell in London, and Winston Churchill smoked big cigars as he walked in rubble giving the defiant V for Victory sign that became the peace sign 25 years later. It was hard for a little boy to know the players without a scorecard. In baseball there was no such difficulty in sorting out good from bad guys: the Yankees were good: the Giants and Dodgers were not.

I blew "It's Three O'clock in the Morning" in a kazoo band in a school production, made my First Holy Communion, and was photographed in a booth. (I have a picture of me in a white suit with my ears sticking out as I gaze piously at a white prayer book I probably couldn't read and almost certainly did not understand.) During the Consecration in the liturgy of the Mass, bells are rung by a server, but I didn't know that when I was little and tucked into a pew with big people between me and the priest. I thought the priest's act of kneeling worked the magic of the bells as he worked the magic of the Consecration.

I carried a brown paper bag containing an egg salad sandwich and Yankee Doodles to school every day. (Yankee Doodles were three chocolate muffins filled with something sweet that passed for cream.) *Every* day. Lunch meant egg salad and Yankee Doodles. For one cent I got milk in a tin cup in the basement of the St. Colombo School where we ate at fold-up tables surrounded by pipes, boilers, peeling paint, and loving nuns. I noticed that some kids got free food at school and asked my mother why I didn't. "That's for poor people," explained my wealthy mother.

I played on the floor of a railroad style apartment (from back to front a kitchen, bedroom, bedroom, living room) with an oatmeal box containing clothespins. More linoleum. (I don't know what the poor kids played with.) Although there must have been some variety, supper was ham, cheese, and potato casserole, light on the ham and cheese—and hold the caviar. Breakfast was oatmeal in winter and cold cereal in summer. I don't know what poor kids ate.

The iceman called from the street: "Eye-sa-man!" Mothers leaned out of windows, mine on the 4th floor, giving instructions regarding size of ice and destination to the man whose wagon was drawn by a horse. The iceman had a thick hemp mat over his shoulder for a big block, and with his other hand he carried another block in pincers. By holding just one of the pincer handles, the ice block hung from one arm, pinched in the pincers. I didn't understand what prevented the ice from falling. That was a miracle like the fireman's coffee miracle. One of the men from the firehouse down 29th Street passed our building to buy coffee at the cafe on the southwest corner of 9th and 29th. The coffee was in a topless tin container. On his way back to the firehouse he would swing the open container by its handle in a stiff-armed 360 degree arc without spilling a drop. Life was filled with similar wonders known to Isaac Newton and firefighters but mysteries to me.

Another man shouted from his horse-drawn wagon, "Froota-veggie!" Mothers leaning from windows would order their apples and beans with a shouted order. Kids would be dispatched to get and pay for the order, or the froota-veggie man's helper ran up steps. There was also a knife and scissors sharpener with grinding wheels on his wagon who appeared in the same way with a sing-song announcement of his services.

Generations influenced by Doctor Spock will note with disapproval, perhaps with alarm, several aspects of my parents' childrearing. If Mom expected to be running errands when I returned home from school, my instructions were clear, and I complied. I went to the rooftop from inside the building, climbed down the ladder to the fire escape on the 4th floor at the back of the apartment, and then crawled through the window left unlocked by a thoughtful mom. That this required me to hang on for about a dozen rungs down the ladder to the fire escape was not a problem to the agile lad, but finding that first rung backwards was always a scary step into the unknown.

Crossing 9th Avenue to get to a grocery store on the other side was yet another adventure worked out between Mom and my guardian angel. When sent for milk or bread at the age of six or seven, I traveled under strict instructions. They were to look back at the critical moment to the 4th floor window where my Mom established an observation post for the purpose. On her signal, I dashed across the near lane, with traffic approaching from my left, to the protection on the lee side of one of the El's large steel supporting members. Another glance back to mom's observation post was rewarded with a wave authorizing me to dash the final steps to the other side. The same technique was employed to return me. It was only years later that it dawned on me that mom's field of vision from that window a half-block from the crossing point allowed her to see oncoming traffic about two car lengths to my left and zero to the right. Beyond that was my guardian angel's responsibility, a responsibility executed in the best tradition of that Corps. However, as a part of the contingency plan, I wore clean underwear to avoid family embarrassment in the event I was run over by an auto or a truck.

One day as I walked under the El to school, the routine was heightened to little-boy-adventure by the sight of marching soldiers in formation, wearing coats like army blankets with buttons and with rifles on their shoulders. It may have been 1940 when some reserves were called up and the first peacetime conscription was enacted. About then brother Jerry was born, the third of what would become a seven-child outfit strung out over twenty-seven years. Same parents!

The 29th Street days included the miracle of the goldfish (the small fish bowl froze in the front room, thawed, and the fish celebrated by swimming happily about); being bitten by a dog and repaired at the French Hospital (I still have the scar on my hand); puncturing a finger with scissors (ditto that scar); seeing *Snow White and the Seven Dwarfs* (mom laughed when I called them dorfs), *The Wizard of Oz*, *Fantasia*, *The Great Dictator*, *Grapes of Wrath*, *The Philadelphia Story*, Fred Astaire and Ginger Rogers in *The Story of Vernon and Irene Castle*, and *Gone with the Wind*. Mom never tired over the years of watching and rereading *Gone with the Wind* and watching *The Story of Vernon and Irene Castle* into her eighties. Her dad was a vaudeville song-and-dance man, and she grew up watching show biz types who visited his candy store when for reasons of health he had to get out of entertainment. She fancied herself a show-biz person. Her specialty was singing off-key with gusto.

One day it was time to go on The Great Trek. Infant brother Jerry was put in a dresser drawer padded with pillows and blankets to join us in a convoy of two cars and one truck that proceeded to 59th Street, over the bridge crossing the East River to Astoria, and on to our new digs in Woodside, Queens, just two blocks south of Queens Boulevard on 69th Street. We had gone overseas. What an adventure! I was in the back of the truck with my uncles and the furniture. The new neighborhood was country where one could climb trees and play in an empty lot. Saint Mary's was my school. The playground was cinder ashes. The toilets were outside in a shed with a trough for a urinal. Our apartment was on the second of two floors; the landlady said, "Make out the light," and her teenage daughter wet the bed. The bus that stopped in front of our apartment killed the Chinese man who worked in the laundry across the street. He was in the habit of ducking out of the cold while waiting and springing forward as the bus appeared. When the bus driver failed to see him in time, his nocturnal lurch became his last. The next morning we kids studied the bloodstains on the street.

At about the time of the attack on Pearl Harbor, we were a five-person family. At one point all of us but my father were very sick for some time, long enough for me to lose a semester at school. My sister and I had the measles, little Jerry had pneumonia and almost died, and Mom had something else. That was a bad time for us and the country as we left the Depression to find war.

Big War, Small Boy

On December 7, 1941, I went for a Sunday ride out to Long Island from the apartment in Woodside with my friend and his parents. The fellow eight-year-old was an only child. I was brought along to keep him company while adults did boring things, like visiting other adults and talking. We played and were called at ice cream and cookies time. In the evening I was returned to my front door.

I entered a dark apartment, surprised to be greeted by my father's voice. He was sitting at the kitchen table in the dark. Alone, except for the bottle of beer. He asked about my day, but something else was on his mind.

"Henry, the Japs bombed Pearl Harbor."

He was solemn. This was serious stuff.

"Where's Pearl Harbor?"

He told me. Then he said,

"That means we'll go to war."

Then he told me other things. He told me that warships at sea salute foreign warships by lowering their colors and then raising them. When he was in the Navy in the mid-1920s he learned that American sailors didn't like to salute the Japanese. The older men grumbled, saying that one day we would fight Japan. Well, the time had come. My father's seriousness made a deep impression. I didn't know what it meant, but I did know that it mattered a lot. He spoke to me for the first time as though I were an adult.

In the days that followed we listened to the radio as President Roosevelt asked for a declaration of war on Japan, and then Germany declared war on us. Then somehow Italy was an enemy. It was a wildly exciting time to be a little boy. The Navy took Uncle George, and the Army took Jean Kremer. When he visited us before going overseas, he wore the shiniest boots I'd ever seen. He was a paratrooper.

All the big guys from the neighborhood went off to the Army, Marines, and the Navy. My Uncle Bill, the failed babysitter and George's young brother, went into the Army later, when he turned eighteen. The dumb kid from the icehouse and beer distributor across 69th Street came home wearing a winter coat that might have passed as a horse blanket. He looked like a pile of doo-doo. But he was somebody. He was a soldier.

Kate Smith sang "God Bless America." Patriotic songs were everywhere, songs like "Praise the Lord and Pass the Ammunition." The Andrews Sisters sang peppy songs about rum and Coca Cola and bugler boys from Company C, leaving no doubt that American energy would overcome all and win. We sang those songs on Saturdays as the lyrics and a bouncing ball appeared on the big screen, joining the now-marathon matinee of double feature, cartoon, serial, previews of coming attractions, and "Time Marches On," a news feature that became war propaganda. Lunchtime to suppertime was movie time for hundreds of us screaming children.

Magazines were filled with neat pictures of guns, tanks, and ships, most in bold colors and all with our side winning. The pictures of aircraft, particularly fighter aircraft shooting up tanks and trains, were most popular with me and my friends. I clipped them and filled scrapbooks, lots of them. I could identify almost all of the American, British, German, and Japanese aircraft.

To win the war there were Victory Gardens, and we had to eat everything on our plates for the starving people in Europe. We boys collected tinfoil, newspapers, and all kinds of metal for "the war effort." Mothers saved melted fat and returned it to the butcher shop. The traffic lights in New York City were blackened so that only half of the light shone through. Automobile headlights were also half-painted black in cats' eyes to reduce the light. "Blackout" drapes and curtains were tested in blackouts as "block wardens," some conscientious citizens and some crypto-Hitlers, checked the windows from the outside and reported slackers. My father had a white helmet with CD on it. That meant Civilian Defense. Buckets of sand were spotted around in multistoried structures.

Rusty ships lined the Hudson for miles up the river, and then they would be gone one morning, gone in big convoys. The French luxury liner *Normandy* was kept in New York after the Germans whipped the French in June of 1940. When it burned and rolled over, spies were blamed. Old men walked Long Island beaches on the lookout for German spies. An ammunition ship blew up at about 7 a.m. while loading in New Jersey and rattled our windows as I prepared for school miles away in Queens, NYC. American ships were being sunk by submarines along the East Coast from Canada to South America as they left Halifax, Portland, Boston, New York, Norfolk, Charleston, Savannah, and Miami.

Lucky Strike cigarette packages changed from green to white as it was noted with great drama: "Lucky Strike green goes to war!" Gasoline was rationed. So was sugar, coffee, and other commodities that either came from overseas or were required in vast quantities by the military. Auto factories stopped producing cars and built tanks, jeeps, and trucks. At the Saturday movies, "Time Marches On" told us how good-just-effective we and our Allies were and how bad-unfair-stupid the enemy was. Liberty ships, tanks, and aircraft rolled off assembly lines like hotcakes. Women wore pants and worked in factories, now called "defense plants." Feature films reminded us that we were at war and that our soldiers were prepared to vanquish evil by being child-loving, good-humored, chocolate-and-gum-dispensers. The European enemies were bad, but we discovered that the Japs were God-awful. One day my pal, Ronnie, addressed a serious issue with a question:

"Henry, could you sneak up on a guy and push a knife into his head?"

"Yuck! I don't think so!"

"The Japs can."

"Really?"

"Yeah. And they only need to eat a handful of rice a day!"

The Japs were different. And mean!

Maybe that's why we cheered when we saw film of a Japanese soldier aflame and running out of a bunker. We also saw film of Japanese soldiers who had killed themselves to avoid capture, sometimes by putting rifle barrels in their mouths and pulling the trigger with their big toes, or stabbing themselves, or blowing themselves up, or jumping from cliffs to the rocks and surf below. Bombed out cities in Germany and Japan were lustily cheered as we saw the good news between double features. Film of subs being attacked drew raves from the audience, particularly from the kid-filled movie theaters on Saturday afternoons. Best of all was the film from gun cameras, registering the disintegration of a Zero or Messerschmidt into a falling pile of junk or a smudge in the sky. War biz was show biz for Saturday afternoons.

Comic books were mobilized as Captain Marvel, Superman, and the others did their bit for victory over evil. When Billy said Shazaam!, the enemies of America were about to suffer a bad hurt. And watch out Krauts and Japs when Clark Kent stepped into a phone booth and removed his glasses!

Houses and apartments were proud to advertise with a blue star in the windows that a man was serving in uniform. A gold star told us that a family had a dead son or father.

We also learned that loose lips sink ships. Propaganda films showed soldiers calling home to mention a sailing date. Spies listened and told submarines. Of course, the subs sank old blabbermouth's ship. And if an American soldier in a bar bragged about some really neat weapon, there was that same guy who talked to the submarines, listening with big ears. The bad guys would copy the neat weapon and kill GIs with it.

Our Allies outdid one another in bravery, decency, and love of us. Joe Stalin was a benevolent pipe-smoking uncle to the brave people of Russia, who would rather kill Germans than eat. The only difference between Russians and Americans is that we have short names. They have long names. All Frenchmen pretended to get along with the Germans in the daytime, but nights were spent blowing up bridges and sending messages to England. In England Winnie walked among the ruins smiling, smoking a big cigar, and flashing the "V for Victory" sign. The Germans were bombing churches, schools, and old people, but Winnie cheered the British people with his cigar and the victory sign. The Chinese were the sweet people Pearl S. Buck had described. Thousands of them carrying little baskets of rocks would dump the rocks and go to get more to build airfields and roads. We had the impression that they liked being useful. And little Chinese kids formed gangs to ambush the Japs in China and to blow things up. There was a lot of blowing up. Bad guys flew through the air. Good guys usually had time to utter a few patriotic words about victory, freedom, mom, and the rosy future being won by the sacrifice of good guys dying, usually with a smudge of dirt on the forehead or cheek and moving music in the background. Even the most God-forsaken places and smallest foxholes housed large orchestras to underscore memorable last words like, "Get a Nip for me," or "Tell mom I love her." The other guys listened and were inspired by the noble deaths and words of their friends. They were determined to kill a German or a Jap for freedom, democracy, Betty Grable, and The American Way.

Well, it worked. May of 1945 meant V-E Day, and August meant V-J Day. The big guys came home and got married. Refrigerators, stoves, and cars rolled off assembly lines the way tanks had. Dumb-happy-nonsense songs were sung about three little fishes, pronounced "fiddies," that swam and swam (prounced "fam" and "fam") all over the dam; shoo fly pie and apple pan-dowdies made your eyes light up and your stomach say howdy; mares eat oats and does eat oats and little lambs eat ivy, a kid'll eat ivy too, wouldn't you? They replaced the longing for peace and the craving for personal pleasures heard in songs like, "When the Lights Come On Again All Over the World," "I'll Be Seeing You," and "Lili Marlene." Soon there would be bluebirds over the white cliffs of Dover, just you wait and see.

Uncle George, Jean, and most of the other big guys were back. They were at the kitchen table at our house, drinking whiskey with my father while I, now twelve or thirteen, sat with them and listened, enjoying every minute of being with real men. Jean, who had been through the mill as a trooper with the 101st Airborne Division, called the human body an incredible machine. He, along with George Patton and some others, believed that we should have gone after the Russians as soon as the Germans were whipped. He pointed to me and made a pronouncement:

"Henry will have to fight the Russians."

I never did fight the Russians, but I was kept gainfully employed fencing with their kissin' cousins in Korea and Vietnam. Memories of the Big War remained alive as the small boy became a big guy and then a geezer.

Growing up in my America was marked by well-established milestones and rites of passage: first day at school; First Holy Communion; "working papers"; first cash jobs for delivering newspapers and cutting grass; confirmation; high school; driver's license; registration for the draft; voting.

Mine included getting a haircut.

3

Pete the Barber

Pete tolerated no foolishness from the grade school boys who filled his shop daily, except Sundays and Mondays. The big plaster eagle above the mirror clutched a snake in his talons. "E Pluribus Unum," said the inscription on the base of the eagle's perch. The flag of the United States of America hung here as it hung in school. This was a serious place.

A glance from the slight man of sixty-plus years was usually enough to settle down the restless natives. His glance aimed at the mirror never failed to find the offending party, who saw Pete's bent back and his eyes in the same photographic instant. The offender ceased disorderly conduct immediately and signaled contrition by pushing his nose into the comic book or magazine in his hands. Once or twice in an hour Pete actually turned to face the row of boys aligned in chairs behind him like so many pots of hot water threatening to boil over. Scissors held high and outreaching like the palm of the Pope in mid-blessing, but uncharacteristically still, punctuated the steady accusing glare of the unsmiling small man with the white hair, white mustache, and white jacket, the latter like a doctor's. Rarely did he find it necessary to say anything but, "You next." On those rare occasions when the reflected glance in the mirror escalated to the direct scissors-stopping glare without result, he spoke.

"Go home. Tell your mother no haircut today."

There was no court of appeals for excommunication. Pete's pronouncement carried the same weight as a decision by Sister Superior at Saints Joachim and Anne or the principal of P.S. 34. The condemned slunk out, already inventing the alibi to explain to his mother his unshorn locks after a visit to the barber.

There were unspoken rules in Pete's domain. Men went before boys. Always. Each of the dozen waiting boys would approach Pete's throne by an invitation that was also a command: "You next." A man was automatically next. Men didn't wait for boys.

Another rule never spoken was that Pete cut hair; boys shut up and sat

15

still. Mothers bringing very small boys operated under an understood subset of rules. Mothers were the only women ever seen in the shop. No one needed to explain that mothers were special. They caused seas to part and children to heal. They were always next, and they were authorized to tell Pete how to cut the little boys' hair. Otherwise Pete just knew. Instructions were unnecessary and unwelcome.

At some point, about the time I was a high school senior, I was next as soon as I entered the shop. It probably happened as a consequence of the summer job I had as a construction laborer rather than recognition of some birthday. In any event, it was Pete's decision that I was a man. Instead of "Next," I became "Hendry."

I went to Korea during the war there and returned to New York in one piece to go to college. Pete had kept track of my adventures by interrogating my younger brothers, presumably granting them special status and dispensation from customary silence, since they were still boys. He and I chatted about all sorts things, but the first duty of the boys remained: to be quiet before and after Pete said, "You next."

I went away to graduate school and returned to the land of Pete to teach and to have my hair cut. I looked in the mirror when Pete had finished and found a new look. When I asked Pete what he had done, he responded, "Teach haircut." And that was that.

He had been cutting my hair for almost twenty years and was about seventy when I asked him if and when he planned to retire. He must have been thinking about just that. He stepped between me and the mirror to fix his eyes directly on mine. This discussion was too serious to be trusted to mirrors.

The eyes fixed on mine unlocked, drifted, and took on a far away look as he thought back to his boyhood in Italy. He said that in the old country old men sat on a bridge as children passed by on their way to school and their parents went about their business. The old men played checkers and cards in the morning sun on the bridge. At midday they went home for lunch and a nap. In the afternoon a glass of wine or grappa was in order before they returned to their station on the bridge to monitor the community's comings and goings as they played cards. When the days were long, there was time to assemble on the bridge for another hour or two after dinner. Pete said that the old men had been schoolboys together in the town sixty or seventy years before they took up their duties on the bridge. Then they had been apprentices, soldiers, married men, fathers, grandfathers, and pensioners.

The far away look faded as Pete asked, "Hendry, in this country, where's the bridge?"

My career as a soldier allowed me to sample barbers around the world, but I'm still stumped each time I'm asked how I'd like my hair cut. I think I say "medium." Aren't barbers supposed to know? Boy, boy haircut. Teach, teach haircut. Soldier, soldier haircut. Old man, old man haircut. But finding the bridge in America . . . not so easy.

At the time I wasn't sure precisely what Pete meant with his question, but after eleven years in Europe and three in Asia I think I understand. In traditional societies, one knows "the way." What to wear to the theater; when to bring flowers to one's hostess, and what kind; to look in the eyes of the person whose hand you are shaking; when to avoid eye contact; the use of titles. "The way" is clear to adults in a traditional society.

The universally understood social reference points are fewer and less clear in our American society. Newness, mobility, the constant influx of immigrants, egalitarianism, and readiness to adapt: these attributes characterize a society ready for constant change. Some immigrants never find the map and compass to guide them through the slalom course of daily American life. A simple old man, even after many years in "this country," notices such things as he contemplates retirement, another milestone in our march to mortality.

Native-born Americans take for granted values inculcated early in life by parents and teachers. I find it difficult to overestimate the importance of the teachers who have been the models for the kind of man I wanted to be.

4

Teachers

I n 1945 Sister Mary Rose was a tomboy. She was also a semicloistered nun of the Sisters of Notre Dame, my dedicated 6th grade teacher, and a dozen years older than her charges. I see her on roller skates during the lunch hour, black habit aflutter as she flew around the schoolyard of Saints Joachim and Anne as the ten-to fourteen-year olds marveled at her exuberance and skill, not to mention the pure novelty of a nun giving every indication that she was a fun-loving human being. I recall her encouragement as I attempted with bad jokes and abuse of the language to inject wit and charm into the weekly writing of themes that were carefully read, thoroughly edited, and promptly returned. A face-to-face critique at desk side, always sympathetic and supportive, supplemented the blue pencil marks that were more encouragement than corrections. Though I was probably just being "a wise guy," she treated my work seriously as I responded to What I Want To Do In Life with an expression of my passion for being a garbageman, pushing a broom and cart as I studied the literature amongst the refuse in the gutters of New York City, or admiring my pal's invention of a lawnmower with square wheels, better for cutting grass in tight corners. Because she was attentive to my work, I took it seriously. Because her order was semicloistered, she did not attend our class team baseball games, but she was there in spirit—literally: she provided religious medals for each of the players. One marvels at her constant presence in the lives of her charges, particularly since her life was spent almost entirely in the convent or in the classroom. Not all saints are in cemeteries.

Part of one afternoon per week in her lesson plan was free reading time. We were released by pairs to go to a storeroom where, among the dusty furniture awaiting repair, books could be found in the disused room at the end of the corridor. There I discovered *Bomba the Jungle Boy*, Tarzan books, Jack London, and O. Henry. The pure hero books, most of them repaired by the nuns with scotch tape, were supplemented by the wit of Ring Lardner and mordant Poe tales. Because of her, I took pleasure in the reading and writing, and she took delight in inspiring her pupils. Since Bill Hundt, my best friend from the 4th grade through high school, and I were "acting up," Bill's mother suggested that we be "broken up." I'm not quite sure how one does that, but no matter. Sister Mary Rose was having none of it. She declared that Bill and I had a beautiful friendship that should be nurtured. She was right, as usual, and Bill and I remained friends until he died an untimely death. Sometimes we visited her during our high school years. Our visits clearly pleased her, and we were pleased that she was pleased.

I wrote a letter to her in 1972 from the Armed Forces Staff College in Norfolk, Virginia, while in my cups, reflecting on the people who had positively affected my life. The letter was never delivered. Later, after reestablishing contact in the mid-1990s, I learned from her of the turmoil in the religious orders in the aftermath of Vatican II, turmoil of which I was, in my selfishness, only dimly aware. The old black habits were replaced by more contemporary street clothes, nuns were relocated, and my letter was probably lost in the shuffle or simply withheld by her "superior" in a system far more rigid than my army.

Sister Mary Rose emerged from the revolution from above as Sister Kathleen, the given name of the Irish girl from the Bronx. New name, same modest and loving giver. She and her friend from my grade school days, Sister Marguerite (the girl from Brooklyn, I later discovered, and my inspired 7th grade teacher), both in their 80s, caring for aging nuns in Maryland. It is not surprising that these teachers of the 1940s are the caregivers of 2001, but they are slowing down. One expects unreserved giving from the beloved teachers who kept lists of all their pupils and prayed for each of them daily for over half a century. But how hard it must have been to maintain direction through American materialism, secularism, and hedonism in the decades from the 1940s to the new millennium, particularly as the Catholic Church was and remains divided along the lines of tradition and change. How difficult it must be for them to witness the Church scandals of 2002. Sister Kathleen cheerfully refers to her latest need for managed care by other nuns as being "in the vestibule of Heaven."

The first word we freshman heard as we sat in the gymnasium at Chaminade High School in January 1948 for our orientation was "Gentlemen." Until then we had been "boys." We looked around and giggled nervously as we realized that we were the ones addressed. The Marianist brothers and lay teachers of the faculty continued to address us in this manner, disregarding overwhelming and clear evidence to the contrary. We were filthy little beasts. The psychological effect of the consistent and deliberate misapplication of the word was not immediately evident, but by degrees over the four years we became apprentice, if not journeymen, gentlemen.

On a faculty of good men, Mr. Joseph Thomas stood out as the model Christian gentleman. He coached and taught. I had the benefit of observing him closely as one of his students in English classes and as one of his players on the football field. His style was to avoid long speeches, preferring succinct expression. He looked us in the eye and made pronouncements that were at least as memorable as the 10 Commandments. Once, during a scrimmage at football practice, I returned to the huddle to meet those eyes and an admonition delivered without passion in a calm, low voice: "Henry, you didn't do the job." A bolt of lightning would not have focused my attention more than those words. I had displeased Mr. Thomas! Clearly on the next play, I was a man on a mission, and I did it right.

Upon reflection, I suppose he was something of an understated stoic. Prominently displayed in his locker room was a sign announcing: "Football is fundamentally a rough game. Boys who bruise easily should not participate." Another showed a picture of a pyramid with the caption: "The secret of stability is a broad base and a low center of gravity." I returned from an examination of my banged-up ribs by a doctor to report the results to the coach. "Contusion, Mr. Thomas," I reported, thinking that would be good for a day away from the practice field. "A contusion is a bruise. Suit up for practice," said the coach. I did. On Fridays, because Mass was celebrated before class and fasting rules were in effect, we older boys didn't get to eat any food until late in the morning. We stirred and squirmed as the bell rang, terminating our English period. Mr. Thomas observed, "Boys, we don't live to eat. We eat to live." The stirring stopped, and I had reason to recall the meaning of that moment of fifty years ago often enough in my adulthood.

He had been an infantry officer, a company commander in Europe in the recently concluded World War II, but, except for response to a specific line of questioning from me, he didn't talk about his combat experience. Once, quite out of the blue, he taught us to march in a PT class, and we practiced a few times. We didn't know why. As a matter of fact, we found it rather amusing. I think the Korean War that had broken out during our high school career was the reason for the drill. He just wanted us to be ready, ready for the draft or ROTC. He also had us doing what I later as a soldier recognized as the "daily dozen," the twelve standard exercises of the Army's physical training program. With the passage of time, it has become clear to me that without fanfare he continually tried to anticipate the challenges we would face in life. He prepared us for the long haul. That's what good teachers do. He also produced winner after winner over the years. His "gentlemen" revered him, his colleagues respected him, and his rivals said of his school: "Chaminade doesn't rebuild. They just reload." I have seen him no more than a half dozen times in fifty years, but the last time, at a reunion of several classes, I approached him as he spoke to another graybeard unknown to me. Without skipping a beat he said, "Ed, this is Henry Gole. End. Tough kid. A step slow." I don't know how he does it, but he got that right as he has gotten most things right for a long time. A step faster and I could have. . . .

Returning from the war in Korea to study at Hofstra College (now University), I found my extraordinary luck with teachers continued. Dr. Chalfant made Shakespeare, Marvell, Pope, Swift, and Johnson my friends. He made learning fun, and he encouraged and improved my writing. He once told me to take a second language. When I asked why, he informed me that I would one day study for a doctorate. I didn't know that. He did.

John Rawlinson was pleased, surprised, and amused when I showed up in his office one day to talk to him about his Chinese history course. At one point, as he realized what I was doing, he asked, "Are you interviewing me to decide whether to take the course?" When I affirmed that, he invited me to the faculty lounge to continue our chat over coffee. He said that that had never happened before in his experience as a professor. He taught me Chinese and Japanese history, how to drink Martinis and how to establish personal and intellectual bonds with my students.

Dr. De Luca was one of the most cultivated and learned men I've known. Studying Spanish with him was far more than a language lesson. He was a model I followed to comparative literature, starting with his Renaissance course, to learn that Machiavelli, among other things, wrote a very amusing play, that Benvenuto Cellini was a marvelous braggart, that Boccaccio and Rabelais can reduce me to incoherence beyond my normal incoherence and to tears of joy and laughter. Because of him and his love of things Mediterranean, I was inspired to eat it all up and later branched out to French Classicism and German Romanticism with his colleagues from the foreign language departments. He was more formal and distant than Professors Chalfant and Rawlinson, so I also learned that great men do not conform to cookie cutters.

Still later, after my adventures in Korea, I was privileged to sit at the feet of Sigmund Neuman at the Fletcher School of Law and Diplomacy. He was one of several German socialists and Jews who got out of Hitler's Germany in time, to my advantage and Germany's loss. Karl W. Deutsch and George Halm were others. Still later at Stanford I enjoyed the friendship of the erudite and charming Gordon Craig, a great man. And Russell Weigley, one of several military historians who brought that field respectability in the academic community, guided me to my doctorate.

I recognize my debt to the men and women named in a very personal way. They will never know how often I have thought of them and how often they have pulled me through crises. The ripples they stirred in the pond of my life have not yet reached the shore. They filled a gap my father could not.

5

Conversations with Dad

B orn in 1909, my father was the youngest in a large family in a remote area in an interesting time. Several of the children died at birth or shortly thereafter. One died in World War I serving the Hapsburgs, and in World War II the family was the very model of an equal opportunity victim. Family members died at the hands of the usual suspects: German and Italian armies, British and American air forces, Tito partisans and royalists. There was no mention of neighbors using the war to grab the back forty of someone else, but it would be surprising if that were not the case. Little people don't concern themselves with big politics, but they do care about property lines.

My father was happily oblivious to most of this when he died an American patriot in 1985. Except for one visit I made to his homeland, everything I know about his youth came from conversations with Dad. He had little notion of a broader context of his time and place. That's another way to say that my source was an uneducated man who left Europe at fourteen and never returned, a man who forgot his native German from disuse, a man born in Slovenia who went to his death considering himself to be an American who was once Austrian. It wasn't until I began this book that I learned that he was a part of a German community that had preserved its identity in a Slavic sea for centuries, until, ironically, Woodrow Wilson's idea of national self-determination ensured that the patchwork Yugoslavia would attempt to erase German language and culture in Slovenia. That's what happens when make-believe nations address concrete realities.

Dad's father scratched out a sometimes subsistence existence for his family by working wherever he found employment. Some winters he led a team of horses dragging logs through town to level the snow, and he kept dynamite in the house to blast rocks in the summer to keep the same improved dirt road clear when the snow melted. My father said his father spoke Italian, German, and "Slavic languages." Presumably the barely lettered man had to communicate in the languages of his employers. In his part of the world, not far from the head of the Adriatic Sea—near Trieste—Latin, Slavic, and Germanic cultures converged. They still do.

In bad times my grandfather got on a boat to Amerika—alone—worked in factories (at least once in Brooklyn, New York), saved his money, and returned home, a part of the Austro-Hungarian Empire until 1919, and thereafter the northwestern chunk of Yugoslavia abutting Italy, Austria, and Hungary. Of course this option shut down during the Great War, but he was permitted to send his sons to die for "Kaiser und Koenig."

In 1923 my father visited the United States with his parents. He was fourteen when he ate his first banana on a ship. (He had sampled oranges at Christmas and Easter at home to celebrate very special and holy events.) He told me that when he saw the engine room of the ship that took him across the Atlantic, it was love at first sight. That was also his reaction to Maryland and Washington, D. C., where his much older brother (Rudolph, a hero and veteran infantryman in the service of the Hapsburgs) and sister (Antonia, married to Harry Evans, a sailor in the Spanish-American War; I really had an Aunt Toni) had settled. When my grandparents returned to Europe, my father refused to go. As best we could figure it, that was my grandfather's third time in America, and the first time for my grandmother. My father never saw either of his parents again.

Circumstantial evidence—and close observation much later—suggests that my father was a headstrong, undisciplined kid. He spent some weeks in each grade in the local school, from the 1st through the 6th, to learn English. It worked. When he joined the U.S. Navy at sixteen, he lied about his place of birth, saying he was born in Maryland. Many years later I met a schoolmate of my father's who called him "Dutch," the first time I heard that. It had never occurred to Dad to tell us that he had once been "Dutch." I always knew he was an immigrant, but apparently neither he nor I thought of him as being an immigrant.

He had a falling out with his sister, a consequence, one suspects, that repeated the ages-old challenge of youth to the rules-responsibility-thou-shalt-nots of authority. The details of this incident and the entire story of his early days is necessarily fuzzy, relying as it does on childhood memories, his and mine. It was my probing that caused him to search his memory for incidents that, it seems to me, he was quite willing to chuck out with the trash. For example, when I pressed him about his school days, he told me about the post-1919 transition from German to what he called "Slavic"—I think he meant Serbo-Croatian—in the new Yugoslavia. He laughed as he recalled the resentment among his family and the neighbors: the first time the Slav teacher struck one of the boys, not unusual in that spare-the-rod, spoil-the-child era, big brother came to school and beat the hell out of the teacher. Apparently the hearts of the German minority were in Austria, but their bodies, property, and means of livelihood were in the then-new, now-defunct Yugoslavia. Bad luck. So, neither your source nor mine is absolutely reliable about what it was like to be ten or twelve in Slovenia before 1923. The outline of Dad's stateside adventures became the stuff of family folklore, but details get fuzzy.

He left his sister's house, got a room in "the District," somehow got an Indian Harley-Davidson motorcycle, delivered telegrams, stole milk and buns for breakfast before the Washington shops opened, crashed the bike, and joined the Navy, lying about both age and place of birth. He served aboard the USS *Denver*, a coal-burning four-stacker beauty, off the coasts of Central America. He drank warm water, was in the middle of a riot in a boxing ring in Nicaragua armed with a 1903 Springfield rifle, patroled ashore in navy whites dyed brown with coffee, shot a lunging dog with a .45 caliber pistol, and buried the dog in the jungle as punishment directed by an ensign leading the patrol. Sounds like he was at the cutting edge of American capitalism in the banana republics.

I think he was kicked out of the Navy. He never said that, but why would a guy who saved papers and pictures from the good old days not frame and show off his honorable discharge, if he had one? He did say that after the Navy—presumably 1927 or so—he went to Florida to make his fortune in a boom there. One day looking at the ships dockside in Miami, he tossed his salesman's sample case into the water before signing on as a merchant seaman.

The irresponsible young man became responsible. Somehow, with long division his highest achievement in mathematics, a total of six years of schooling, some five years of English, and one hell of a lot of sweat, he passed the required tests and became a licensed maritime engineer, a junior officer to whose cabin, he was pleased to say, steaks were brought by mess stewards. Sailing for the United Fruit Company between Central and South America and New York City, he was smitten by my mother, the fair, red-headed Irene Catherine Finn of Greenwich Village.

My mother, born in Greenwich Village in 1913 to a former vaudevillian, a song and dance man who ran a candy store, told me about the sometimes gifted and usually eccentric characters who graced the premises with their presence; of outhouses in the Big Apple; of delivering newspapers to Jimmy Walker, the charming and sticky-fingered Mayor of Gotham; of my uncle who swam in the Hudson River; of dock-wallopers, athletes, jailbirds, and other wondrous things. My favorite was Buttsy, who could blow a cigarette butt from his lips so that it stuck to a ceiling, still burning, a stunt no doubt admired by the NYC Fire Department.

St. Vincent's Hospital and staff welcomed me to the Village in 1933, the very nadir of the Great Depression. Dad, frustrated to be out of work and embarrassed to be on Home Relief, was forced to go to sea again to support his new family, me and Mom. He might have just kept sailing had he known that I was the first of seven bouncing babes that would fill his dwellings, the last of whom is twenty-seven years my junior, all of us a testament to scrupulous family planning.

Dad became, in about this order, a long-time payer of bills, a worry wart, a building superintendent in Manhattan, a hard-core union man, a loving disciple of Franklin Delano Roosevelt, a proud homeowner, a serious drinker, and a superpatriot who contended that the best day of his life was the day he got on the boat that took him to the Statue of Liberty. I get maudlin each time I seek out 134 West 37th Street in the garment district on my treks to the big city. He ran that building for many years.

In 1970, almost fifty years after his departure, I finally got to his hometown. The American jokes about the town so small that you'll miss it if you blink might not comprehend the small town missed with your eyes wide open; the town with big and deep holes in the road and large rocks to be avoided (since my grandfather, fixer of roads, apparently had no successor); the town with four or five visible houses; the town whose most distinguishing characteristic is a bend to the left as you descend slightly before the road straightens. It was good to see the place, but, as usual, the people made the visit memorable: a neighbor called Jaglich and a cousin called Pepe.

My father listened in open-eyed wonder, more the four-year old on Santa's knee than the grizzled geezer he was. Because I had read history, because I had just been there, because I was number one son, he listened attentively and asked the right questions.

He said he was Austrian. I put that in perspective for him. His people were ethnic Germans and Slovenes by location. They were loyal to the man in Vienna—true to things German—and, when able to choose, they remained within the Austrian border, as much of his family had done after World War II, relocating to the north. However, the place he left when he left it was Yugoslavia, a place like Galicia, like Poland where it meets Germany and Russia, like Schleswig-Holstein and like Alsace-Lorraine: places without neat frontiers and places cursed by competing cultures.

We had this conversation in 1970 while I was in the United States for a few weeks between another tour in Germany and another one in Vietnam. It gave him much pleasure and seemed to fit together some missing pieces, perhaps because his number one son, the college guy, was the authoritative messenger.

He lost contact with his family during the Second World War. When postal service resumed after the war, it is ironic that he turned to German-Jew Americans in the garment industry to read to him the letters written by his mother in German script as indecipherable to him as Arabic or Chinese. In his desire to be "a real American" he had succeeded in unlearning his native language. One by one his father, mother, brothers, and nephews died. He and his American-born son saw the world through different lenses.

When I returned from Korea at the end of that war, he asked about my plans.

"I'll go to college, Dad."

"Good idea. A year or two of college really helps."

"I plan to graduate, Dad."

"Yeah, yeah. You'll get married and need a job."

The depression and World War II guy spoke Sanskrit to his son.

"Watch me, Dad."

On graduation day in 1957, he was proud. Nice cap and gown, diploma, pretty speeches, good weather. What more could a father want of number one son?

"Now waddayagonnado?"

I was afraid he'd ask.

"I'm going to graduate school."

"Waddaya mean? I mean after you graduate?"

"Dad, I'm going to get a Master's degree, an advanced degree in another school."

"But you're getting married. You're a college graduate. You're getting married and going to school?"

I nodded. All of the 1950s was improbable to him: my B.A. in English, marriage, more school, the study of history, my insouciant glance at the wolf at the door as my wife supported me, something called an M.A. He did what I expected. He shook his head as though there was a death in the family.

When I was a teacher in Baldwin in 1958, his reaction was:

"No money in it. All that school and no money."

Three years later I told him I was going back to the Army.

"You were already in the Army."

"Right. I'm going back. This time I'll be an officer."

Unmollified, he asked:

"Why?"

"I liked being with men. It's like being with good guys in a bar, or fishing, or on the job. Besides, I think there's gonna be a war in Asia."

"You want to be in another war? I don't get it. You're a teacher. You were in Korea."

The picture of "my son the teacher" had grown on him. Now something else. He shook his head. Again.

When I was promoted to colonel in the early 1980s, he was there, beaming. He had recently learned that an Army colonel was the same military rank as a "four striper," a Navy captain, a big deal to the former sailor. Not many opportunities to refer to me as "the colonel" were missed, even when I was present. It sounded pretty good to me as well.

Discussions of "diversity" benefit from the fact that Dad is in his grave.

One suspects that he would alternate fits of Olympian apoplexy with vigorous vomiting as victim after victim parades across the stage in our time filled with self-pity, lamentations, and serious oh-woe-is-me. His solution to unemployment: take the shitty job and work yourself up. To learning English: Get outta the goddamned ghettos and talk English. But a sense of social justice and fairness emerged from time to time.

Over drinks in his house in the early 1980s—we were doing damage to the bottle of Chivas Regal I gave him—Dad groused about the beefs of unemployed non-speakers of English. In his usual diplomatic manner, he said of the latest crop of new immigrants:

"Keep the goddamned bums out."

"Who should keep them out?"

"The government."

"Who should they keep out?"

"Goddamned foreigners."

"What about you?"

"Waddaya mean?"

"You were a foreigner. The USA came like a ship and threw you a line. You raised seven kids. You got a nice house. You give me good scotch. Now you look down at some poor bastards and you won't throw them a line? Are you gonna pull up the line, leave 'em?"

He paused, thinking, smiled, and said:

"Nah. You're a smart boy."

"Must be my genes."

"Nah. You're right. Throw the bastards a line. Let's have another drink."

Ours was a loud, angry, affectionate family, and Dad was the heavy-handed leader. I've often tried to imagine what it must have been to muddle through the 1920s as an ignorant boy in a strange country, and to weather the Great Depression and a world war while herding seven kids over dangerous terrain, the first born in 1933 and the last in 1960! All of this armed with a sixth grade education in the rat race of New York City. Memories of conversations with Dad surface from time to time, providing some useful insights, but I did not walk in his shoes.

Thank God.

6

Geopolitics

I n 1952 I left college after one semester to have my war as my uncles and the "big guys" in the neighborhood had had theirs in the 1940s. Ascribing personal motives for that decision and other decisions made long ago is a tricky business. With the rest of the human race, I prefer to find nobility in actions more probably taken out of a desire to escape boredom or a longing for experience beyond the horizon. Observing the eighteen-year-old prototype of me permits an objectivity that comes rather easily, since that me joins Mickey Mantle, Harry Truman, Marilyn Monroe, Dwight D. Eisenhower, *Guys and Dolls*, and Senator Joe McCarthy as a relic neither forgotten nor a hot ticket item. I think I wanted to be a war hero, but there were other reasons. Almost thirteen years in school had filled my nostrils with chalk dust; I was in love and didn't know what to do about it; far-away places with strange-sounding names beckoned; it was time to leave the nest in which I was the eldest chickadee. The truth might be found somewhere in that haystack.

The war in Korea was two years old and the big guys were coming back home, our role models, the bigger boys who had chased us younger boys from the baseball field when they were ready to play.

"Justice" applied only among peers as I grew up in New York City. Among us boys was a strong sense of justice. The charge of not being "fair" was serious and could lead quickly to knuckle drill if another boy didn't do "the right thing." Big guys, teachers, parents, priests, nuns, and adults in general were guided by an unseen star that allowed them to be totally arbitrary. Under no condition was it acceptable for a boy to give lip to the absolved class, essentially all adults, those directly addressed politely as Father, Sister, Mister, Miss, or Mrs. If sufficiently rankled by anyone exempted from the rules of fairness, I was to tell my father, the final authority on earth. He then did "the right thing." Since lawyers were seen only at house closings and when someone ran afoul of the police, remedies in the neighborhood were swift and independent of outside influence. My mother dealt with the school and my father dealt with the world. My father polished his technique in a series of interpersonal experiences. Male offenders were punched. Ladies were shouted at. Big kids were slapped and invited to send their fathers to see my father. Small children were warned off by a kind of growl perfected by my father.

Since I am 27 years older than my youngest brother, and since six of the seven of us are males whose sense of propriety was learned from our father, it is no exaggeration to say that my mother had an extensive and not always amicable experience with school authorities. Ripped shirts and bloodstains on the boys as they returned from school had two consequences, one certain and one probable. For sure Mom whacked us with a hanger where it did the most good. That didn't do much for the ripped shirts and bloodstains, but it made Mom feel good and didn't bother us at all. Alas, too often was Mom invited to make a trip to school for a chat with established pedagogical authority. Visits to school had to be difficult for her, since fierce loyalty to her children, already whacked with the hanger, collided with her respect, mixed with a bit of intimidation, for the black-draped agents of Holy Mother Church. A nun could, in theory, be wrong, but she remained a nun. The Irish Catholic girl born in 1913 in Greenwich Village had at one time quite naturally considered entering the convent, so nuns were a lofty category set apart from the flotsam and jetsam of base humankind. Affection for her little beasts who, sad to say, regularly threw sand in the machine maintained by God's shop stewards, made interviews with the sisters, indeed at times with Sister Superior herself, difficult. Love wrestled with justice in Mom's bosom.

In any event, since I had been chasing little kids from the baseball field when I wanted to play, and since Pete the Barber took me right away, I had become a big guy. In August of 1952, I went to my draft board in Jamaica, New York. To "enlist" meant three years or more in one of the services; to volunteer for "the draft" meant two. I figured I could win the war in one.

Arrogance played no part in my assessment. Any detached observer considering the evidence would arrive at the same conclusion. I was American, played football, went to Mass regularly, had seen most of the World War II films, and America protected the weak. If John Wayne could defeat the Japs while Patton beat the Germans, how hard could it be for me to win a "police action"? My decision was not sudden. I had been thinking about fighting in a war for two years.

When the *New York News* headline screamed WAR IN KOREA! that warm June day about the time school let out for a boring summer, we nodded sagely before asking where Korea was. The only Korean we knew was Kato, the Green Hornet's driver, but we sensed that the war news might prove more important to us than the Yankee, Giant, and Dodger scores. At that moment in the summer of 1950, however, Rockaway Beach on Long

Island's south shore beckoned as we sipped on our cherry Cokes. (Coke in those days was a reference to a soft drink.) Of course, it was quite likely that our soldiers would settle the hash of those rascals, whoever they were, in a few days.

When the war dragged on, there was talk of joining the Navy. Folk wisdom had it that you could count on showers in the Navy, the importance of which eludes me since we ran around grubby and ripe though showers were already available to us. The Air Force would teach a young fellow to fix airplanes, a skill that might prove useful later at the nearby La Guardia and Idlewild (later J. F. Kennedy International) Airports. Dummies went to the Army or the Marines for two dummy years. Smart guys would be clean in the Navy or turn wrenches in the Air Force, both for four years.

Seminars on the subject continued under streetlights on hot summer nights from 1950 to 1952 as bad news from Korea was discussed and big guys three or four years older started to appear in uniforms. Changes in the international constellation took some talking out. The Chinese turned bad, a description inconsistent with the picture in our heads of really nice peasants who were pushed around by warlords and communists before somebody in Washington "sold them out." Until then they had flocked to the Catholic Youth Organization we supported in Sunday collections, which were sent to Gregory Peck, a missionary in China. They were on our side against the Japanese. Chinese women interrupted harvesting for just a few minutes to give birth behind a rock before returning to the rice paddies, and the laundry guy was a nice man. We thought they were OK, so when Chinese troops entered the war in Korea against us, we were confused. Somehow the Russians got the Chinese to help the bad Koreans—there were two kinds—when some disloyal Americans sold out China.

Since the end of World War II, the Japanese were OK. They played baseball, made cheap watches, and were nice to Americans in Japan. Some of the big guys even came back with Japanese wives. We stopped calling them Japs, and they stopped saying, "Marines, tonight you die."

The Russians and Germans really knocked over the apple cart. Uncle Joe went bad after World War II, and we confirmed that the Germans were just like the people we knew who were running the bakeries and delicatessens around New York. None of them ever said, "Achtung!" or "Ach!" or "du Schweinhund!" or "Vee haf our vays" or held their cigarettes that funny way with thumb and first finger as they squinted through smoke while menacing captured Allied agents.

Two factors decided me on volunteering for the draft: the failure of the League of Nations and my scrapbook filled with World War II aircraft. The world was screwed up, and it was up to the United States, the United Nations, and me to fix it.

Despite Latin, Algebra, chemistry and other obstacles thrown in my path by my teachers, in my senior year I was still in Chaminade High School, a Catholic prep school that actually required students to read whole books. I figured that World War II happened because the United States was not a member of the League, which permitted the Italians to defy the League of Nations and the Germans and Japanese to thumb their noses at the League, thus making it impossible for the world to be like Queens Village, my hometown. Queens Village was a blue-collar community in the Borough of Queens, City of New York, Empire State, USA—in brief, the center of the universe. Now the Russians were getting the Chinese and the bad Koreans to beat up the good Koreans. If we didn't stop them, there might be another big war, maybe even with atomic bombs. It was up to the United States and me to use the UN to make Korea a kind of Queens Village East. All of this was possible because one day a Russian didn't show up for work at the UN. He could have prevented the UN from intervening in Korea, but he blew it. It was up to me to help out, but I couldn't until I was graduated from high school. I was prepared to face the hordes of Chinese without flinching, but only after high school. High school would not make me a better rifleman, but it was clear to me that if I left school before graduating, my father would snap off both of my legs at the hip. Then I'd limp, never be a rifleman, and never be a hero. First I had to pass the New York State Regents Examinations. Then I could win the war.

The scrapbooks taught me the differences between a Zero, a Messerschmidt, a Wildcat, a Spitfire and a Mustang. That was all right for a boy, but a man should take his cue from *Battleground*, the movie about a rifle squad near Bastogne, and from Jean Kremer, who was there, and from John Wayne, who was always ready to go hand-to-hand with America's enemies on-screen and with Hollywood starlets off-screen.

I had to be a rifleman.

7

You There, Personnel

My white bucks, blue shirt, and chino trousers was the preppie uniform of 1952. The hood uniform was black leather jacket and hair combed into a DA, or duck's ass. Mine announced to the lady behind the counter at my Jamaica, New York, draft board that I was a college boy, probably a student in danger of losing his draft-exempt status. When I told her I was there to volunteer for the draft, she pulled out a file and announced that I was classified 2-S (student, deferred), a status resulting from a test I had taken at the advice of a college deanlet at Freshman Orientation. She explained that I need not defend freedom at that time and seemed surprised when I persisted and signed a release. When, I asked, would the next bunch go off to the Army? Upon the morrow, said she. Too precipitous, thought I. That did not allow time for gay parties ("gay" meant happy, light-hearted fun in 1952) and touching partings (like Humphrey Bogart and Ingrid Bergman kept from a rendezvous by German troops marching into their 1940 Paris and separating again in Casablanca, thus demonstrating how great events affect private affairs—I knew my drama). When would the next bunch march off to Victory and Defense of The American Way? In two weeks, said madam. Count me in, said I.

On 17 September 1952, I became US 51177493. Later I became 093040, and yet later I became my Social Security Number, my bank account number, and my email address. Maybe I'll be my DNA code before I become my burial plot number in Arlington National Cemetery.

The induction process is familiar to the millions of American males who turned 18 from 1940 until conscription ended in the 1970s. Recalling it will bring a smile to their lips, partially for the memory itself and partially for imagining the youth of today explaining their rights to the sergeants and petty officers of 1942 or 1952.

We were herded into a room in the Induction Center on Whitehall Street in downtown Manhattan. A sergeant-shepherd welcomed us: "You there, personnel! Get off the wall!" The object of his attention, a slouching self-pitying lamb, allowed some space between his body and the baby-shit-yellow wall, and I learned that I was a personnel, an enlisted personnel, not to be confused with a gentleman. After a blur of Army talk and milling about, we became a file of men naked except for shoes and socks, each of us clutching a fistful of forms that were initialed, stamped, and signed as we wended our way through a slalom of "stations" that comprised our "physicals."

My eyes were checked by a young man in a white coat whose own were never unglued from the pocketbook he was reading. We were informally introduced when he shouted, "Next!" I presented myself in all of my natural splendor, stood next to where he was seated, read the lines he told me to read, and gave him my forms that he initialed without a glance at me. I departed when he shouted, "Next!" We did not become friends.

Others inspected my various body parts in a similarly detached manner.

One poor lad couldn't urinate on command, so a friendly neighbor peed in his little bottle, presumably establishing the military bonding one hears so much about.

The most uncomfortable and dehumanizing twenty seconds of that busy morning—and of my short life—took place in the presence of two men at a long table, one allegedly a medical doctor, the other his spokesperson. "Next! (pause) Come to the table, give the doctor your papers, turn right, bend over and spread your cheeks."

Yes! Those cheeks!

I complied, humiliated, aiming my anal orifice at the doctor. The doctor growled, "Spread 'em!" before signing the papers without a glance at my eyes or any other irrelevant orifices.

I recall thinking of the gray-haired old doctor's hard work at medical school and his many years of practice and how he had become an asshole checker, doomed to an eternity of viewing the dark side of life. Dante made no reference to asshole checkers in his description of the inferno, so we don't know the circle to which the doctor was assigned. What a terrible fate, even if he had failed medical school or cheated on his Boards! At the rate of 200 assholes in the morning and a like number after lunch—could he eat lunch?—that would be 2,000 assholes per week. Even figuring in leave time and holidays, that would be 100,000 per year, give or take a few assholes. And who knows? He might have been at that table since 1940. It is an indisputable fact that New York has more assholes than places like Des Moines and Ithaca, even including the faculty at Cornell. It could be that I was examined by the all-time asshole checker champion, with the possible exception of some Chinese doctor. But my ruminations were interrupted by a call to the next station, the one marked "Psychiatrist."

"Do you like girls?"

"Yes, doctor,"

"When was your last date with a girl?"

"Last night, doctor."

"Next!"

Since all the papers were initialed, we took the oath and got on the government bus.

As we departed New York a transformation took place in the once-again fully-clothed veterans of thirty minutes of Military Service. Before we even had uniforms, the good manners and socialization monitored by loving parents and teachers for so many years simply vanished. My bus mates became GIs. All females, including those barely on the brink of puberty or matrons long safe from mashers, became the object of whistles and catcalls from this foreign legion denied companionship of the fair sex for minutes, even hours. The ride on the New Jersey Turnpike from the big city to Camp Kilmer, New Jersey, took on the ambiance of an audition for players who would perform as one of the stock figures in a World War II combat film, the Big City Wise Guy, as each young man on the bus tried to top the others with very unfunny one-liners. This attempt to camouflage nervousness was followed by silence as each of us realized that this was "it."

Whatever "it" was began in New Jersey and led to Korea.

8

Camp Kilmer

everal days at Camp Kilmer confirmed that the Army was in charge. "We" were disoriented. "They" knew the game. Chased from early dark to late dark by agents of surprise and arbitrariness, we focused on short-term survival: how to get through this day, this task, this problem. Fear concentrated our attention on routine tasks. Initially I think we expected a smile, a wink, or a nod, some kind of recognition that they were kidding us, this was a big joke, an initiation. There was an other-worldliness in the absurdity of clearly ignorant men with seemingly unlimited power over us, controlling if, when, and where we ate, slept, and spoke. On the first night at Kilmer (the irony of naming the dreadful place for the hero-poet did not strike me at the time, since I was more focused on bad manners than bad poetry), an officer told us about military justice, providing examples, probably invented, of bad soldiers living in dungeons into their dotage on bread and water for minor infractions of not-yet-understood rules. The point: do not challenge military authority; shut up; do what you are told. Everything about the body language, jargon, and place said, we got the whip.

Upon our first wake-up in the Army, we were told to make our beds by oh-dark hundred and to fall out in the company street on the whistle. We did, providing the sergeants with the opportunity to shape the amoebae we formed into four ranks. We were sent back to the barracks, warned not to sit or stretch out on our beds, and told we would have one minute after the whistle to form four ranks. I'll never know if we were "trained" or simply forgotten as we waited for two hours on our first full day in the Army for someone to blow a whistle and take us to the mess hall. One by one we dozed off. It was still dark at 4 or 5 in the a.m. Bodies were strewn about the barracks under the beds, beside the beds, and in the center aisle. "They" had gotten our undivided attention. Not a single body was in or on a bed. In the blur of several days, we were intimidated, issued clothing, inoculated, and tested. I still wonder how much of the Kilmer experience was planned for psychological impact and how much resulted from dull intellects simply forgetting us.

Emerging from a warehouse with duffel bags literally overflowing with clothing, we giggled as we held up long-handled underwear, that we city slickers had seen only in films, until a corporal drawled that we'd " 'preciate the woolly things in Frozen Chosin," the first of many references to Korea. I would recall the corporal's laconic comment as I wintered in Korea, sometimes in a hole in the ground and sometimes in a sleeping bag wearing every bit of clothing I possessed.

Tips about breaking in our boots ranged from taking showers in them to alternating our two pairs of boots daily. Despite tips, most of us went through a period of blisters until that simply stopped.

World War II films left out at least two parts of Army life that were omnipresent and universal: blisters and nagging colds and coughs in the first weeks in uniform. Morning formations were a cacophony of spitters, gaspers, and coughers auditioning for a TB ward.

We filed through a dispensary wearing too-green uniforms that announced "new guy." If the green newness didn't give us away, the fit did. We were mobile sacks with hurting feet who bared arms punctured by bored young men in white jackets. By the next day many of us had low-grade fevers and the general miseries, reactions to one or another of the several shots administered to the fresh meat. A corporal advised doing push-ups to alleviate the reaction to the shots. While no one died doing the push-ups, it was noted that those doing so were the same men who showered in combat boots—and did poorly on the mental tests.

Memory of mid-September 1952 at Camp Kilmer features coal and chill. A fat sergeant put the fear of God in me as he directed me to tend several stoves in a consolidated mess hall that fed thousands of hungry young men. Should the stoves not be burning brightly at 0430 hours, I would die. Suffering from shots and oversupervision, I staggered through the night from warm snooze on the kitchen floor near the stoves to filling my bucket with coal piled outside in the chilly New Jersey night. At 0430 I was dismissed. Eyes glazed, muscles aching, I took my coal-dust covered body to the barracks, anticipating the voluptuousness of a hot shower followed by sleep between clean sheets.

Alas, the irony! I took a cold shower, an icy shower. The fireman for our barracks had fallen asleep. He was neither shot nor hung. Half frozen and still unclean, I tumbled into my bunk for an hour or two. Nominally "off," since I had worked all night, sharing a bedroom with twenty-five men milling about as I shut my eyes was not quite a snooze at the Waldorf Hotel.

The institution that had trained many millions of men chose to administer the mental tests that would determine our military futures when we were sick, tired, and disoriented. One wonders why. In a post-test interview I was told I was eligible for Officer Candidate School. Then I was told to get on the bus. The test, based upon an enormous sample and vast experience in human assessment, was absolutely critical to sorting us out to determine our futures. Somehow it put us all on the same buses to the same place. The test result must have said: SEND THEM ALL TO CAMP PICKETT. One suspects that in the absence of a test we all would have been sent to Camp Pickett.

I learned the immutable rule—not of the Army but of life—that explains and makes it all bearable: I lose. Understanding this, everything falls in place. Not always neatly.

One draws a practical lesson from the conscript experience that might be considered by those eager to see a return to a draft army: conscription devalues and dehumanizes people, leaders as well as conscripts. Forced labor seems to produce an unintended negative consequence: poor leadership. Treating ordinary soldiers as objects may teach conscripts stoicism, but it teaches leaders to be arbitrary and wasteful of human resources.

I met few good leaders from 1952 to 1954.

9

When I Say Squat

The books and films about the basic military training of Americans for World War II got it right, particularly the bad books and films that rely so heavily on clichés and stereotypes. Too bad. Scribes prefer to expose, reveal, discover, uncover. I merely lived the clichés.

The barracks were the two-story wooden structures built in 1942 and 1943 "for the duration" of World War II. "For the duration" was itself one of those clichés. The barracks can be found in their beige drabness in Army camps around the country into the 21st century. The red clay surrounding the barracks from Virginia to Georgia is also real, not the fanciful distortion of a film director who had a back lot sprayed for the right color effect. Nor did the Southern sergeants disappoint. They seemed to come from central casting. Perhaps the good ole boys became the film versions that became the models for the NCOs who trained me, a kind of art imitating nature imitating art. The folksy speech patterns, swagger, and genuine contempt for us urban, northern, "whaz" asses were captured in the films and books of World War II and played out in 1952 in Camp Pickett and in that caricature of a southern town, Blackstone, Virginia. We may have been the biggest collection of Catholics and Jews seen by our captors, except for films of World Series crowds at Yankee Stadium and Ebbets Field.

Korean War weapons, clothing, and equipment were mostly World War II vintage, further contributing to a feeling of stepping onto a movie set in mid-production. The story was old hat to me and to most Americans until the early 1970s when conscription ended and military training ceased to be a shared American male experience. Nevertheless, playing out the old script was new to each of us as a personal matter.

Off the bus. Tired after a long bus ride. Hot for late September. Duffel bag on shoulder. Walk onto a company street. Yep, red clay, standard barracks. Sweat. Sun. Four ranks. A captain with a gaggle of NCOs, wolves watching raw meat. The corporal actually said it. Really. "When ah say 'shit,' ya'll squat 'n try!" Then inspection in ranks by the captain. One of us was sentenced to KP for boots not laced right. What's right? Rat races. Run into the barracks. On a whistle, run out and form four ranks. Run into the barracks. "Hurry, hurry! Ah don't wanna hear ta screen door close!" Empty your duffel bag on bed. Whistle. Load duffel bag. "Hurry, hurry, hurry y'all!" Outside with the duffel bags and beds.

We were turned over to our platoon sergeant in the open barracks. A non-Rebel, slight build, thin blond hair, bespectacled, soft spoken. His body language and demeanor said, I am a shy man with no desire to torment nor to be bothered by rookies. Later we learn that he is a veteran of close combat in Korea, waiting for the end of his term of service, no happier to be there than our saddest sack. During his lesson in how to make a bed, a wise-crack came from a New York City jokester who hadn't gotten the message. Without a blink or change in his tone of voice, the sergeant says, "Report to the mess sergeant for KP." We learned that meant a very long and joyless day in the mess hall.

The first week at Pickett consists of work details: KP, police call, patching targets. We learn to melt into the middle of formations to avoid being put on details normally taken from the left, right, front or rear. If one's eyes adapted quickly enough, scoot into the shadows. If the sergeant doesn't have your name, hide.

When the sixteen-week training program began, we had gotten accustomed to the constant shouting, hurly-burly, regimentation, and arbitrariness of generally dull-witted bullies in authority. Should I be ashamed to admit that it was fun? We ran obstacle courses, jumped fences, climbed ropes, marched, and fired rifles. I discovered a new and personal attraction in the absurd, but mostly I enjoyed the freedom of physical activity and the mindlessness of my new life. Feelings of camaraderie more than compensated for frequent inconvenience and deliberate injustices. I had asked for it, I was innocent enough to marvel at the diversity of my fellow man, and I sensed that training was just the beginning of what would be a great adventure. Directed mindless irresponsibility was new, and it was fun. It was also fun to be nineteen, healthy, and uncomplicated.

At the time, I was not fully aware that my company of some 250 souls was unusual in its composition. About half of the men were college graduates. With the exception of some 20 or 30 Seventh Day Adventists from the West, we were mostly from Boston, New York City, Philadelphia, and New Jersey. Noo Yawkers all to our southern trainers to whom the sin of being Noo Yawkers was compounded by being educated. We didn't like that, but it was less offensive to the young men of 1952 than to succeeding generations with a far more heightened awareness of fairness.

The fickleness of authority was as normal to me as the law of gravity. Things fell down. Authority was arbitrary. The Sisters of Notre Dame called the shots. Sister Mary of the Blessed Sacrament said, "Look at me when I speak to you" and, "Lower your eyes, you bold creature," and I had to comply. In a mano a mano between the athletic Corporal Flo and Sister Mary of the Blessed Sacrament, there was no doubt in my mind that she would kick his ass. Her left hook was inferior only to her right cross. Eleven nuns would devastate eleven corporals in a football game, because the nuns played dirty and had God on their side. Adults, nuns, brothers, and corporals held the whip and were in charge. None of this struck me as being unusual or unfair. It was the way of the world.

Memory filters out the ugly and retains the giggle-producing scenes from one's youth. That's probably what attracts geezers to the American Legion Hall and the VFW.

I see Jack S. Berkowitz clearly. When called by our last names, we were to respond with our first names and middle initial. His Jewish lilt and accent on the second syllable made "Jackess" of "Jack S." He was built like a beer barrel and as strong as a mule, or jackass. He attached highest priority to frequent weightlifting, saving his energy for the gym. As a consequence, work details or strenuous activities by Jack's squad found scrawny rascals wrestling with heavy objects as Jack watched and rested. Responding to my challenge, he once did thirty push-ups with 180 pounds of me sitting on his back, saying, "OK, Gole. Get off. I don't want to tire myself." When he flexed his pectoral muscles, they leaped up with a start, almost bumping his chin.

The Army was at its best in training us to use the M-1 rifle, a skill developed in the process of training millions of rookies in the previous decade. I've forgotten much over the years, but not getting my rifle and firing it. It is right up there with the other rites of passage of the early 1950s: driver's license, Selective Service Card, the right to order a beer, voting the first time, and groping in the parked car. The young of the 21st century may find these ruminations strange or quaint, but I think my feeling was shared by the other young soldiers as we accepted the nine and a half pounds of wood and steel that was the lethal M-1 rifle.

The desire to fire our rifles was whetted by the tedious process of preparing us to do so. Required to memorize the long serial number stamped on the rifle, we were punished for failing to do so immediately. Even the least mechanical of us took the weapon apart to its many bits and pieces and reassembled it so often that we could do so quickly while blindfolded. Dropping a rifle was a punishable offense. Calling it a gun was a sin. The sinner was required to run around the company formation with his rifle extended above his head while shouting at the top of his lungs:

> This is my rifle.
> This is my gun. (grabbing at his crotch)
> One is for killing.
> One is for fun.

We spent a very boring week at the PRI (Pre-Rifle Instruction) circle dry-firing our rifles, learning the proper sight picture necessary to hit a target, and rehearsing breathing and body position. Finally going to the range to live-fire our rifles was accompanied by the pomp and circumstance of a Bar Mitzvah or Confirmation. We fired from various positions at targets as much as 500 yards away, surprising ourselves by being able to hit a bull's eye that was a microscopic speck on a tiny matchbox. City slickers who had never fired a rifle qualified as experts, tempting some of us to consider for a moment the unlikely proposition that the Army knew what it was doing. In the 50 years since, there have been but several instances in which I was similarly inclined.

Two hundred-plus of us, still city slickers to the malevolent country boys who herded us about, were provided the opportunity to enjoy the delights of communing with nature in a week-long coming-out party late in basic training. The intent of duly constituted authority was to deny the apprentice heroes civilization's amenities so that we might emerge as hardened soldiers prepared to strike a blow for freedom on the field of honor. The intent was executed, however, by men whose boyhood was spent focusing the sun's rays on ants through a magnifying glass. Now we were the ants.

The adventure began with a long march, each of us carrying too much of what the Army had issued us. [Note: The combination of combat pack, cargo pack, horseshoe roll plus various belts and straps was clearly designed by someone never required to carry it. A rucksack fitted snugly to the upper back is a vast improvement, but all armies overload infantry soldiers.] Darkness fell on sweaty drones directed to set up their tents in a pattern prescribed but deliberately incomprehensible. In brief, we could do no right. The comedy began.

Soldiers tripped over tent ropes, tents fell, equipment was misplaced in the enforced blackout, and soldiers collided with one another when not tripping over tree roots. Curses filled the air as suspicion grew that the disorder was designed to illustrate our ineptness. An oaf caught me on my cheekbone with the barrel of his rifle as he floundered about, rendering me temporarily sightless and prepared to kill the next SOB coming within three feet of me. Then a whistle summoned us. Again.

We assembled in light emanating from the tent in which our keepers drank whiskey and played cards when not toying with us. Organized into patrols and sent to the four winds, we were led by a sergeant whose function was to take us into ambushes where his gleeful playmates machine-gunned us as our mood slid from anger to frustration to hopelessness. Then we did it again.

Upon our return to base camp in the wee hours, we formed four ranks to hear that we were useless. Dismissed, it became clear that we had been deliberately disoriented. We could go beddy-bye and snooze in our little houses—if we could find the damned things! The search for our country houses, left in disarray as we were hastily summoned from our nocturnal housekeeping to conduct fun and games on the heath, would have made a fire drill in a whorehouse look like a precision drill team on parade. Searching for tent and tentmate, we jack-knifed over tent ropes and tangoed with trees while gnashing teeth and engaging in some serious self-pity. But all good things come to an end.

Boots off, head on combat pack, stars in the sky, order in the universe, peace reigned and we dozed off. Hardly noticed shit-kicking music and bawdy tales in the sergeants' tent provided background to our snugness and content. Until the shrill whistle interrupted initial deep sleep. Again.

Form four ranks. Something serious had happened during our earlier nature walk. There was a thief among us! But let Sergeant Dodson explain it to you as he did to a mob of sullen Yankees fifty years ago in the dark woods of Virginia in the wee hours.

Men, I bin ast if Ahm fum ta north or ta south. Well, Ahm fum ta north an ta south: Ahm fum north Texas. In north Texas theys nuthin worst than a horse thief. In ta army they ain't nuthin worst than a barracks thief. Private Abromowitz done reported his stole salami. We don't allow no thieves in this here company. We gonna have a investigation.
(Pause. No confession.)
The man what stole Private salami gotta confess.
(Pause. No confession.)
Private Abromowitz, git up here and describe ta stole salami.
(Description followed.)
So ta salami is a foot long 'n three inches fat. Last chanst. Who stole Private Abromowitz's salami? (Pause.)
We ain't gonna rest until Private Abromowitz is satisfied.
Platoon Sergeants, form a skirmish line. Conduk a thura search a ta area.

Over 200 men floundered in the dark, some two yards between men, falling over rocks and plowing through brush for about a mile to the north. Then to the south. Then east and west. The whistle brought us back to base camp, tails dragging.

Thus spoke Sergeant Dodson:

Private Abromowitz, ta salami ain't bin found. No one in ta company done took ta salami. So ta investigation finds ta foxes et the salami while the company was trainin. But we ain't satisfied til you satisfied. We can conduk another search of ta area. Are you satified with ta finding a this here investigation? Ta foxes et ta salami.

Plaintiff Abromowitz saw his options clearly—surrender to duly authorized military good order and discipline or total alienation of the company.

He indicated his satisfaction with military justice. Sergeant Dodson, flushed with the satisfaction of having done his duty and God's will, dismissed us, went to his tent, and presumably et ta salami.

A dozen of us were told to report to the dayroom, a community room with pool table, Ping-Pong table, TV set, soda machine, and magazines, to which we were normally denied access, except to clean it. The company commander was to make one of his rare appearances. We saw him at Saturday inspections and paydays, when he counted out our cash in a ritual no longer practiced in the hi-tech Army. I don't know how he occupied himself, but training was left to our sergeants. I think he was a dummy, a World War II vet resurrected for the unpleasantness in Korea, but he was treated with respect. When he entered, we jumped to attention at the command of a sergeant who then departed. The captain told us that we were eligible for Officer Candidate School. To that point the military experience had been more the vengeance of the dullards than an attempt to attract talent, so I was one of the few nitwits who volunteered for OCS. Three or four of us remained at Camp Pickett to train troops in the company in which we had been trained.

As the next cycle of training began, it became apparent to us new trainers why our sergeants had been so hostile to us. The new crop was from Alabama. In their desire to please duly constituted military authority—that meant me—they were putty, begging to be molded by the system and its instruments. My mob had been dubious, contentious, resistant, always searching for ways to beat the system. The southern boys were docile, trusting, the Labrador Retrievers of the species Homo sapiens. Now standing in front of a platoon or company, instead of in ranks, it became clear that my job was made infinitely easier by those prepared to lubricate the system rather than sabotage it. The difference was analogous to dealing with a loving puppy instead of a trial lawyer. The greatest danger was the possibility that the new troops might pee on my boots from pleasure or lick my hand in their desire to please.

My duties were easily accomplished, allowing time for thinking, mildly subversive in young soldiers and dangerous to the Republic in senior soldiers. With pretend corporal stripes on my arm, I taught the most rudimentary soldier skills: dismounted drill (Army talk for walking), weapons assembly, physical training, preparation for inspections, and general housekeeping in the barracks routine. They were an orderly lot requiring little from me. My primary function was to have them at the appointed time at the appointed place so that the various committees could teach subjects like weapons, tactics, and first aid. Often I'd leave the troops to the tender mercies of the committees and return to the barracks where, in my newly elevated status, I had a private room. I read voraciously. That was when I read

From Here to Eternity, The Naked and the Dead, The Young Lions, and the general outpouring of World War II literature. In the background was music: "Oh Happy Day" with its happy lyric droned in a lugubrious monotone; Jo Stafford singing "You Belong to Me" and "Jumbalaya"; Patti Page singing "How Much Is That Doggie in the Window?" and "The Tennessee Waltz"; and a steady dose of shit-kicker music that grew on the Yankee boy, songs like Hank Snow's "Movin' On" and something called "Wedding Bells Are Ringin' in the Chapel," a lament on young love gone awry.

Blackstone was The Generic Southern Town on the other side of the Generic Front Gate of The Generic Army Post: a bus terminal, bars, loan sharks, dingy beaneries, and bargains for cars and car insurance. In that bus terminal in 1952, the New York boy was stunned to find signs for "colored" and "white" water fountains and toilets. Until then segregation had been a word in a vocabulary test. Tasting the cultural delights of the town was a promenade of some three hundred yards before one fell off the edge of the earth.

The bus ride from barracks to Blackstone ended in a bar whose charms matched the metropolis in which it was found. I once asked a bar maid in all innocence if pizza were available. By her reaction I saw that she had completely misunderstood my inquiry for food as an expression of my carnal desire for her body. Upon reflection I concluded that she must have heard "piece a," finishing the sentence with images of her bottom bouncing on springs. Perhaps the poor thing's verbal skills went no further than "check, please" and "uh-huh." In any event, a couple of trips to town accomplished what I would not have believed possible that first day at Camp Pickett. The barracks and red clay had become home.

After several weeks with the trainees, I decided that I'd better get to Korea before the war ended. This was probably a consequence of having too much time to think. I had been before an OCS board and was led to believe I'd be off to OCS, but I could get no further information as to where and when. I had survived an auto accident in which with three others we rolled a car at high speed; I had chewed tobacco in Richmond on pass and vomited; I had drunk beer with buddies in town and gotten sick. I was a crusty old vet of five months and ready to win the war. In February of 1953 I asked the First Sergeant to withdraw my application to OCS and send me to Korea. He did.

Part II

Khaki in Korea

. . . in which our narrator travels to faraway places with strange-sounding names, fails to win the war but leaves the Army knowing that he will miss the locker-room, barroom, foxhole feeling of being with the guys.

The Zeitgeist and My Little World

The first year of the Korean War was a war of movement and sudden reverses. In June 1950 the North Koreans attacked South Korea, the United States intervened in support of the United Nations, and UN forces barely hung on by their fingernails in the Pusan perimeter. The American amphibious landings in Inchon in September, in conjunction with an offensive from the south, destroyed much of the North Korean Army. Allied pursuit north of the 38th Parallel toward the Yalu River resulted in Chinese intervention and a series of bloody UN defeats as the Chinese attacked south. Possession of Seoul changed hands several times before a front was stabilized by the contesting forces roughly along the 38th Parallel, where the shooting had started. Armistice negotiations begun in July 1951 resulted in an armistice in July 1953.

Fighting in Korea, while at the same time providing U.S. troops to the North Atlantic Treaty Organization established in 1949, strained an army severely reduced after World War II. That explains both initial unpreparedness for war and why we were an unskilled army even after two years of combat in Korea.

Interest in the static phase of the Korean War waned as the American people, who understood "a war to end all wars" or a "Crusade in Europe," failed to understand war as a "police action" or "limited war." Samuel Hynes, in *The Soldiers' Tale: Bearing Witness to War*, was right in calling World War I, World War II, and the war in Vietnam "the myth-making conflicts that have given war the meaning it has for us." He dismisses the war in Korea as "a war that came and went without glory, and left no mark on American imagination." That sounds about right to me. I think we plunge into new adventures with great enthusiasm, but we seem to tire or become bored if success requires long-term plodding—and the blood of our young. Perhaps that explains why we are more successful in sprints than in 5K, 10K, and marathon races. Indeterminacy also frustrates us. We prefer the stop-plan-execute of American football to the free flow of soccer. We want the knowability of science in a world whose course flows by the nonrules of art and unknowability.

A hydrogen bomb was "successfully" tested on the Pacific atoll of Eniwetok in 1952. Dwight D. Eisenhower defeated Adlai Stevenson for the presidency. Gamal Abdel Nasser led an officers' coup to seize power in Egypt. The Mau Mau raised hell in Kenya. Mr. Jorgenson went into a sex-change operation George and came out Christine. King George V of England died and was succeeded by his daughter Elizabeth II.

Diary of Anne Frank, *The Invisible Man*, *The Bridge on the River Kwai*, *East of Eden*, and *Charlotte's Web* were published. *High Noon*, *Singin' In the Rain*, *Come Back Little Sheba*, and *The Quiet Man* were on the big screen. *The Seven Year Itch* was on Broadway. I sang *Don't Let the Stars Get in Your Eyes* along with Perry Como as I swapped white bucks for combat boots.

10

Wasn't That Just Yesterday?

I turned 70 years of age in 2003, fifty years and a week from that hot day I learned from a radio in a squad tent in Korea that the shooting would stop in twelve hours. Did I hear it on Gypsy, Vagabond, or Nomad, the Armed Forces Network stations we listened to when I was an indestructible infantry soldier in a rifle company?

Korea. The word releases a stream of unsorted images that flow through my mind on automatic fast-forward, stop, and reverse. Some of the pictures cluster as in a film clip; others are single still photos, just there, unconnected to a story line. Despite the years between shooting the film and the private viewing, some of the images are clearer than those from last week's events.

Among them: three weeks below the water line in compartment 4C en route from San Francisco to Yokohama to Pusan on the good ship *Montgomery Meigs* in the company of 4,500 young men, most of them seasick and homesick; a delay of two days near Tokyo to draw an M-1 rifle and fire it for zero at Camp Drake, where man-size copies of Bill Mauldin's World War II caricatures of dogfaces Willie and Joe were painted on barracks walls; over twenty-four hours of stop and go on a train with wooden benches and missing windows from Korea's southern port city, Pusan, to the 25th Infantry Division's Replacement Center as dirty children at sidings hustle pornographic pictures and cheap rings through glassless windows for GI food or funny money scrip; the chilly reception of the new guy to Company C, 27th Infantry (Wolfhound) Regiment, suggesting that he had crashed a private party; accommodating to life "on line" in bunkers furnished with rats, mice, and beds constructed from engineer stakes, commo wire, and C-ration boxes; dense clouds of tiny gnats landing on sweaty bodies in May and June; sorting out the battle noises into the background music of outgoing or distant fire, and the attention-grabbing solos of incoming and close; the first patrol, a scene from World War I, except for the rice paddies, dikes, and the all-pervasive smell of human feces; the dull stupor after being awake for 48 hours on the squad-size outpost (OP) a mile forward of the

Main Line of Resistance; momentary shock at the sudden movement of pheasants noisily departing the sandbag-lined trenches on the OP at first light; white-tail deer the size of a large dog moving in stunted vegetation in little valleys; the first dead American, a young man like me, a person with a name and round eyes; the coziness and fellow feeling of chow time, even if the meal was eaten in the great out-of-doors while sitting on one's steel helmet.

Among the still photos are young American and Korean faces: Plunkett, Pepper, Nixon, Talbot, Devine, Smitty, Romano, Um Chuk Sup, Jones, Thornton, Kim Yong Hawn, Green, Kim See Yong, Noble, Catlow, Pak Yong Wu (where are you?), Haynes, Duchaies, Ninni; bare hill tops scarred with rusting barbed wire and gashes in the earth around the military crest; much of Seoul a pile of rubble in the streets; pull, push, tap, aim, fire if the BAR malfunctions; sore hips chafed by web gear heavy with hand grenades, ammo, and water; warm wet Mickey Mouse boots making sponges of feet in winter; snow, ice, and cold—again cold; hills, always hills to climb; itchy forehead under the pile cap; neck rubbed and irritated by the olive green wool shirt; ham and lima beans, pears in a can, 101 rations, two beers a day on line; kimchee, go han, yakjew, dried squid; lister bag and water trailer; water from rice paddies doctored by iodine or halizone tablets, picking out the larger "foreign objects" fertilizing the paddies; SOS and technicolor eggs; stop the bleeding, protect the wound, treat for shock, prevent tongue swallowing; Marilyn Monroe on a red velvet blanket in an early Playboy centerfold; Sinatra in *From Here To Eternity*; Mickey Mantle; *The Caine Mutiny*; Willie Mays; *The Cruel Sea*; Duke Snyder; *Stalag 17*; Jackie Robinson.

Tunes punctuate recollection, an inseparable part of experience. "Dear, I thought I'd drop a line, the weather's fine, PS I love you"; "Dear John, oh how I hate to write . . ."; "Wedding bells are ringin' in the chapel, they're ringin' there fer you an' fer me"; "They's a big eight wheeler comin' down the track, it's your sweet lovin' daddy, he's a-comin' back, he's movin' on" modified to "hear the pitter-patter of little feet, its the 1st Division in a full retreat" or "there's an old mama-san movin' down the track with a GI baby strapped on her back." Hank Williams sings "Your Cheatin' Heart" and even city boys succumb to country music. But we city slickers rejoice in *Wonderful Town*, recalling that the Bronx is up and the Battery's down, and people ride in a hole in the ground.

Then I left the company that had treated me as a stranger and become family, returning to parents, sister, brothers, and friends a "veteran" not yet old enough to vote and still eager to do important but indeterminate things. Or maybe I could just Rock Around the Clock.

The youthful soldier still living deep in the core of me, as the outer portion loses its war with gravity and a bearded old man glares at me from the mirror, views 1953 Korea through the eyes of one who later saw infantry combat in Vietnam, gentler assignments around the world, and vast changes in himself and in his country. But the memories of the fellow who turned 20 the week after the armistice announcement linger on Korea just a bit longer than on other events. It may be that memories etched early are deeper than those that come from later life. Maybe it was the intensity. Whatever the reason, lucid memories linger.

And getting there was half the fun.

11

Fun and Games at the Replacement Center

F lying from New York to San Francisco early in 1953 was a great adventure for the nineteen-year-old working-class kid turned soldier on his way to war. It transformed him, in his mind, from naive waif to sophisticated man of the world. San Francisco was Shangri-La; going to war was exciting stuff; being nineteen is enjoyed by each of us once. For a year. Being alone, untethered, and unsupervised was liberating and just scary enough to make it exciting. God, it was good to be alive!

We landed early in the day. Since my orders required me to report to Camp Stoneman before midnight, I checked my duffel bag and AWOL bag—now called gym bag—in a locker in a bus depot to conduct a ten-hour odyssey of walking and gawking in the city by the sea. Leaving New York City in a snowstorm, the mildness of the climate, the colors of eternal spring, and the attractive young women—who ignored me—were most appealing, but the excitement of being on my own in a strange place was absolutely seductive. In almost infantile innocence, I struck out boldly on my wild adventure—to send a postcard home, to visit the library, to gaze at the fabled bridge and the vast Pacific. Perhaps I had five dollars in my pocket. My cup was full. The near-truant child climbed aboard the bus to the camp.

This camp was a mirror image of the other camps 3,000 miles away. Why not? The wooden buildings were built to the same specifications, at the same time, in the same colors, in the same relative position to one another.

REPORT HERE!

I did. Impersonal stare from behind the counter. Stuff plopped on the counter. Sign here. Move out. Next.

Armed with blanket, one each, pillow case, one each, sheets, two each, and burdened with my bags, I stumbled about in the dark and found a familiar metal bed in a familiar baby-shit yellow wooden barracks built in 1942 "for the duration." It was late. The little man had had a busy day. Sleep came quickly.

In the morning we discovered that there were only two or three of us downstairs in our barracks and none upstairs, while other buildings bulged with prime beef awaiting shipment to Korea. My companions in ignorance joined the others, but, noticing sergeants shouting the soldiers into formations, I decided to review the situation, as Oliver Twist's mentor, Fagon, would. When a sergeant organized a gaggle to march them off, I followed by a parallel street, curious to see if good things or bad things happened. They entered a mess hall to eat. That was a good thing. I ate.

Grasping the obvious, I noted that I was one of thousands of anonymous young men in identical green clothing milling about in a landscape of hundreds of barracks. I knew no one. More significantly and, most happily, no corporal or sergeant knew me. There was what one might call a control problem, which to me became a control blessing. I determined to observe activities without putting myself under the thumb of those capable of causing unpleasantness. Surely, to maintain this mob in transit, unpleasant work was needed; privates would do that work; I was a private desiring relaxation and reading while awaiting onward movement. Sergeants were the enemy of tranquility. Ergo, sergeants were to be avoided. Syllogisms were not wasted on me. Logic has a place, even in the Army.

By listening and snooping, I discovered that the names of those scheduled to ship out were posted on a board with notes indicating where and when one was to report, "bag and baggage," for the bus ride to a ship. Some men had been waiting in the replacement center for a week or more. There were indeed dirty jobs to be done by the privates foolish or slow enough to allow their identification and herding. My task, gleefully accepted as fun and games, was to remain anonymous in my private barrack so that I could nap and read. When discovered outside, drifting from library to PX to cafeteria to mess hall, I ran like hell from any sergeant who said, "Hey, you" in a tone of voice exuding authority and suggesting work. My nineteen-year-old legs ensured a pleasant stay at Camp Stoneman.

The San Francisco Bay area was lovely by day, chilly by night. My part of it was characterized by a military abounding with fat sergeants who became apoplectic when evaded by a smiling private who seemed to enjoy the chase. Perhaps that is why the Army put name tags on its soldiers after the war in Korea. In due course a nocturnal visit to the bulletin board revealed my name and the time and place of my departure from Camp Stoneman, California, and the United States of America.

Sailing the Bounding Main

roopship cruises in 1953 failed to make it to the *New York Times* Sunday Travel Section, where Caribbean and Mediterranean cruises are featured. As a matter of fact, my Pacific cruise remains right up there with root canals and mathematics exams on my short list of unpleasant events experienced over the past three-score-plus-ten years. I should have known that when the steward failed to take me to an outboard cabin on the promenade deck. Making a note to take up this oversight with the purser on the morrow, I boarded.

Compartment 4C provided snug accommodations for me and several hundred of the 4,500 souls on the *Meigs*, the ship that sprinted from San Francisco to Yokohama at nine knots per hour, a rate of speed that compares unfavorably with that of submarines in World War II. Our location below the waterline established a further kinship with submariners. We were told that the engine room was to our immediate rear, astern, as we card-carrying Rulers of the 180th Meridian say. (Be it known that our scribe has both that card and a certificate from the Domain of the Golden Dragon signed by David Jones and His Scribe.) The constant throbbing sound from that direction comforted those of us who thought the ship was sinking.

We were stacked five high in pipe racks onto which canvas was secured by ropes woven through the grommets in the canvas and around the pipes. The bottom bunk was undesirable. The only way to the upper bunks was to climb the pipes, which meant the creation of a trampoline-like effect as one's companions weighted the bottom bunk and suddenly unweighted it. Being bobbed awake in this manner was disconcerting. Even more disconcerting was vomit splashing on the floor inches from one's face. Vomit was launched by the soldiers stacked directly above at eighteen-inch intervals, and by the five men similarly stacked on the far side of the three-foot-wide aisle.

The top bunk had its hazards, chief among them facial or cranial damage caused by sudden sitting up. Sudden contact between cranium and steel

Camp Drake

The pamphlet on each seat of the passenger cars in the train from the port of Yokohama to Camp Drake were new to me, but since then I've read the message upon arrival in Japan, Germany, France, Vietnam, Italy, Korea, and other lands to which my Army has delivered my body. The message is the same:

WELCOME MR. AMERICAN AMBASSADOR TO X!

X is a land with a long history and ancient culture going back to before the invention of bubble gum. The people of X are friendly and hard working. They have long-standing and harmonious relations with the United States, except sometimes when they bombed us or sank our ships. They like polite people. You are an ambassador of the United States. Be polite. Don't pat their children on their heads, don't pat their women on their butts, respect the elderly, and don't stick your head out the train window or it will be knocked off by the telephone poles close to the tracks.

Welcome to X, Mr. Ambassador.

The cover of the booklet shows a picture of a smiling family of Xes. The insights, advice, and the picture on the cover of these publications got millions of American soldiers through their overseas tours. Scrupulous adherence got me through a long, if not distinguished, military career.

Several images of my two days at Camp Drake remain. The first is of my reaction to a show put on for our benefit as we passed through Japan on our way to war. After a month in transit, including the incomparable delight of a Pacific cruise, anything ashore short of a beating with a big stick was gleefully welcomed. We were a happy and receptive audience to the entertainment provided. Asked to greet a country and western music band with applause, my general sense of well-being turned to mad mirth as I joined in the applause for a band of a dozen Japanese, none of whom was more than five feet tall, as they filed onto the stage in Western garb, replete with silk shirts, shoe-string ties, cowboy pants, and ten-gallon hats. That sight and their rendition of melodies revered by the shit-kicker, fanned the embers of my whimsy to a bright flame. The apparition was a memorable entertainment, being as congruent as Mona Lisa watching television or driving a bulldozer. It was perfectly wrong.

Bill Mauldin's "Up Front" caricatures of Willie and Joe adorned the walls of the barracks we occupied for our two nights in Japan. That was right. Mauldin's original panels, drawn for newspapers, were lovingly reproduced and rendered man-sized. They evoked smiles then and now as I think about Willie and Joe, those icons of American infantry. They are *perfectly* right for young Americans going to war.

We zeroed our M-1 rifles with live ammunition and turned in our Sunday-go-to-meetin' clothing, keeping five sets of underwear and socks, two sets of fatigues, a field jacket, and a soft cap. Then we were issued combat and cargo packs, helmets, helmet liners, pistol belts, first aid packets, canteens, and other go-to-war equipment, including that M-1 rifle and a bayonet. The dimmest among us realized that this was serious stuff.

I accepted without a great deal of reflection that being herded about was the Army's tried and proven way of administering its individual replacements. The presumption was that "they" knew what they were doing. This was the Army that had won World War II by mobilizing over eight million men and getting them to the right place at the right time with the right stuff—more or less. I was nineteen. It was my first time.

Mature reflection upon a career including three experiences "in the pipeline" to war causes me to conclude that rarely has your scribe been lonelier than he was as an individual replacement in 1953. Dehumanization may not have been the intent, but it certainly was a consequence of a system better applied to spare parts than to human beings. It didn't change very much for the privates going to war in Vietnam. Transit by air was faster, but institutional depersonalization persisted. That's why GIs called the army The Green Machine.

We were taken by train to the port, boarded another ship for the overnight trip to Pusan, and anxiously scanned the horizon for the Land of the Morning Calm.

14

The Last Leg

hen you hear your name, sound off with your first name, middle
initial, and last four," intoned the voice coming from the ship's
public address system as we milled around on deck with rifles and
duffel bags; we were coming to the end of a trip from Yokohama to Pusan
that had lasted about twenty-four hours. The passage was tolerable because
it was brief, because we were pensive, and because of new sights and old
scents.

The early morning light revealed small boats propelled by one oar that
was also a rudder. Out of sight of land, the skills of the Korean or Japanese
fishermen impressed us. We wondered about how they navigated. We
passed small and isolated island groups consisting of tiny, remote bits of
land, each with a strip of beach, some boats, a few houses, and a mountain
looming above the signs of human habitation. The sights were exotic.

The smell was familiar. Long before we saw Korea, the scent of a rural
outhouse wafted to us, competing with fresh sea breezes and eventually winning. The smell was offensive, but within days ashore, perhaps hours, one
lost awareness of it.

"Gole."

"Henry G. 7493," I shouted back to the man with the clipboard at the
bottom of the gangplank.

We were marched on cobblestones through a port area that I would discover later to be indistinguishable from any other port area, except that a
glance at the people and signs told me I was in Asia.

The train that would take us from Pusan to the war looked all right from
the outside, except that the windows were not covered with glass—or anything else. The inside had wooden benches, like a New York City streetcar,
and they had been built for people considerably smaller than the current
passengers. In the middle of the aisle at one end of the car was a large galva-
nized metal container with water and an emerging heater in it. We recognized that standard field-mess gear, and the boxes of C-rations and five-

gallon water can told us we'd be heating cans there and eating canned food while stuffed into the cramped benches next to permanently open windows. This was another kind of Orient Express.

My initial impressions were confirmed. The train burned coal; there were lots of tunnels; remember the windows? Within a couple of hours we looked like players in a minstrel show. Indications of our relative status in our new world were the frequent and protracted periods spent on sidings as important cargo, presumably bullets and beans, chugged by. When the train stopped, children would crowd around the windows, begging, selling pornography, and using gutter English that would make a pimp blush. Alternating freezing our butts at siding stops with listening to mind-numbing clickity-clack, we spent more than twenty-four hours en route to a destination unknown to us. I cannot say if our mode of travel was a step up or down from the forty-and-eight boxcars of World War I—forty men or eight horses. Given clean hay, I think I might have preferred the earlier windowless travel to the 1953 trip in a mobile refrigerator in frozen Chosen.

The arbitrary decision by a functionary at the 25th Tropic Lightning Infantry Division (the best division in the best army, etc.) pleased me as it was announced to us in formation: "The following named enlisted men, change in MOS from 1666 (medic) to 1745 (rifleman)." I was an infantryman.

On to the 27th Infantry Wolfhound Regiment (the best regiment in the best division, etc.). To the 1st battalion (the best—you get the idea). Directed to Charlie Company, I was spared "the best" incantation and sent to the 1st platoon. Told to report to SFC Lemper, last tent on the right, I trudged through mud in the rain with rifle, duffel bag, steel pot, and other bits and pieces to the designated tent. My clumsy entrance was greeted with a growl, "Close the BLANKING flap!" The adjective was alliterative. Variations of the multipurpose stem served as gerund, verb, noun, and adverb. I did as directed. I was home.

The train ride following the crossing of the interminable Pacific and constant movement, made me eager to gather some moss. Any home would do. The bunkers and tents of the following months were a vast improvement on the means of getting to the war, primarily because bonding with the men of my rifle squad and platoon was infinitely better than the isolation of travel as an individual replacement. That suggests that I am a social critter, who attaches higher value to social than physical comfort, a thesis tested and confirmed often in the half-century beginning with my preparation for war in Korea.

15

That First Night on Line

The amplified voice came out of the darkness to the front, beyond the trench line, bunkers, and barbed wire. "Welcome Chary Company! Welcome Woofhounds! Her-ro Rootenant Kramer!"

Our efforts to ensure the secrecy of the move from the reserve position to the main line of resistance came to naught. We had moved at night, torn all Tropic Lightening shoulder patches from our uniforms and covered the truck bumper markings with tape or mud, but the Chinese welcomed us nevertheless as the First Platoon led C Company forward to relieve the ROK Marines below Hill 155, between Panmunjon and the Han River. The nineteen-year-old replacement, who didn't even know the names of all the squad members, was struck by the enemy's identification of the regiment, company, and one of the platoon leaders. By name! The new guy didn't know that leader of one of the other platoons in C Company. The enemy did.

Nothing in my reading, basic training, or the brief combat familiarization before we moved up prepared me for the battlefield noise and pyrotechnics that characterized night combat in Korea in the early spring of 1953. Soon I would find it as normal as the vibration unflinchingly experienced by people living next to railroad tracks. But not on that first night.

The rookie soon determined that the repeated booms to the rear were caused by friendly outgoing artillery, and that the thunks behind us were our mortars. It did take some time, in the absence of instruction, to realize that not each illumination round fired meant that some good guy saw a bad guy in the neighborhood. The lazily rocking flares suspended from parachutes did shadow tricks. They were fired irregularly by friendly mortars and artillery to reveal the enemy—and to keep rookies wide-eyed!

And why didn't someone tell me about the quad fifties? In the coming days I would see the half-track with four .50 caliber machine guns parked on the reverse slope of a small hill near the mess tent. But on that first night I heard the nerve-jangling scream of four heavy machine guns firing from nearby, and I didn't know what—or more significantly, whose—they were.

Whether theirs or ours, I assumed that they were engaging an observed target uncomfortably close to me. I didn't know that in modern combat the overwhelming mass of fire is directed at unseen suspected enemy locations, not at observed targets. The source of my immediate discomfort, the quad fifties, fired indirect fire to harass the enemy, interdict his movement, and terrify me. Their target was probably a trail junction or a bridge used by the enemy. Fifty years after the event I am angry that my chain of command failed to warn the new guys that the God-awful scream of that weapon firing directly overhead was no danger to us.

Anderson, Amborn, and I, all new guys, were put in the same bunker, a clear case of the blind leading the blind. None of us had the foggiest notion of what was going on. One was from Minnesota, the other from Wisconsin, and they each really said things like, "Throw the cow over the fence some hay," and not just to amuse the city slicker. One of us peered to the front through the aperture of the bunker, one of us watched the cave-like entrance to our new home, and the third sat glumly between the other two wishing the sun up.

Our squad leader came by once to tell me that I would man a machine gun in another bunker from 2 to 4 a.m. At the appointed time I was awakened and led stumbling in the strange trench to the appointed place to relieve another soldier. In the next two hours I stared at no-man's-land over a .30 caliber machine gun, a world of concertina wire, and spooky shadows intermittently distorted by light from descending parachute flares. The swinging flares created an eerie light show and loss of depth perception, almost sea sickness. Every thirty minutes, I whistled into the sound-powered telephone to give a negative report. Then I took a prisoner.

Hearing stealthy movement in the trench to my left, I moved back from the machine gun with my M1 rifle to a dark corner of the bunker. My prey never knew such helplessness as I pounced and slapped him against the sandbag wall of the trench! Hands behind his back, my bayonet in his lower ribs, he froze in terror as I reported my victory on the telephone.

"Ask him for his name," directed the disembodied voice of my platoon sergeant.

"Kim Yong Hawn," I reported.

"Congratulations. You just captured a KATUSA from your platoon."

Kim, one of many Kims, was a Korean Attached to the United States Army. I released him, allowing him to complete his appointed rounds as trench guard that night and to spread the word about the dangerous new guy in the First Platoon. Had Kim known, he could have added that the new guy had had no training on the .30 caliber Browning machine gun, had never before used a sound-powered telephone, and was seriously rethinking the wisdom of his desire to experience war. It wasn't what he expected.

Anderson survived his combat tour in Charlie Company unscathed, and

Kim was alive and well when I returned home from Korea after the guns stopped in July of 1953. But Amborn lost a leg to a mine while on patrol about a month after our first night on line.

I retired from the U.S. Army in 1988 after a career that provided many adventures in faraway places with strange-sounding names, but that first night on line is etched more deeply in my memory than other nights, perhaps because it told me how not to treat soldiers. The "old guys" in that Army took pleasure in watching the "new guys" reacting to the otherworldliness of a dark place where men killed one another.

Where was the leadership? How, in God's name, had I found my way to that place where "friends" were as hazardous to me as the enemy?

16

Rios

My platoon sergeant made me tent guard. I think he did so because I was the newest replacement in the rifle company on that day in the late winter of 1953 as the other men went to chow. When one of the others returned, I could go to the mess tent for lunch.

I looked for something to read the way a thirsty man seeks water. I was without a pocket book, an unusual circumstance. Early in basic training I had learned to keep something to read available for the frequent waits that characterize a soldier's life. On one of the fifteen cots in the squad tent was a newspaper. I found myself reading *El Diario*, a Spanish language newspaper. My three years of high school Spanish was up to the task.

Ismael Rios Rodriguez, returning from lunch to relieve me, noticed what I was reading.

"You understand?"

"Yeah. Most of it."

"Read to me."

I did.

"Tell me in English."

I did. Reading was within my competence, but little emphasis was placed on conversational skills when one studied foreign languages in the 1950s.

We became pals. He taught me the BAR and survival fieldcraft, but most of all he taught me a spontaneous generosity. On a small outpost—OP to GIs—he drank half of the cocoa he brewed. Then he looked for me. The other half was mine.

By day, as we improved our positions by deepening trenches, filling sand bags, and checking commo wire, barbed wire, and mines, the distinctive sound of incoming caused me to drop my shovel and dive over a trench for a bunker entrance. Rios and I arrived at the entrance at the same time, in a tangle of arms and legs. We looked at one another and laughed as a mortar round landed close to the bunker.

Lemper, the platoon sergeant, visited the OP. He demonstrated his circa thirty-year-old maturity and World War II experience with a very dumb joke. Unknown to us, he had removed most of the black powder from a hand grenade. While we were assembled in a circle for a pointless pep talk, he pretended to drop the grenade accidentally, shouting, "Grenade!" He laughed as we dove for cover, and picked up the grenade. There was just enough powder stuck in the grenade, the way some flour or cement sticks to a paper sack, to cause a small explosion, enough to cut his hand. His little joke was a demonstration of irresponsibility and incompetence typical, unfortunately, of our "leadership." Rios was hit, but his skin was not broken.

One night we had to fire from the OP in support of a friendly patrol in contact. It was in this time of immediate need that the "leader" learned that the machine gun oriented in the right direction could not depress sufficiently to bear on the enemy some 500 meters away. Obviously that gun could not be brought to bear on an enemy much closer. Rios addressed the situation by taking up the slack with fire from his BAR, a weak substitute for the firepower of the Browning light machine gun.

One day on the same OP, someone bullied Rios, I took up his cause, bleeding on and punching the bastard who had rewarded my nobility by hitting me with an entrenching tool. At the aid station where a few stitches repaired the damage to my head, the assumption was that I had been hit in a mortar attack on the OP. I "corrected" the situation by saying the injury was the result of a fall on a shovel.

One night while our squad was on line, we returned to friendly front lines from a badly led patrol exhausted and soaked in sweat. Rios, Anderson, John Plunkett, and I fell to the ground near a lister bag, a water bag. Rios said to me, "Buddy, get me some water." Tired and irritated, I said something brusque. The voice repeated the request adding, "I mean it, Gole. I can't move."

I got the water.

Memories of moments like that brought me back to the Army eight years later, after a seven-year break in service. Of all the joys in life, one is the elemental fact that regular and sustained proximity to good men is supremely important to me. Men like Plunkett. And Anderson. And especially Rios, a scrawny native of Puerto Rico who was my teacher of military and survival skills in accented English and the personification of buddy, mate, and Kamerad in an unaccented universal language.

One night we almost died together.

17

The Gas Cylinder Retaining Pin Assembly, Sir

ong after the dawn ending the first night on line in Korea in 1953, the same fellow—in a slightly used body with a few miles and a bunch of combat dawns on it—can testify that morning in combat is salvation. Puppies, birds, chipmunks, and young soldiers greet the new day like the frisky critters they are. This frisky private was greeted one dawn with a pronouncement by his platoon sergeant. "You're a big kid. You are now a BAR man. Rodriguez, teach him the BAR." With that he tossed me a weapon twice the weight of my M-1 rifle.

Rodriguez, at 135 pounds, was the other BAR man in my squad and clearly not a "big kid." He taught me the intricacies of the 19.4 pound Browning Automatic Rifle and became my friend. So did my BAR.

The three of us went on dozens of patrols together, manned a squad-size outpost for four weeks, shared cigarettes, coffee, goodies, stories of home, photographs, and dreams. I took care of my BAR, and Rodriguez took care of me. Half of all he had became mine, and I reciprocated as I learned the meaning of camaraderie. We also shared filth, fatigue, and fear as we looked out for one another and became veteran combat soldiers before we could vote.

Rodriguez noticed it as our patrol prepared to cross the Line of Departure as night fell. As we approached the opening in the barbed wire, he touched my elbow and pointed to a hole in the gas cylinder assembly under the barrel, a hole that should have been filled by the smallest part of the BAR with the longest name, a little pin with a crescent-shaped handle. My weapon was old and severely worn. I cleaned it at least once each day, and no one knew how long, nor how many soldiers had rubbed and oiled it, nor how many wars it had seen. The part was so worn that it had fallen from its place without permission. It had been there an hour earlier when I scrupulously checked it and the rest of my patrol equipment.

I reported the fact to our platoon leader, Lieutenant Cook, who was the patrol leader this night, and I asked if I could dash to a bunker where I knew I could borrow a pin.

"What is it?"

"The gas cylinder retaining pin assembly, sir." He didn't know what that meant, but he looked at his watch.

"No," he said.

"I could borrow another weapon."

"No. Join Sergeant Martell and the alert squad."

That was that. An alert squad was held ready in a bunker "on line" to reinforce whenever a patrol was out in no-man's-land. Cook didn't want to delay the patrol. Charlie Company patrol leaders hit the Line of Departure on the dot! I joined Sergeant Martell, the alert squad leader, in his bunker, as directed.

The night was uneventful. For me. The patrol, however, was ripped by an artillery round rigged and detonated by the enemy as a mine. Amborn lost a leg. Two others were slightly wounded by steel splinters, and another was temporarily blinded by the flash. The platoon medic, a crude and simple man, saved the life of the amputee by somehow finding a vein, getting saline solution into his bloodstream—thus preventing severe shock—and supervising the movement of the badly wounded man back to friendly front lines. All of this was accomplished by a young conscript in darkness, dirt, and confusion as the patrol prepared for an enemy assault to exploit the shock of the detonation. The enemy did not assault. I have no idea why the alert squad was not committed. It existed for that purpose. The patrol returned to the company with its wounded.

In the morning Rodriguez came by so that we could walk the mile to the company mess tent together and talk. I had greeted the dawn in youthful aliveness before he arrived, and I had scraped off the peach fuzz that passed for manly whiskers. As we walked and talked he told me what had happened, concluding, "Buddy, you got eight lives left." My position in the formation as we had rehearsed it on the previous afternoon was taken by Amborn.

The God who notices the sparrow falling to the ground also notices the falling gas cylinder retaining pin assembly and protects puppies, chipmunks, and young soldiers, at night and in the dawn.

18

Listening Post

I t went about like this.

"Gole, come with me. You gonna take out a four-man LP tonight. I'll show ya where to set up."

I grabbed my Browning Automatic Rifle and followed my squad leader down the steep hill to where it met a road some 300 meters below the outpost. The road roughly paralleled the MLR, the Main Line of Resistance, known to civilians as "the front." It was about a mile by foot and 1,000 meters, if you were a bird, from the road to the MLR.

At the road we turned around to face the OP that had been home for more than a week.

"See that little knoll 50 meters off to the left of the trail we just came down?"

He pointed. It was close, about thirty to forty meters above the road and not quite as high as the OP.

"Yeah."

"See the path to it from the road?"

I looked off to my left and saw the path.

"Yeah."

"Take that path to the knoll. That's your LP. There's commo wire up there on the ground. You can't see it from here. Take TLs with you. Hook the double-E-8 to the WD-1."

TLs were a kit consisting of pliers for cutting wire and a folding knife used to strip the black rubbery-plastic protective covering from the wire underneath. It attached to one's belt. An EE-8, called "double-E-Eight," was a field telephone in a form-fitting canvas bag with a carrying strap. WD-1 was black commo wire designed for communications, but GIs used it for dozens of purposes, including fabricating beds in bunkers by weaving the wire to engineer stakes to form mattresses.

"OK."

"Go through the OP wire at 2200. Return at first light after a commo check with me."

"Got it."

"After you hook up, gimme a commo check. Then commo checks every thirty minutes on the hour and half-hour."

"OK."

"Take Andy, Amborn, and Adams."

"Hah. Triple A and the G-man."

"What?"

"Our names. The guys are all A for Able, and I'm the G-man."

He wasn't known for his quick wit. In fact, he was a stupid son-of-a bitch.

"Mission?"

"What?"

"What's my mission?"

He gazed at me to indicate that I was the dumb SOB.

"Y'know, LP."

I nodded sagely.

"Right."

When we returned to the OP, I told the guys about our nocturnal mission, resenting the fact that the squad leader hadn't told them that they were going and who was in charge. We were all privates, new guys. I had been on line for a couple of weeks, on several patrols and on the OP for awhile. I guess that made me a veteran. But the squad leader simply failed to understand the most rudimentary aspects of both human nature and something called the chain of command. He should have told the others what was expected of them and who was boss. Little did we know that Amborn would lose a leg within a week or so.

At 2200 we pulled the concertina wire aside, passed through the opening and closed it, starting down the hill. We heard the men still on the OP placing tin cans and flares on the concertina wire.

It wasn't a bright night, but it was light enough to find the road, then the path to the LP on top of the knoll, and then a shallow hole with room for the four of us. One learned to read the shades of darkness from gray to black and blacker.

I gave each of the other three men a segment of our perimeter to observe and cover by fire, indicating left and right limits by pointing to rocks, bushes, and trees. I gave myself the position closest to the road, since I could do the most damage to the enemy with my BAR.

I adjusted the height of the bipods and, burying them just a bit in the soft soil that formed a lip around our hole, I sighted left and right along the road, noting again the bushes, rock outcroppings, and trees to my front. The idea was to cover the target area without exposing myself to fire. Removing two twenty-round magazines from the twelve in my belt, I placed them next to my weapon within easy reach of my right hand. Andy had another eight magazines that he carried for me. All twenty-one—one in the BAR, twelve I carried, and Andy's eight—were loaded with nineteen rounds each to spare the magazine springs. Rios Rodriguez and John Pepper had taught me that. Then I placed two hand grenades a little to the right of the magazines.

I connected the phone to the wire and made a commo check, telling the squad leader we were in place. Loosening my belt so that no magazines were under my belly, I scrunched around on my poncho to find a comfortable place. The other guys settled in without conversation. I had told them the form for the night on the LP: two guys on for the three hours from 2200 to 0100 and two guys on from 0100 to 0400. Since it would get light shortly after 0400, all four of us would be bright-eyed and bushy-tailed as we prepared to leave the LP for the OP at the end of our little mission. That was the deal. The night was pleasantly mild after a hot day. It would be damp during the night as it had been for a couple of May and June weeks, but we were grateful that it wasn't raining. Andy and I took the first shift.

I had made the 1230 commo check and was looking forward to a little snooze-time at 0100 when I heard the unmistakable sounds of infantry troops on the move at night. A combination of boots on the ground, trouser legs rubbing, weapons brushing against the belts and straps of canvas equipment-carrying gear with canteens, ammo pockets, bayonet scabbards, first aid pouches, grenades, and commo wire. Steel helmets made contact with brush or trees, and, from time to time, a whispering voice might be added to the other sounds. None of this carried very far, but once heard, one immediately recognized the sound of combat troops on the move.

Andy heard what I heard, but the other two men were sleeping. I touched each of them carefully, waking them without startling them. Then I indicated my intent by "dumb-show" for each man, cocking my head in the direction of the sounds with a hand cupped behind my ear. They responded with nods of assent. I put my finger to my lips. More nodding. I took a hand grenade, pointing to each man and motioning as though to throw. Nods. I touched each man's M-1 rifle, shaking my head the no-no way. Nods. They got it.

Reasonably assured that they understood my intent to initiate contact by tossing our grenades and not revealing our position with the flash and bang of rifle fire, I whispered onto my field telephone, hoping that the rest of the U.S. Army was not sleeping.

"OP, LP."

"OP."

Someone in the Army was awake. It was my squad leader on the OP.

"Got troops on road. Maybe thirty, forty."

Pause.

"Are you sure?"

Pissed at the knucklehead, I wanted to reach through the wire and strangle the dumb son-of-a-bitch who put me in harm's way and now wanted to play Twenty Questions. I controlled the impulse.

"Troops on the road. Moved from your right to your left. Now stopped below LP."

Pause.

"Wait. I'll contact platoon."

The platoon headquarters was on the MLR, a mile to the rear.

Longer pause as troops below us stirred a bit. My finger to lips. Nods.

"LP."

"Yeah?"

"Platoon says ain't supposed to be friendlies there. Checkin' with company. Wait."

Company was about a half mile behind the bunker and trenches of the MLR. Since nobody on the LP had a date that morning or tickets for a ballgame, we waited. Meanwhile, I felt for my magazines and hand grenades and sighted along my weapon to be sure I could bring effective fire on the men below us. The others took my cue, placing grenades in handy places and checking their weapons.

"LP?"

"LP."

"Company says they ain't ours. Checkin' with battalion. Wait."

"Roger. Waiting."

While waiting, I played generalissimo. My four against their forty, if they were bad guys, was not as bad as it looked at first blush. We had a lot going for us. Surprise, for one thing. We could put a dozen grenades on them to begin the fight. Tossing the grenades downhill was easy, and they'd bounce around among the soldiers below, causing all kinds of confusion and sudden terror out of nowhere. They wouldn't know our exact location. By the time they figured that out, I was sure I could personally kill most of them with my BAR. And the other guys firing M-1s at this short range would tear them some new assholes. The poor bastards were caught in the open, and we were in a hole. They'd need lucky shots to hit us, and I was betting they could not organize an assault on us. Even if they did, they would die as they tried to rush us. Uphill. And they'd probably worry about our artillery and mortars. Yeah, I liked the odds of the four against forty, all things considered. We'd kill or wound all of them, probably without ill effects on us. Except for peeing in our pants. All things considered, I'd rather be in college sweating out an exam.

This was my unspoken estimate of the situation. Either grenades and then all weapons, or grenades and call in artillery and mortars. Hmm. Kinda close. A friendly mistake could easily do us more harm than the enemy might.

Decision was spared by the call from the OP.

"LP?"

"LP."

"Don't shoot! Don't shoot! Do you read?"

"Yeah. Don't shoot. They are good guys."

"Roger. It's a patrol from B Company. They wandered into C Company area. Don't shoot."

"Roger. Out."

I had no intention of revealing the LP to the lost souls below. In due course they moved back to the right, got home safely, took wives, and spend weekends with their grandchildren.

That was my first experience in combat leadership. I learned that in an environment of fear, tension, fatigue, and violence, it is as easy to have one's body perforated by a friend as it is to be injured or killed by a foe. Making mistakes in the dark while scared shitless is the norm, not an aberration. Reentering friendly front lines is always a very tricky situation, since you are approaching from the enemy direction, and sleepy nineteen-year-olds have automatic weapons in their hands with license to kill. More specifically, the testosterone-laden teenager, more id-driven than candidate for canonization in any event, has license to kill me. If a kid squeezes off a burst in the middle of the night, almost certainly his playmates will join in, making me the target of what seems to be most of the U.S. Army. One Nervous Nelly can do that. So can poor land navigation and stupid pills.

Those who are snug abed, as their young kill one another in faraway places, can pontificate about fratricide or friendly fire and conduct investigations in cozy rooms, but it has always been a part of the dangerous game called combat. One suspects that the number of incidents of fratricide reported is a small drop in a large bucket. For a good reason. Combat soldiers are inclined to accept it as a normal cost of doing their abnormal business. Despite the many undeniable advantages of hi-tech and coalition warfare, one of the costs is that the same systems that produce impressive results will also multiply the effects of mistakes in combat. The constant is that friendlies will kill friendlies.

A Teenager's Theory

Sitting on an outpost in Korea in the company of a dozen other teenagers—the speed bump to a billion Chinese menacing the U.S. Eighth Army—I was aware of death at an early age. I was not without imagination. And I read books and newspapers. The prospect of my mortality flitted through my mind as something quite real.

There were moments in basic training during which killing and being killed ceased to be abstractions. That was, after all, the purpose of combat training. Sometimes it worked.

Throwing that first "live" hand grenade got my undivided attention. After the blah-blah of safety instructions, each trainee was required to pull the pin and hold the grenade, squeezing the spoon until the safety NCO told us individually to release it and get rid of the evil thing by throwing it and ducking behind the logs and sandbags of a bunker. It was a technique like so many military skills: simple, but you had to get it just right—or pay an enormous price. A neighbor back home in Queens Village, my father's drinking buddy, Larry Mahoney, had two hooks for hands and one glass eye, souvenirs of his World War II hand grenade training. Larry was much on my mind whenever I held a grenade in my hands. This was not theory.

Bayonet training consisted of mastering a ballet culminating with the bludgeoning of the enemy's head and face with butt strokes before finishing the job by slashing with the bayonet and pressing it into his abdomen, con gusto. This was rough stuff, not entirely foreign to the city slicker, but he had never wrung a chicken's neck or killed a rabbit. The disparity between knuckle drill, punching and kicking in a fight, and the use of what Victorians called "cold steel" was, in the vernacular of 1950s soldiers, serious shit.

Training on the rifle range with an M-1 rifle was the essence of infantry soldiering for millions of us from 1940 to 1960 as we sought accuracy. The live combat assault courses were visceral. Firing at close range kicked rocks and earth about and showed the shooter the effects of his shooting in a way that a hole in a paper target did not. May God forgive me, it was also great fun.

Conversation with my basic training platoon sergeant made a profound impression on me that I recalled frequently as I had my experiences in wars. He had recently returned from Korea where he had served as a combat medic with the infantry. He wanted to tell us about his experiences to help us, but he knew not how. We city brats saw a slight, quiet, and inarticulate man from upstate New York, but we had no idea what went on in his head. He wanted to help.

I became teacher's pet because I tried so hard to be a good soldier. He had me marching the platoon to training and acting as an important fellow, a corporal. One day he summoned me to his room, one of the two cadre rooms on the second floor of the standard two-story barracks that offered their occupants some privacy. (We trainees slept in open bay areas, some twenty-five downstairs and twenty-five upstairs. Toilets were also doorless: one section for showers; one for sinks and urinals; one for commodes.) He told me to be seated. In a very agitated and tongue-tied manner, he expressed his concern for our lack of seriousness. He said what happens in close combat, how cold it was, how frightening. He said that "we" had to do something about it. Then he reduced his message to a few very intense words, staring at something far away. "Gole," he said, "you . . . you . . . could reach out . . . and TOUCH THEM!" He meant the enemy in Korea. I hadn't the foggiest idea what to do about his concern, but it was apparent that he cared about us, his innocent charges, very much. He was permanently marked by his flirtation with early demise. Scary stuff, I thought, in my role as recruit, confessor, witness, and/or shrink.

Between basic training and arrival on the outpost, I'd had other insights into the dangers ahead. Some of the men on the boat were returning veterans of Korea or World War II, and I listened to their versions of the truth of combat. Being delivered to Charlie Company like a package from home focused attention on the business at hand. Moving up on line that first night introduced me to battle noises and concentrated all senses on here and now. I learned to distinguish sounds as dangerous, benign, and neutral, as have all infantrymen before and since, and I learned when to scramble for cover and when to note and ignore the nonthreatening noises in the background. As the days passed, I experienced for the first time the death in combat of a young person I knew. He was on patrol near my OP, and I saw the firefight with a Chinese patrol as a kind of light show. My BAR position was close to the squad command post with our radio and telephone, so I could monitor the talk between the patrol leader and our company commander as I watched the exchange of tracers and heard the differences between friendly and enemy infantry weapons. We fired in support of our patrol. The mine injuries on patrol were recent. Dr. Johnson once noted that the prospect of hanging tends to focus one's attention. These events got my attention. I knew the KIA and the WIA. I realized I might die.

That's when I developed Gole's boyish theory of concentric circles, a theory that has successfully escaped discovery for almost a half-century. Four weeks on an OP is a lot of time for introspection. The nights were long as I alternated standing and sitting in the notch in the trench that was my home away from home. My task was to cover the entrance to the OP with my Browning Automatic Rifle. At night we dragged concertina wire across the path that led to the OP, to which we attached flares and tin cans as early warning devices. Of course the wind and the plentiful rats could and did set off the warning devices, so periodically during the night my heavy eyelids would uncover eyeballs bigger than pizza pies, scanning the front like laser beams to uncover hordes of Chinese soldiers on their way to Pusan, San Francisco, and, their final objective, the George Washington Bridge and (the few) New York virgins. The monotony of staring at the likely avenue of approach into our position was relieved by the trench guard making his rounds, the tinkling of C-ration cans—either wind-, rat-, or Chinese soldier-induced—popping flares, exchanges of indirect fires between friendly and enemy artillery and mortars over my head, and reflection on my impending death. From time to time a firefight nearby would enliven our dull domesticity, but most of the time it was simply boring. The wag who said that combat was 99% tedium and one percent terror had it about right in this instance. Abundant time devoid of homework, dating, and sports—my civilian activities—permitted me to work on my theory. Now it can be told.

Premise: Henry G. Gole dies. So what? First consequence? Easy. The Baltimore Catechism was clear on that. Since I hadn't had time to be a really major league sinner, I would "be happy with Him" in the next life, in Paradise. For eternity. (Now that's a long time!) Given a few more years, I might have put this outcome in doubt. Lucky me, to die young. OK, so I'm happy in The Big Fish Fry in the Sky. I've got it made in the shade. But what does my death matter to others? This gets tricky, but I had enough time to work it out, so take notes. I estimated how everyone I knew might react to my death, and I put them in the appropriate circle. My first thought was what a fine fellow I was, rather like Jud in the musical *Oklahoma*, who sings of himself, "Poor Jud Is Dead," regretting that he's "a-molderin' in his grave." NOW they'll miss him! NOW they'll miss ME! The business at hand, since I was safely tucked away in Paradise, was: How is the world taking the bad news? The letters have gone out, the phone calls have been made, the body is in transit to the States, and the soul has been delivered to my Maker. (Later, in another war, a friend and I wrote a singing telegram death notice for Special Forces KIAs to be delivered by a leggy dancer, jiggling butt and bosom for grieving loved ones. It opened with the kind of movie music that anticipates really big scenes and an upbeat happy-talk announcement: "Your son is dead!" But 1953 was a gentler time, and I was a gentler piece of work.)

A girl who said she was going to love me forever got married a few months after I left New York to defend freedom. She opted out of the inner circles. *Sic transit Gloria mundi.* Let's take it from the top, I thought, the way Galileo, Newton, and Einstein would, and, like Plato, Augustine, and Aquinas go about the truth business. Who would remember me for how long? That would determine relative centricity, with the weepiest and most shattered in the inner circle, near me, the star of this production. (What the hell, it was my production!)

By the time I worked it all out, I placed my mother and my sister in the first circle. They would remember the dearly departed me on my birthdays, at Christmases, on anniversaries of my death, and when photos of me fell out of the album as they posted new ones of grandchildren (as yet unborn). That would go on for ten years or so, maybe even longer when something triggered their memories of me, such as someone failing a math test or bed-wetting. Then I worked through a short list—those who didn't make the cut were and remain damned ingrates!—of people who would remember good old me for a couple of years. Maybe two to five. Then I assigned others to the one-year package, considering bonus points for tears, dewy-eyed toasts at The Track, The Hatbox and Kelly's—bars in the old neighborhood. I assigned points for letters of condolence to the bereaved, but I gave up on the point system for technical reasons. For example, I couldn't decide if my mourners should get more points for thinking of me while they were drunk or sober. *"In vino veritas,"* said the Romans, but who wants to be remembered by drunks hanging out in New York bars? And how could I know if the writers of condolences were sincere, just doing it pro forma or to cadge free beers from one of my brothers? Should I give half-points? The lists of people who noted my demise with equanimity or feigned sorrow was much longer than those positioned in the first and second circles. The bastards! Then came those who were indifferent but basked in the reflected glory of the fallen young hero, saying, "Hey, I knew him!" as they read the four-line obit in the *Long Island Daily Press*, complete with misspelling of the family name and an incorrect count of siblings.

I think the concentric circle exercise of the nineteen-year-old me, only slightly exaggerated in the retelling, was useful in my later calling as a professional soldier. Realism never goes out of style. Only a handful of people notice the passing of a soldier, especially a young one whose footprints are few and shallow, but that's OK. A soul leaves no footprints, everybody dies, and the point is to die well, with and for friends.

20

Report to the Company Commander

An arm and a head came through the flap of the squad tent of the third squad, first platoon, somewhere in reserve in Korea. The head said,

"Gole, report to the orderly room."

"What's up?"

"Dunno," said the retreating voice.

I reviewed my most recent sins as I brushed down my well-worn fatigues, gave my combat boots a quick wipe, and plopped my cap (field, one each) on my head. Soldiers were not summoned to the orderly room for social calls. Ten-to-one something bad was about to happen, I thought, as I made a bee-line for the tent that was our headquarters, the workplace of the company commander, first sergeant, and company clerk. Any one of them might have sent the runner for me. I couldn't think of any gross transgressions against good order and discipline, great crimes against humanity, infringement or violations of the laws of the United States, or spitting on a sidewalk. Recently. But delay would imply guilt. It would never do to keep the captain waiting.

I banged on the door of the orderly room. This tent was "winterized," meaning it had a wooden floor and a door.

"Come!"

I did, and the first sergeant, noting my presence, said:

"Report to the company commander!"

Hmmm? I was expected. No fanfare. No indication of mood by voice, nor smile, nor scowl. I was still in uncharted waters as I navigated, hat literally in hand, to yet another door, leading to the captain's inner sanctum. I banged, the "enter" came, and I reported "as directed." The company commander looked up and said,

"At ease."

A good sign. Ass-chewing form would have been to keep me uncomfortably at the position of attention.

My only impressions of the captain to this point were that he was a digni-

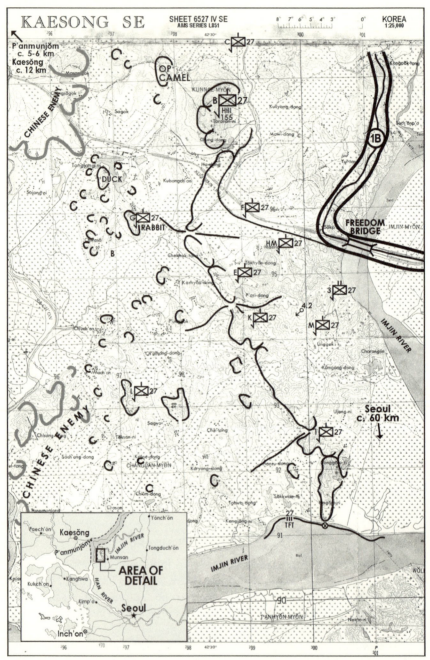

KAESONG SE   SHEET 6527 IV SE
AMS SERIES L851
KOREA
1:25,000

In 1953, the author summered on or near OP CAMEL as a BAR man, C Co, 27th Infantry. When
not on OP or on patrol, Hill 155 was left and CAMEL to the front of Lakeview Manor, our bunker.

Map, courtesy of U.S. Army Military History Institute. Graphic adaptations by Jim Kistler, USAWC, Visual Information Division.

fied man, not a member of the apoplectic school of military ranting, a West Pointer and a ripe twenty-nine. He really was "the Old Man."

In the early 1950s, NCOs led soldiers in the hands-on tasks, and officers did the thinking, such as it was. Soldiers had very little direct contact with the company commander—unless they screwed up very badly. The First Sergeant had great authority and generally kept anything short of homicide from the officers.

Apprehension evaporated as the captain's demeanor and tone indicated that I would not be going to jail. Now.

I relaxed as he explained a bit of military small print previously unknown to me. The Army selected some men from the ranks to attend the United States Military Academy at West Point. He had checked my scores on the standard tests administered to all soldiers upon entry on active duty, and, he said, he had been observing me. After discussing me with his officers, he thought I was a likely candidate. What did I think of that?

The truth was that the sudden transition from possible miscreant to potential West Point cadet caught me off balance. I bought time on the principle that clinching was OK if you caught a good shot and needed time to clear your head.

"Sir, do I need to decide now?"

The captain smiled at that, aware that the callow lad had been ambushed by a burst of rationality in the midst of the almost total arbitrariness of life in the lower strata of a rifle company.

"No. No hurry. Think it over, and come back to talk with me."

"Yes, sir!"

Salute, about face, march out. Back to the tent to think.

The young man, now a sergeant who had just turned twenty, recognized a once-in-a-lifetime opportunity and had some heavy thinking to do. That night I reviewed the bidding that led to a decision duly reported to the captain. Time blurs memory (generally making the young us better than we were), but I am quite certain that I pondered as follows. Flattered to be the only man from the company given this special opportunity, I reasoned that while I knew a bit about the Army, I knew little of life beyond it and school. I knew that I wanted to read literature, philosophy, and history in a place like Princeton. I wanted freedom, to chase girls, to escape the heavy-handed control of others, to sample *la dolce vita*. The picture in my head of life as a cadet at West Point included other young men regularly screaming at me, I saw myself feeding someone a knuckle sandwich. I declined.

My decision appears ironic in retrospect. Ultimately, I spent a career in the Army. In 1953 I knew there was no way I could afford an education at Princeton; I knew even then that I really liked the powerful fellow-feeling of life as a soldier. After seven years, a college degree, two graduate degrees, and three years of teaching in a high school, I returned to the bosom of the Army.

What the hell. I was twenty in 1953.

21

4 IQ

Shortly after the shooting stopped in Korea in July 1953, the Army decided to bring all soldiers to at least 4th grade educational level. I committed the common sin of generalizing on my personal experience by assuming all Americans could read and write. Not so. Not only was I wrong, but, interestingly, some of the men exposed as illiterates were not the duller soldiers in Charlie Company.

Red, a mortar man in the weapons platoon (not the mess sergeant Red, nor the company drunk, also a Red), was an alert and intelligent man, a little older than most of us at, perhaps, twenty-three. When he returned to the squad tent we shared after his first day "at school"—half-days were spent learning the three Rs, the other half doing normal duties—we discussed the experience. He was matter-of-fact about it, and I let him know that I could help him with his words and numbers. Only after we settled into a tutorial pattern did I ask him how it came to be that an American raised in California in the middle of the 20th century couldn't read or write. The answer: he was raised by his grandfather in a remote lumber camp far removed from schools. Furthermore, he informed me, he had none of his teeth, the result, he assumed, of a diet consisting of a lot of sourdough and not enough of whatever it takes to grow healthy teeth in kids. The fact was that he was never a child; he was a little man. All of this was a revelation to a New Yorker, who had the advantage of parochial schools and a fine prep school.

Bozo (I'd rather not use his real name for reasons that might become clear) was another interesting case. He was from a Portuguese fishing family in Rhode Island. Boys in his family didn't go to school; they went to sea with the men at ten or twelve. One day he and I were alone in a tent when I asked how he was doing in school. He was proud that he could add and subtract and willingly demonstrated those skills for me. Since he had had some success, he was an enthusiastic pupil, ready, he said, for the next challenge: multiplication. Did I know anything about that? I told him that I was one of America's great multipliers.

First came theory. Multiplying saved a lot of adding. I demonstrated, for example, how one can avoid adding 7 to 7 to get 14 and then adding 7 to 14 to get 21. I knew a better way. I knew that three 7s were 21. Always! My pupil thought that was neat, correctly recognizing my genius. Next came demonstration.

I cut a C-ration box with a bayonet to make a handy-dandy multiplication table, just like the one on the outside back of my old copybooks, the black and white marble ones. The numbers 1 to 12 were neatly copied down the left side and across the top of our training aid. The lines forming boxes were straight as arrows. Then I filled in the blanks. Bozo watched, fascinated with the result, mightily impressed. All those numbers! And right out of my head, full-blown like Botticelli's Birth of Venus stepping from a clam shell. Next came the exercise.

"Pick any number from 1 to 12," I said. "4," responded my pupil. I pointed to the 4 in the left column. "Now give me another number from 1 to 12." "3," he responded, warming to the game. I pointed to the 3 in the horizontal line at the top of our C-ration cardboard, numbers lined up like soldiers in formation. Then, like Harry Houdini, I drew my finger down from 3 until I got to the box that was the junction of 3 and 4. Presto! "What is the number in the box where 3 crosses 4?" "12," he announced triumphantly. I congratulated him for his perfect first step as a multiplier and intoned solemnly, "3 × 4 = 12. Always. And so is 4 × 3. Always." We then added up four 3s. Sure enough. 12. Then we added up three 4s. Damn! 12 it is! He smiled.

"Give me two more numbers between 1 and 12." A sly expression came across his face as he tried to trick the Great Multiplier. "5 and 5." A smile accompanied his words. Bristling with confidence I traced my finger down, down, down until the first 5 met the second. "What is it?" Barely breathing, he looked at me, saying, "25?" as a question. "Twenty-five!" I asserted with the boldness of certainty. "5 × 5 is *always* 25!" Then I asked him to tell me what 4 × 4 might be. I got a tentative 16, but when he consistently got the correct answers, the tentativeness vanished, as he assumed the brashness of the Great Multiplier himself. His feeling of accomplishment was so evident that he would have jumped into the air clicking his heels, had he thought of it. Alas, joy turned to sorrow, as is too often man's fate in this vale of tears.

His innocent "What's next?" evoked a response that reminds us of that human condition, heads in the sky, feet stuck firmly in the mud. "Now," said the Great Multiplier, his tent mate and beloved teacher, "now you memorize the tables so that you can write it out the way I did. The good news is that we'll start now with the twos for tomorrow."

His instantaneous transformation from gay caballero to surly ingrate was striking, particularly as it was accompanied by an imaginative and explosive combination of blasphemy and profanity, an indication, I believe, of his chagrin. "All that?" he asked pointing to the number-laden C-ration card-board, just recently honored as Moses' tablets. It was ominous, but a good multiplier is a friend of pain. I endured his recalcitrance with the nobility and generosity of spirit befitting the bearer of Truth. But when he stepped toward the tent flap and announced, "I ain't gonna do it," I set aside my newly acquired professional attitude as pedagogue and wise man.

I grasped him firmly by his throat, lovingly but firmly, and bent him over our multiplication tables and the waist-high table upon which it rested, strangling him slightly while explaining my disappointment and desire that he continue his good work. One cannot be sure if it was my words, his good nature, or God's intercession, but by the time I left Korea, Bozo knew his tables and could recite them the way he could the names of his family members.

Both Red and Bozo achieved the minimum requirements of the 4 IQ Program. And I found a career as a teacher.

22

Chimpo Charlie

Sex and humor loom large in the thoughts and deeds of species Homo sapiens, subset Americus Yungus. In 1953, every GI in Korea knew that "chimpo" was the word for the primary male sex characteristic. We didn't know if it was a Japanese or a Korean word. I learned that the can of beans and frankfurters in our C-rations was "beans and chimpo." Of my growing and increasingly exotic vocabulary, that word would play a central role in my revenge for taking me from my home in C Company and sending me to D Company.

Someone in a high place—even higher than the first sergeant, maybe the Pentagon or God—decided that the specialty learned in weeks of training would take precedence over what soldiers did in months of war. That meant that as fast as I could say it, I was a medic. In Army-ese, the order said something like: ". . . the following EM, Gole, Henry G., US 51177493, MOS changed from 1745 to 1666 effective as of this date." Presto! From trigger-puller to angel of mercy by a short burst on a typewriter.

I was less chagrined at the job change than I was at being sent away from my friends. Since the shooting was over, it might be more fun being a medic than carrying the BAR with little prospect of using it. I was sent to something called the Clearing Company, a gaggle of medics at regiment in the rear. But I was returned to my battalion when I said I liked it there. Apparently, not many of my new colleagues were eager to go to a line company. The only problem was that I was sent to Dog Company, not Charlie.

In Dog Company, I was surrounded by nice men who treated me royally. They didn't know the details, but they did know that I wasn't a new guy. Combat infantrymen take good care of their company medics, so I enjoyed the status of both old guy and medic. Further, there was less walking in Dog Company, since trucks and jeeps were required to move the 81mm mortars, the 75mm and 106mm recoilless rifles, and the heavy machine guns of a rifle battalion's weapons company. We rode almost everywhere, and when they made me a sergeant, I was a big shot. But I missed John Plunkett, Rios

Rodriguez, Charlie Romano, Smitty, Andy Anderson, Sam Talbot, Cowboy Green, Ed Ninni, Buel Nixon, John Pepper, Pak Yung Wu, Um Chuck Sup, Kim Yuk Kil, Kim Yung Hwan, and Solomon Haynes.

From Dog Company, I could see Charlie Company a half-mile distant as I walked to the mess hall each morning. Hell, I couldn't miss it. The white-painted rocks announced CHOPPIN' CHARLIE in six-foot letters on the hill behind the first platoon, my alma mater. They were there, and I was in Dog Company. It must have been as I walked to breakfast that the Holy Ghost descended upon me with inspiration, His specialty. I wrote the following words in my note pad: CHOPPIN' CHARLIE and under them I wrote, CHIMPO CHARLIE.

A few letter changes and the job was done.

It would be done at night, scrambling up a steep hill. Because of a guerrilla threat, our guards were armed, a problem that would be overcome by those willing to assist in the Lord's work. It would be an inside job. I consulted my learned colleague, John Plunkett, whose broad grin signaled approval. He was in. Buel Nixon similarly indicated conversion. We plotted and assigned responsibility for the I, M, P, and the O. The company commander and the first sergeant would be mightily pissed. That was, after all, the idea. They would do dreadful things to us if they learned of our apostasy, but this was not the first protest in the tradition of Western Civilization. Only three men knew the plan. But Lenin, too, started with a small cell, and Christ had only twelve guys, one of them a stool pigeon.

There was one glitch—the guard. But as Buel and I did the deed on the first moonless night, John found a plausible reason to swap guard duty, putting him at the base of the hill for operation switch. So it wasn't the end of the caper when one of us sent a stone rolling down the hill. Some eager beaver might have shot at us, but we could count on John. We finished the job and vanished into the night.

The next morning as I walked toward the D Company mess hall, I stole a glance at the hill behind C Company, but it was too dark to read the sign. Later, as I climbed into the back of a deuce-and-a-half truck for a dental appointment and my first visit to the 25th Division Rear, I barely suppressed a joyous yelp as I saw the successful result of our nocturnal efforts. No one else had noticed. Yet.

I was in the dentist's chair when another dentist greeted mine with a hearty laugh and an announcement. "Somebody moved the big white rocks above Charlie Company of the Wolfhounds to spell out CHIMPO CHARLIE. You can see it for miles. Everybody in the division is laughing about it."

They chortled in unison, showing the brilliant teeth caps they had done for one another. I maintained the respectful silence and serious demeanor appropriate for a sergeant in the presence of distinguished medical professionals who were also officers and gentlemen. But I smiled broadly on the outside, sharing their amusement, and swelled with pride and joy on the inside for a successful military operation. And, in due course, I schemed my way back to Charlie Company.

23

Chow Down

I entered Charlie Company's mess hall an hour before the announced time for supper, sat down, accepted a cup of coffee, asked where the mess sergeant was, and learned that Red Allen was at the garbage sump.

"Yeah, Doc, he wanted to inspect it. He should be back any minute."

Red and I started our Charlie Company careers almost a year earlier as riflemen on a squad-size outpost where we spent several weeks. There were nine of us on the OP, 100% alerts were commonplace. We got to know one another well. By day we dug to improve the trenches, wire, mines, and bunkers. By night we stared into the darkness from our fighting positions, because higher headquarters expected an enemy offensive.

The physical exertion and the darkness made it difficult for nineteen and twenty-year-olds to stay awake, so we welcomed exchanges of artillery that sailed high above us as both sides fired on the other's suspected locations and known fortifications. Friendly rocket fire provided an entertaining light and sound show as it went over us, not on us. We were like officials at a tennis match, except that we were in holes instead of on tall chairs. From my fighting position, I saw a protracted glow from behind friendly lines as a World War II–vintage rack of rockets was fired. Seconds later, I heard the firing. Another few seconds and I heard the swishing sound of their passage above me. I turned 180 degrees to see a glow where the Chinese were. Then I heard the explosions, entertaining myself by counting the seconds from flash to bang and estimating the distance from the firing to me and to the target. From time to time, a firefight on an OP or one involving a patrol broke the tedium of staring at the darkness. I learned to smoke C-ration cigarettes under a poncho to stay awake. Within a week I had gone from nonsmoker to two packs a day. Combat was exhausting. The dirty secret is that it is also very exciting.

During the day, when we weren't digging or sleeping, we entertained ourselves by reading, preparing food, and conversing. That's how I got to know Red. He was a bright and sensitive guy. We talked about our dreams and aspirations, the way young men do, and we shared some adventures on the OP and later on patrols. He was from Miami, he was an honest-to-God civilian cook, and he was eager to get out of the hole in the ground and into the mess hall. I had been trained as a medic, but I really wanted to be the Audie Murphy or Sergeant York of the Korean War. We were an odd couple, but we seemed to understand one another.

Red was assigned to the mess hall after a little more than a month in the squad when the old mess sergeant discovered him. I always got the royal treatment from him and the other cooks. In the social pecking order of a rifle company, Red and I were minor eminences.

I sipped my coffee, noting the rain outside and observing the cooks scurrying in the Quonset hut as they prepared to serve the evening meal. Before the Quonset hut went up, the cooks prepared our food in a squad tent, and we ate seated on our helmets, rain or shine. Now we had tables and benches.

As soon as Red entered, I knew something was very wrong. His normally fair complexion had turned chalk white, and he teetered on the verge of shock, a condition with which I had become too familiar. I took him by the arm and seated him, saying:

"Give Sergeant Allen a cup of coffee."

And to him:

"What's the matter, Red? You look like hell."

He paused, wrapped both hands around the cup to warm them, and stared at me. His lips moved:

"I feel like hell."

He told me this story.

Each day the slops from the mess hall made a trip of about two miles in a ³/₄-ton truck to a place where a large hole was dug. The slops were dumped there. Normal practice was to dust the surface of the slops with lime each day, and eventually the hole would be covered over with earth. That was standard military field sanitation for latrines and garbage sumps. But a Korean family had gathered scraps of canvas, sticks, and flattened beer cans to build a shack near the hole. They ate the slops. Field sanitation gave way to Red's compassion.

Another family joined the first, and then another. In strict accordance with the law of supply and demand, when demand exceeded supply, price rose. Price took the form of constant alertness and readiness to pounce. The sound of the slops-bearing truck caused jockeying for position. Its arrival caused a scramble for the slops dumped from soldiers' trays into the large drums now on the truck.

The rain and mud caused a Korean father, climbing to the slops that sustained his family, to slide under the wheel of the backing truck. The truck crushed him. He died.

Red finished his story in a shocked whisper as the troops arrived, jostling one another in youthful play as they enjoyed locker-room fellowship and anticipated the good food they would soon chow down. Fifty years after the incident, there are other anxious fathers in too many corners of the world searching for slops to feed families living in shacks made from flattened cans, scraps of canvas, and sticks.

24

Good-bye to All That

eaving C Company was an emotional experience whose intensity came as a surprise to me. Home for over a year, the company had undergone just about a 100% turnover. I was now an "old guy," probably the oldest guy in service in Charlie. To the degree that I thought about it at all, I thought my reaction to departure and homecoming would be a feeling of unreserved joy. We all fantasized that we would somehow snuggle in the bosom of the beneficent United States, an anteroom of Paradise, a place where there were no sudden wake-ups, no rice paddies, and hills were climbed in trains and automobiles, a place where it wasn't so damned hot in summer and so terribly cold in winter. Departure would be an unmitigated joy. It didn't work that way.

The company left me. It had gone to an exercise in the boondocks. Only the short-timers—me—and the sick, lame, and lazy were left in the squad tents that were home. On the morning of The Great Day, a runner woke me. I grabbed all of my worldly possessions in one hand, walking the few steps to Andy's tent to bid him good-bye. He would be next to go in a day or two. I woke him up and shook his hand. The big, phlegmatic, simple, good man and I exchanged a few words. We would not have been friends in our other lives, but we had done some growing up together in Korea. The words were ordinary, but I think we both knew it was good-bye forever. Good-bye to that first night on line, to Amborn, to one another, to Charlie Company, to war, to Korea, to youth. I think we both teared up.

Then a jeep ride to the personnel people for the usual paper shuffling, where I got another surprise. My former company commander, now an adjutant and one of the very few leaders I respected in my two years as an enlisted man, thanked us for our service. Because of what he represented to us, the unwashed herd, it was not bullshit. It was a direct thank-you from him. As the deuce-and-a-half carried us away, he stood at attention outside his Quonset hut saluting us. He held the salute until he disappeared from our view.

The rest of the trip from soldier to civilian was the usual stop-wait-go over a three- or four-week period. The truck from the 27th Regiment took us to a train. We spent the night in a tent near the port. I simply have no recollection if the port was Pusan or Inchon, but I do remember the kid.

It was morning. I was watching two- and three-year old kids on the other side of the barbed wire as they played with a sled in the deep dust of July. (Yes. A sled.) One of them was blue-eyed and blonde, a Korean-Caucasian kid. I wondered then how he would make it in Korean society. He's now over fifty. I wonder how he made out.

The only differences in the boat ride were that I was going home instead of to war, I was a chief instead of an Indian, and authority was less abusive. In Yokohama, where we picked up some more passengers, the longshoreman really hustled. In Seattle, where we debarked, the workers moved at a deliberate, if not leisurely, pace. Had I had two coins to rub together, I might have read the signs and gotten rich by investing in Japan, Inc.

We got the legendary steak and ice cream that we had heard was served to returnees, had a few free hours that I used to buy some cheap civilian attire, and boarded a train that was home for five days. The highlight of the cross-country trip was waving to farm ladies who interrupted their wash-hanging to wave to us. Somewhere around Minneapolis-St. Paul, a few of us dashed into a track-side bar to gulp down a beer before running after the train that was literally leaving the station.

In the middle of the night, I arrived back in Camp Kilmer where my military odyssey had begun. We repeated the mooing and herding, at which I had become adept, and crashed into a GI bunk that looked a lot better in 1954 than it had in 1952. One never forgets living in holes in the ground. Beds are appreciated even many years later.

I still fail to understand why it took several days to stamp, bend, and mutilate the records I had carried from Korea to New Jersey. Perhaps the unlimited source of labor provided by conscription creates the general climate of gross inefficiency found in the Army and in soviet societies at that time.

July, Year of Our Lord 1954. On my last night in the Army, I seethed with resentment. My name appeared on a duty roster, appointing me the noncommissioned-officer-in-charge of a vital mission: supervising six soldiers who swept out a movie theater after the last show. I was so angry at the clerks and jerks, veterans of duty in New Jersey, who sat on their duffs while the animals from Korea spiffed up the movie house, that I almost killed one of the soldiers on my detail who chose to find the enemy in me! The next day we had to endure the silly, self-satisfied twits as they "out-processed" us in a curt and abusive manner. I headed for New York City happy in the knowledge that I had made it through a rite of passage, pleased that never again would I suffer the mindless whims of military bureaucracy.

Years later I read Robert Graves's account of how he reacted to his much longer and harder experience as a junior leader for almost all of the Great War. Toward the end of his book, he writes that he would never again subject himself to the orders of others. He said Good-bye to All That: authority, convention, bourgeois values, and to England itself. I was neither an elitist nor had I suffered the war Graves had, but I did reject authority, mostly because the "leadership" I saw was arbitrary and mindless. At the same time, I was more than dimly aware that I had seen that place in the human experience where the base and the glorious, the profane and the noble come together in a kind of muddy purity, where sins of the flesh and heroism blended with my Roman Catholic sense of sin and redemption. I felt an indeterminate yearning, but for what I did not know.

College, graduate school, marriage, teaching, and home ownership awaited before I returned to the Army. I was not yet 21.

Part III

Interludes and Reflections While Safe

. . . in which our narrator takes a wife, studies, teaches, leaves home and hearth once again, this time in response to his President's call, enjoying Germany before, between, and after tours in Vietnam.

The Zeitgeist and My Little World

Korea disappeared from newspaper front pages after the first year of fighting, becoming a forgotten war while it was being fought. America continued to move to the suburbs, spinning Hula Hoops and later doing the Twist. Despite plans to tend its own garden, America learned that a superpower is too big to hide, even in the biggest garden in the neighborhood. The outside world required constant watering and weeding.

French troops left Vietnam after the battle of Dien Bien Phu, but the smell of defeat clinging to them since June 1940 followed brave troops to Algeria and into the 1960s. In 1956, Eisenhower refused to back military actions by Israel, Britain, and France after Nasser's Egypt nationalized the Suez Canal. Then the world watched as the Red Army put down the Hungarian Revolution. Castro consolidated power in Cuba, Mao allowed many flowers to bloom before snipping them off, and Sputnik orbited earth, to the chagrin of Americans puffed up in their conviction of technological superiority over the backward Russians.

Newsprint was spent on: Papa Doc Duvalier, Martin Luther King, Thalidomide, Willi Brandt, Charles de Gaulle, Arafat, Ho Chi Minh, the St. Lawrence Seaway, Xerox copiers, JFK, the U-2 and Francis Gary Powers, war in the Congo, Adolf Eichmann's capture and trial, the Quebec separatist movement, the Berlin Wall, America's increasing involvement in Vietnam, Yuri Gagarin's first human space flight, the Bay of Pigs, and the Peace Corps.

Senator McCarthy's witch-hunting career ended, Brown v. Board of Education found the "separate but equal" doctrine unconstitutional, Rosa Parks refused to surrender her seat on a Montgomery, Alabama, bus and Freedom Riders rode south to register black voters. "Sit-in" entered our vocabulary as young blacks and liberal whites challenged practices in public places generally accepted in the American South.

Bill Haley and His Comets exploded with *Rock Around the Clock*, Fats Domino crooned *Ain't That A Shame,* and Johnny Cash sang *Folsom Prison Blues*. A white kid named Elvis sounded like a black kid named Elvis and had some success, but I was with Frank Sinatra, *All the Way*.

In 1957 I became the family-first college graduate with a degree from Hofstra College. Recognizing a scam that required almost no heavy lifting, I refused to leave school, earning another degree from the Fletcher School of Law and Diplomacy before teaching at Baldwin Senior High School. It only took a year of grading English papers to chase me to a department called Citizenship Education in 1959. I taught European and American History, but they were called "Cit. Ed." Presumably, "history" has an old-fashioned ring to it. It was fun. So was coaching baseball and buying a little house a short walk from school.

Listening to John F. Kennedy's Presidential Inaugural Address on a cold and windy 20 January 1961, I rejoiced. Then I voted with my body. The President told me to "ask what I can do for my country." I did.

I went to the Army and said, I am a combat veteran with two graduate degrees and three years of experience as a teacher and coach. Lemme be an army officer.

They did.

25

Volare

The widow Giliberti liked me. She was indifferent to my bride of eighteen months.

We lived in her house, whose second floor had been converted, probably illegally, to a one-bedroom upstairs apartment that was just right for us at that stage of our lives. The living room allowed an adult to stand straight up—if one remained close to the middle of the room. My cup was full. I was a new high school teacher, and my bride had returned to college after supporting me during my stints at Hofstra and the Fletcher School. We were young, in love, and life was good. It was 1958 and I was a teacher at Baldwin Senior High School, a fine school with quality kids and faculty.

Our new neighborhood was Italian. Teenaged boys passing the house deferentially inclined their heads toward Mrs. Giliberti, muttering a sweet "Buon giorno, Signora Giliberti" accompanied by pleasant smiles. Then they left the neighborhood to terrorize gangs just a couple of blocks away. On this side of the highway, they were good boys. On the other side, they were thugs. Mrs. Giliberti accepted the obeisance as her due. This commedia dell' arte informed me that my recently widowed landlady was a grand dame, and not only in her opinion.

She was also an avid wrestling fan. Professional wrestling was available nightly on TV in 1958 in New York City, and Mrs. G never missed a match. As my bride studied and I prepared lessons, our reverie would be interrupted from time to time by expressions of surprise and hilarity from below where our grande dame whooped it up in splendid isolation. Later generations would proclaim her glee by saying that she was really "into it." We were amused by her whoops and gleeful shrieks as she watched and pleased that she took so much pleasure from the watching. She didn't hear well, so we heard everything from the announcer's murmuring and to her enthusiastic response. By 11 p.m. silence reigned.

The budding friendship between Mrs. G and me was strengthened by what the humorless might view as my aberrant behavior. On more than one occasion when music blared and the fruit of the grape flowed in our digs on a Saturday night, my bride would caution me that we were probably being too loud for the grande dame. Recalling Mrs. G's nocturnal cheering, I responded to my bride's admonitions by singing "Volare," an Italian song popular in the United States at the time, *con brio e basso-not-so-profundo.* To get full credit for my efforts, I sang on all fours, close to the hole in the floor for the heating pipe. Mine was a foolish act, combining crude humor and a dash of vindictiveness, just one sample from a litany of mindless acts, but the old lady loved my choice of music almost as much as my singing.

Saturdays my bride was out and about on food shopping chores, trips to the dry cleaners, and whatever else is imbedded in the Saturday morning tradition of "errands." As soon as my bride drove away, Signora Giliberti would summon me with a call to Mr. Go-lee, accent on the first syllable. (She called my wife Lillian. My wife's name was and is Lydia, but the grande dame had apparently never heard of anyone foolish enough to be a Lydia. So she was Lillian.)

My lonely hostess would sit me at a small marble-topped table from which I could admire her precious possessions. We sampled homemade wine in beautiful crystal, ate delicious cookies recently made and elegantly presented, and drank coffee from freshly ground beans prepared with loving care. Surrounded by more plants and flowers than are found in a botanical garden, we chatted about nothing important. I think she simply wanted to show off her special things and to enjoy civilized conversation. That I was a teacher seemed to matter a great deal. I was a somebody: Mr. Go-lee, the teacher. She also thanked me frequently for my enthusiastic rendition of "Volare," yet more evidence that I was a man of the world who respected people of quality. But mostly she wanted company and to show off her valued objects. I reported my princely treatment to Lydia, who had gracefully accepted that she had been relegated to the dust heap of Lillians.

One Saturday morning as my bride went about her plebeian duties and I trained as a diplomat, I was munching, sipping, and nodding in agreement with the grande dame's soliloquy when she stopped as though transfixed by a vision of Heaven or Hell. "Mr. Go-lee, look!" I did. A kid walked by the house. "He touched my tree!" That last was announced with a stage-whispered vehemence more appropriate to witnessing a slaughter of the innocents than to teenage mindlessness.

I did not see the sin, but I clucked sympathetically. Homemade wine, elegant pastries, and coffee fit for a king were not to be forsaken by inattention to the indignation of my hostess. I clucked *con gusto.*

In a flash, my benefactress was on the telephone speaking in an impassioned Italian I had previously heard only on Saturday afternoon broadcasts of the opera from the Met. The offender's mother or father was getting a full report, presumably with a recommended punishment, something short of execution but something that would almost certainly leave scar tissue.

After she put down the phone, she visibly decompressed by degrees, and I rejoiced at her recovery, which was accompanied by a refilling of my glass and a resupply of cookies. The least I could do was to re-cluck with even more feeling.

So went Saturday mornings from 1958 to 1960 in Elmont, Long Island. My bride tended to mundane tasks. I was kind to an aged landlady who chose to see her teacher-tenant as a gallant serenading the lady in Italian song.

Cookies on chinaware and wine in crystal ended when my bride and I bought a little house in Baldwin, Long Island, close to the school in which I taught. We were on track to settle among our fellow New York City expatriates, to raise little suburbanites behind our very own white picket fence, and to live happily ever after in a society that rained consumer goods on us like confetti on a hero's parade down Wall Street.

But John F. Kennedy spoke to me.

26

Me and JFK

President Kennedy's inaugural address knocked my socks off. I was twenty-seven years old and in my third year as a high school teacher in New York in January 1961, when I heard it. George Leonard, guidance counselor at the school and soulmate, telephoned within minutes after the President spoke, and we cited passages from the speech to one another, picking up on the challenge that resounds to this day: Ask not what your country can do for you. Ask what you can do for your country. Sharing our unreserved enthusiasm for the speech, we Roosevelt-boosting, Truman-supporting, Stevenson-commiserating liberals believed that we had just heard an unambiguous call to duty. We were witnesses to history. I took the call literally.

Our cool new President spoke directly to me, and I can see the craggy, white-haired, venerable Robert Frost struggling with the cold strong winds in the bright sunshine to control the pages from which he read his poem written for the occasion. Young president, iconic poet, cold, wind, sun, dignity, lucid prose, these comprised a perfect backdrop, a sense of purpose, a quest, a call for sacrifice. Kennedy's words impelled me to the First Army Headquarters on Governor's Island, New York, to seek a commission in the United States Army. Others, I realized later, responded to the President in various ways. Some flocked to the Peace Corps, some rode buses to the Deep South to register black voters, and others reported to the CIA, the Department of State, or to the military. What strange bedfellows! Idealism, for better or worse, swept the land, kicking off a tumultuous decade of foolishness and nobility. In retrospect, much of the reaction to JFK was rejection of the grasping materialism we had grown up with in the 1950s, itself a reaction to the Depression and war. Economic well-being was assumed by the children of the 50s. To our parents it was the pot of gold at the end of the rainbow, the end, the payoff. We regarded it as a jump-off point from which we would accomplish indefinite but great things. Our pragmatic parents, many of whom had clawed their way out of the slums and ghettos to occupy the new suburbs, found the fuzzy ideals of their children in the 1960s incomprehensible. My father was such a parent. He did arithmetic. I attempted calculus.

When I left the Army as a sergeant in July of 1954, not yet twenty-one, the likelihood of my voluntary return to the Army was precisely zero. The war in Korea had been an exciting adventure, I was happy to have done it, I was proud of my Combat Infantryman's Badge, but it was over. Finished. On to bigger and better things.

I studied, loving it as I never had before, earning a B.A. in English at Hofstra and two Master's degrees, one real—in politics, history, and economics at the Fletcher School—and one fake—an M.S. in Education. Then I enjoyed three years of high school teaching, but I realized that I didn't want to do wear a groove in the slate steps of the new school as I stooped and grayed. There were maidens to be rescued, foes to be vanquished, justice to be served, noble warriors to be joined.

The unvarnished truth is, I was restless and considering a change when JFK addressed his inaugural address to me, personally. This charismatic leader wanted to know what I would do for my country. I wanted to do as much as I could. The call came to me when I was bored. The conversations of our friends, the young marrieds of the late 50s, were about buying furniture, gadgets, and gizmos, when it wasn't about babies and moving from rented apartment to mortgaged house.

My wife of four years confirmed my madness when I told her that I was returning to the Army. Recognizing signs of restlessness in me, she had proposed that I study law, complete a Ph.D., or take a cold shower. Perhaps we might relocate to California. We had bought the house in the suburbs a year earlier, a big step toward upward mobility, a short walk for me to school and a short drive to work for her, where she was enjoying success in a career with Ma Bell. She had been an apartment dweller and really enjoyed being a person of property, even if the house was tiny and the property modest.

After years of studying and part-time work, I finally had a real job, a career, and so did she with new status and rapid promotions. We were on the path to middle-class respectability when I came up with this madness totally out of her experience. She and others thought it was like a techie of the 21st century choosing to sell pencils on a street corner in the wrong part of town.

She knew little of military life, but she knew it was nomadic, something men did in times of national crisis, and she knew its essence was violence, antithetical to her.

My experience in Korea in killing people and breaking things was not a great insight into what it was to be a career officer in times of peace, or in a Cold War that wasn't quite war or peace. In any event, I could not tell her what to expect, because I didn't know what to expect. (It was said of a clubby Brit who served in the Second World War: he wasn't a real officer. He was just in the war.)

Our income was reduced by half when I returned to the Army. Her math skills suggested my career change was a bad move, and our friends, acquaintances, relatives, colleagues, and the village idiot concurred. They were shocked that their rebel without a cause would even consider subjecting himself and his city slicker wife to the arbitrariness of the rednecks who were military authority. The Army they knew was Sadsack, Sergeant Bilko, *No Time for Sergeants*, *The Teahouse of the August Moon*, the Army that had cooks driving trucks and truck drivers cooking. They were right, but I did it anyway.

A board of officers grilled me at Fort Hamilton in Brooklyn. Among other things, one of them asked me what my wife thought about my return to the Army. I told him we had a house with a white picket fence and two good jobs; she thought it was the craziest goddamned thing she ever heard of. That must have been the right answer. Presumably my brilliant responses, combat experience, and education persuaded the Army to give me a direct Regular Army commission. "Direct" meant without benefit of training at West Point, ROTC, or Officer Candidate School. "Regular" meant that I had tenure, a kind of union card that absolved me of the need to shape up daily (as Marlon Brando did in *On the Waterfront*). "Army" meant lots of things, few of them attractive to the general run of *boobus americanus*. I was a Regular Army Officer and didn't know shit.

My initial steps upon receipt of strange orders comprised a comedy born of profound ignorance. I went to the Fort Totten Post Exchange for a summer uniform and to Brooks Brothers in Manhattan for a green uniform, a uniform introduced after 1954 and new to me. My 1952–1954 costume was Ike jacket in winter, khakis in summer. The two new uniforms I bought would get me through my initial reentry, after which I would figure out what else I would need. I later learned that the orders I had in hand were unusual. They were to be effective upon my swearing in. That is, I had an assignment that would be effective if I signed the papers and swore the oath of office.

Since I didn't know how to go about the swearing part, I flew to Washington and went to the busy grand concourse in the very bowels of the Pentagon. There I asked for "personnel." The guard looked at me strangely before he pushed a directory at me. There were pages of "personnel." I found something in the thick book that looked about right and presented myself to an amused officer who swore me in, informing me that any commissioned officer could have done it, as in New York, Georgia, or anywhere. I have no idea why I didn't go to the local college ROTC department at Hofstra, my alma mater, to inquire into the administrivia of reporting to the

Army. That is what those ROTC detachments do: turn civilians into officers. But I didn't ask.

My perfect imitation of an unguided missile continued on a trajectory from Washington's National Airport to Columbus, Georgia, via Atlanta. In order to get the lay of the land, I intentionally reported for the Infantry Officer Basic Course at Fort Benning a week early. A puzzled duty officer informed me that I was early, and I asked if that was a problem. It wasn't. When the next man reporting in was made my roomie several days later, I read his ROTC books to discover that the battalion and regiments of my 1952 Army were no more, having been replaced by "battle groups." I watched my roomie like a hawk. When he set up his uniform, I waited until he left the room to set up mine. Then, one evening, posing as an officer, I went for a short walk in uniform, my maiden voyage, saluting and returning salutes. That wasn't so hard.

The whole deal was something of a paradox, even a charade. My Combat Infantryman's Badge and the ribbons on my chest said that I was a veteran, but I hadn't the foggiest notion of how one did the officer scam; nor did I know how my Army was organized; nor was I current in "milspeak." It had been nine years since basic training and seven since I had last worn my nation's uniform. By watching the others, I bumbled through without disgracing myself—I think. Then came bumbling through ranger and airborne training before reporting to a rifle company in Germany in November 1961. As I sorted out what I was doing, subordinates and superiors saw me as an old soldier. The hundreds of thousands of veterans dubious about the leadership they experienced in uniform should find vindication in the sure knowledge that Gole hadn't the foggiest idea what he was doing.

When President Kennedy was killed two years later, I shared a personal sense of loss with the Peace Corps kids and those who registered black voters, though we would find ourselves on opposite sides of the barricades in the decade that followed as idealism worked itself out. But a deal's a deal. Between 1961 and 1988, when I took off my uniform, I had more or less figured out what I was supposed to do. I did it.

27

Bist du die Lidwina?

W hen the Berlin Wall went up in August of 1961, I was doing
courses at Fort Benning's school for boys as a new but not young
infantry lieutenant: the Infantry Officer Basic Course, the Ranger
Course, and jump school. Recognizing an opportunity for adventure on the
grand scale (and a chance to get off orders to Fort Riley, Kansas, where, as
a Noo Yawk City guy, I dreaded the prospect of watching the corn grow), I
sent a letter to officer personnel at the Department of Army, offering my
services in the struggle against Godless Communism in Germany. Noting
the national peril and my personal merits, the President or one of his little
helpers pulled out all stops so that I could win the Cold War. My orders
were changed and November of 1961 found 2/Lt. Gole in a battle group in
Bamberg, Germany. It would take a while for me to win the Cold War, the
only one I won. Got a draw in Korea and a loss in Vietnam.

In my usual haste to do things now rather than well, I failed to anticipate
that the Army would stop sending "dependents" to Europe. Dependents
were later called "family members," a response to dependent wives who
didn't want to be called, or be, dependent. Wives became "spouses." Blowing people to smithereens became "target servicing." Unless they were civilians. Then they were "collateral damage." My Army thought it was
"progressive," but H. L. Mencken probably hit the mark when he referred
to "greasy meaningless words." Civilians imitated the Army. For example,
they call mayhem "education" and dimwits "intellectually challenged."

The possibility of war was real, to which the American military community in Europe at the time can testify. The good deal for soldiers and their
families in Europe became, at least for a couple of years, rather tense times.
For example, because my rifle company had to respond to alerts by having
85% of the company out the gate of the Kaserne (old clusters of German
Barracks comprising a military post) within thirty minutes of notification
and in fighting positions some miles away within two hours, leave and pass
policy was affected. It was harder to get away, and even while at home base,

soldiers and their families, like Cinderella, had to be off the German streets, out of the bars and restaurants, and in quarters by midnight. To prevent our soldiers from being run in by military policemen, officers and NCOs ran "courtesy patrols," another opportunity to excel by attempting to reason with drunken troopers intent on bedding tender young things or veteran hookers as both hands on the clock tiptoed to twelve.

Further, private travel on certain roads was prohibited, as was presence within five kilometers of the inner-German frontier and the border with Czechoslovakia. Dependents in-country were required to rehearse an evacuation plan with "sponsors," the military members, sometimes by driving hundreds of miles to embarkation points or neutral countries. Survival kits, consisting of food, blankets, fuel, flashlights, and first aid kits for wives and kids, had to be maintained to sustain them during possible evacuation. Life for soldiers in Germany was less fun than it had been, and some family members showed signs of nervousness.

Despite all, my wife joined her slightly daft husband in the winter of 1961–1962, at our expense for both travel and rent. Technically, she was a tourist. As luck would have it, that winter was so cold that GI trucks brought fuel to Germans as canals froze. Record cold winters are a peripheral concern to those tucked into snug houses and apartments. But extreme cold becomes a serious concern when the husband-as-platoon-leader absents himself about 70% of the time, and his bride, also a Noo Yawker, must carry coal in buckets from the basement to the third-floor apartment where pot-bellied stoves were the only sources of heat. In the modest digs at 22 Memmelsdorfer Strasse, taking a bath required building a wood fire in a Rube Goldberg–style stove attached to a water tank above the bathtub. So it was as I defended freedom in the early 1960s, and my wife as Camp Fire girl had a full-time job keeping warm.

There were compensations. In addition to travel to wonderful places we had read about, there was the charm of Bamberg itself, a jewel of a city of some 50,000 souls. There was also the bonus of living close to the village in which my wife's mother was born and from which she had departed as a young lady. Three daughters had migrated to the United States in the early 1920s, but two brothers remained in the village of Geusfeld and a sister resided not far away in Kitzingen. Our first visit to Geusfeld was serendipitous, emotional, and comical.

Wife and car arrived in Germany at about the same time, but not together. When all of us—wife, car, and soldier—were reunited for our first drive on a dreary Saturday afternoon in December 1961, my bride suddenly burst into the high adventure mode, announcing as we entered a market town on Bundesstrasse 22, "Ebrach! Eby! My mother and aunts often mentioned Ebrach in their stories! Eby is Ebrach and Bamby is Bamberg! The village is nearby! Geusfeld is close!"

And so it was. But it took some detective work to find it. The first clue was the woods on one side of Ebrach and the fields on the other side. It was up the hill and through the woods to Geusfeld, my wife declared. It was unclear if her reference was to tales of Geusfeld or tales of Little Red Riding Hood, stories easily garbled in her memory and easily confused, as I would discover, in a Germany rather accurately portrayed in fairy tales. We found a road that looped around the woods and the hill. In due course we passed through Untersteinbach, a place my wife remembered from a childhood apparently spent eavesdropping on her mother and aunts as they reminisced dreamily of the old hometown "on the other side." Untersteinbach, a grand metropolis of two thousand, was called Little Paris by the humble folk of Geusfeld a kilometer away.

We entered a town too small to have a sign identifying it and saw an old crone in dull-colored costume walking on the otherwise deserted cobblestone road. My wife, by now quivering like a filly in the starting gate at Belmont racetrack, said, without ceremony, "Stop!" I was a veteran husband. I stopped. The crone approached the 1958 MGA. I banged my knuckles opening the sliding Plexiglas window designed by our British cousins to bang knuckles. The Walt Disney version of a witch in *Snow White and the Seven Dwarfs* stooped to stare at me through the window on the driver's side as my bride, from the passenger side, addressed her in German known to them but not yet to me. I had a wonderful view of the woman's right ear, wrinkled cheek, and facial hair as she pushed her head past me to engage in conversation with my bride/interpreter.

"Bitte, wie heisst diese Ortschaft?"

"Geusfeld."

"Kennen Sie zufällig die Familie Finster?"

At this point the old gal stared even more intently at my wife, studying her as she asked:

"Bist du die Lidwina oder die Alice?"

Even I could make that out. Forty years after the departure of the three girls from the town, the old lady standing in the rain with her noggin inches from my face had asked if my wife was Lidwina, which she was, or Alice, my wife's sister, which she wasn't. Weepy, but still the filly in the starting gate, m'lady responded:

"Ich bin die Lidwina."

My mother-in-law was a Lidwina as well, and one of her sisters was an Alice. The old crone, never having laid eyes on my bride, recognized her immediately. In later years I saw why. The daughter, then in her twenties, must have looked much as her mother did when Mom left the village for America, just as the daughter looks like the mother-in-law I knew in later years.

"Können Sie mir sagen wo das Finster Haus ist?"

Directions to the house where her mother was born were followed. It was only a hundred yards distant, but by the time we had turned past the school, circled the church, and stopped in front of a modest farmhouse, the family was assembled in the rain to greet us. The local reception had dashed through narrow paths to alert the family that the Americans were coming. It was a happy reunion. The only non-German speaker in their midst felt a strong surge of fellow feeling that day.

Over the years my bride and I enjoyed four tours in Germany, spending eleven years there. We made dozens of visits to Geusfeld, our second home and family. We have an aerial photograph of the village hanging in our Pennsylvania home; we saw some seventy houses become more than a hundred as the "economic miracle" of Germany was realized before our eyes and prosperity came to a small town; we've heard the "Star Spangled Banner" played to honor us as we left the village church after Mass. All of those things remind us of Mom's hometown, but I think of the "once upon a time" introduction of fairy tales, *Es war ein Mal,* and see the old crone on a gray day asking "Bist du die Lidwina?" when I see Geusfeld in my mind's eye. That began my love affair with Germany.

28

Pumpkins and Cobblestones

Jim Fenlon and I would turn into pumpkins at midnight. Among the measures taken by my Army in reaction to Soviet construction of The Wall in Berlin in August 1961, was the imposition of curfew for American troops and their families in Germany. The two of us, infantry lieutenants in the same rifle company, were enjoying a boys' night out for reasons long since forgotten, but the memory of the evening and the walk in the old city refuses to fade.

The exchange rate was four Deutsche Mark to the dollar. The GI's favorite Gasthaus meal was "Schnitzel," as much for the limit of his German vocabulary as for the succulence of the food. That word brought from the kitchen a piece of meat—veal or pork, spiced, breaded, and fried—sufficient in size to hide the plate. It was accompanied by a heap of home-fried potatoes and a generous portion of salad set aside in a separate dish. This was before fat-gram counting, before we all became cardiologists, before my hair turned gray. The cost of that just-right standard fare in Bamberg was DM3,80, that is, less than one buck. A half-liter of fine beer to wash it down was Kulmbacher, brewed not far away. It cost 80 Pfennig, less than a Mark, less than two bits. One beer deserved another. A postprandial stroll was next for the two men in their twenties and in communion with the universe and all God's works on this evening in early spring.

We wended our way on the winding cobblestone streets, noting cornerstones inscribed with dates from the 12th and 13th centuries, savoring the moment. A steep climb took us to the Dom, the cathedral in which the only Pope buried in Germany rests, and the home of the Bamberger Rider, the idealized youth on horseback. We wandered in the great cathedral courtyard before descending to Schenkela, the pub with a unique Rauchbier (smoked beer), a gentle transition from the spiritual to the earthy. We sipped our beer, smoky in appearance and taste, in the brown-on-brown old Gasthaus where everything was worn and cozy. The hands on the clock moved toward twelve.

En route to our parked car, we paused on the bridge, looking in the direction of Little Venice at the houses and boats on the far bank of the river some two hundred yards distant. Water rushed white under us. Behind us was the baroque Rathaus with its mural invisible in the darkness. A courtesy patrol jeep stopped in front of a soldier hangout to remind troops that the witching hour was fast approaching. Curfew violations were taken seriously. As we walked to the car, Jim noted there wasn't a street in town that was straight for more than a hundred feet. One of us said: "The Germans are backward. These cobblestones will need to be replaced every two-thousand years."

29

Poncho Annie

Master Sergeant Stalsberg, a highly intelligent man whose size, steely blue eyes, and blond hair made him a Nordic bantam rooster, could have played convincingly in Ingmar Bergman films if he weren't starring as my platoon sergeant in 1961 and 1962. His continuing efforts to keep me out of trouble were much appreciated, as was his deferential manner, which allowed me to feel important as I stumbled from problem to problem in the highly centralized, unimaginative U.S. Army of pre-Vietnam days. I think Stalsberg liked me and was dedicated to saving me from being devoured by the Blimps dominating our part of the Army.

"Sir, let me buy you a coffee."

Translation: Let's go to the mess hall for your tutorial.

In those days, a rifle company had its own mess hall, a kind of home-away-from-home. Mess sergeants outdid one another and competed in making their mess halls comfortable. They prepared coffee and cookies and had them ready for the troops in the wee hours of the morning as soldiers returned from night training. Tablecloths and matching curtains, flowers, fish tanks, and other touches of things domestic made each mess hall a bit unique. Mealtime was social hour. I think the company mess was one of the keys in soldier bonding, the *sine qua non* of a combat force. It was also a place for a junior officer and his sergeant to work out puzzles, tactical, personnel, and personal.

Stalsberg looked at me through the steam rising from his cup and said: "Gleason (not his real name) wants to get married."

I saw Gleason in my mind's eye: a tall, slim, acne-marked, dull-witted ridgerunner distinguished by his addiction to Coca Cola before I'd heard of such an addiction. Curious at the sight of the perpetual case of Coke under his bed, I'd once asked a man in his squad about it. He said that at wake-up Gleason popped and drank a can before getting out of bed; last thing at lights-out was another pop and gurgle-gurgle. He put away about a case a day. Aside from his addiction, he wasn't the brightest bulb in the lamp.

"Who's the lucky lass?"

"A German woman fifteen years older than him."

"A virgin, no doubt."

"She screws anything that walks . . ."

". . . who can pay for it."

"Who can pay for it."

I thought about the big mistake in the making. Then I spoke.

"His squad leader is the best squad leader in the company. Even Gleason should know that. How come Harry didn't fix this thing."

"The kid says he's in love. Harry's the one who brought it to me. Kid won't listen. Says he's about to file the paperwork."

Ponder time.

In 1961 it was still necessary for a soldier to get the permission of his company commander to marry a German national. This was a vestige of the 1945 nonfraternization rules that later became de-Nazification and then became a "security matter" that was, I'm quite sure, a means of preventing some unsavory women from marrying a ticket to the USA. In fact, it was intended as an obstacle to precisely the kind of mismatch Stalsberg and I had in our laps.

Gleason, for all of his faults and stupidity, was not a problem soldier. Further, he was MY soldier, a dopey young man about to make a very serious mistake likely to adversely affect the rest of his life.

I disliked playing God, but I have always believed that up to the point at which mission accomplishment was threatened, the most important task for a troop leader is to look out for his men.

I played God.

"Tell me what you know about the woman."

"Skenk," said Stalsberg, using the GI term of the day for a two-bit whore, round-heel, lady-of-the-night, or whatever the current expression is for a very bad woman.

"The troops call her Poncho Annie. For ten Marks she'll screw in the back of a car, against a wall, on the ground . . ."

"Got it," I said.

Ponder time.

There were several solutions to this problem. I could talk to our company commander. He could prevent the marriage as German police and U.S. authorities investigating the matter would easily establish that Annie was a professional hooker. But this solution would almost certainly alienate Gleason, possibly causing him to defy the Army and all its pomp and works. I think I recognized a kind of proud, if very dull, hillbilly predisposed to find a semblance of "honor" in wrestling with authority for the woman of his dreams. He'd probably dig in his heels, defy authority, and go from being an adequate soldier to a problem child. In the long run, he'd be a serious loser.

I had a better idea.

"Where do the guys in the squad stand?"

"They think he's being a jerk. He's not popular with the other guys, but they feel sorry for him and think he's a dumb kid making a big mistake."

"Hmmm," said the brilliant platoon leader as Zeus or the Holy Ghost descended.

"OK. Here's the deal. I'll meet with his squad in the company commander's office that I'll borrow. Put him on detail so he doesn't notice what we are up to. I want you there. I'm going to let the squad take care of it. I think they can fix it without the Army officially coming down on our boy."

And so 'twas. I sat the squad down and asked what they thought of Gleason's wedding plans. To a man they agreed that it was the dumbest thing they'd heard of lately. I agreed with them, explaining that official action would only piss him off. They understood. I then told them that their squad leader, Stalsberg, and I would stay out of it. I wanted them to fix it so that Gleason would not destroy his life—at least at this early stage of it.

The marriage never happened. I have no idea how they did it, but Gleason dodged that bullet. The squad, already good, got better. I certainly admired the men in that squad.

In my military career, I did two or three things right. Preventing this mistake was one of them. Unfortunately, I was witness to many mistakes, too many of them caused by arrogant leaders.

30

Deaths and White Rocks

oldiers needn't wait for war to die. Mix youth, heavy equipment, aircraft, explosives, realistic training with a dash of stupidity—the usual components of the combat arms in training—and soldiers will figure a way to kill themselves or others. High-speed driving combined with strong German beer also takes a toll. That is not a unique military problem, but it is because they are in the Army that young American soldiers find themselves in Germany. Intelligent leaders, if they can be found, can minimize foolish deaths by paying more attention to the craft of soldiering and less to appearances like shiny floors in garrison and shiny boots in the field. But realistic training will inevitably lead to injuries and deaths. It is small consolation for grieving friends and relatives to hear that scores of combat deaths are saved by their personal loss of a loved one in realistic training, but it's probably true.

Moving armored personnel carriers around at night without a ground guide after soldiers have dismounted is a particularly effective way to kill or maim men. Despite repeated cautioning, some kid will decide to move a tracked vehicle at night to improve a field of fire, to provide for an expeditious tactical exit from the current position, or to relieve the tedium a nineteen-year-old American feels in the middle of the night when he isn't listening to music, chasing girls, or sleeping. Since he intends to move just a few feet, ain't no big thing. No sense bothering nobody. Hell, I know how to drive this thing, and no one is between me and where I want to go—except the guy in the sleeping bag who, unnoticed by the driver, moved to a softer spot on the ground an hour or go. Despite radio announcements, admonishments by junior leaders, and command emphasis, we killed quite a few soldiers that way in the winter of 1961–1962, a particularly cold winter.

Some medics chose death by cozy asphyxiation. The SOP of the U.S. Army in Europe in the early 1960s dictated that tactical wheeled vehicles—jeeps and trucks—not put up their canvas tops; they restricted visibility. But medical vehicles of all types were an exception to policy, since freezing broken soldiers is a bad idea, and cold contributes to shock. Despite being warned that running engines at night to keep warm in a vehicle risked poisoning and possible death from carbon monoxide leaking into passenger space from the exhaust system, cold soldiers did it anyway. They died warm.

Sometimes it's hard to blame anyone for a death. Our infantry battle group was fortunate to have an intelligent man and experienced officer as our observation helicopter pilot. Our aviator and Captain Allen, the Assistant S-3, flew to our field location in the two-seated, bubble-covered chopper. The bird gently descended to land in a snow-covered field near a road. Artfully, the pilot put both skids in the snow before reducing power. But the snow concealed a ditch some three feet deeper than the field. The aircraft dropped at a severe angle to the right, causing the still-turning big blades to smash into the earth. The helicopter was engulfed in flame almost immediately. The pilot got out. Allen did not. That's a hell of a way to go.

Another of our companies blew up some soldiers in a demolition accident. I don't know why it happened, but it cost one man a hand and another, his sight. The incident was veiled in secrecy. Recollection raises a question: Why weren't we told in detail what happened, so that troop confidence could be restored and technical competence enhanced?

At the time, I suspected I was in a rotten outfit. Later experience, including a couple of tours in Vietnam, confirmed my suspicion and put it in perspective. The soldiers were bright and willing; the NCOs were a mixed bag, most of them skilled and dedicated to doing right by the outfit and their soldiers; the junior officers were a gung-ho bunch, generally intelligent and eager; the middle-grade officers, who had survived the reduction in forces after the Korean War, were generally a very conservative, even frightened, bunch. Unimaginative and career-oriented, they endorsed the principle, "When in doubt, yell and shout." I think they bear much responsibility for what happened in Vietnam. I saw it in Germany.

The M-113 Armored Personnel Carrier (APC) was bought all around the world and is still in many armies in the 21st century, but it was new to us in 1961–1962. So were the M-14 rifle, the M-60 machine gun, the M-79 grenade launcher, and other systems that were replacing the World War II family of weapons and equipment that had served us well in The Big War and in Korea. Sergeant Johnson was in another of the rifle companies. His M-113 went to the bottom of the Bug River, taking Johnson with it to his death as his winter clothing and load-bearing belts and straps became entangled in the machine and the icy waters closed over him. I wasn't there, but, since my previous experience was light infantry, I was aware of my ignorance and interested in learning about the four damned machines I had in my platoon. Johnson's entry into the river was a fall from a steep bank with both driver and commander hatches open. The personnel carrier filled and a man died. The manufacturer's instructions said—highlighted in red ink—that the hatches should be closed upon entry. The vehicle would go under and then bob up. Only then should the hatches be opened. Someone knew better than the manufacturer. He should have gone to jail for this one.

We all should have seen a demonstration by people who knew what they were doing, and then we should have entered the river from a spot on the bank with a gentle gradient. Once upon a time, military teaching followed demonstration with a practical exercise, but I found myself in a strange new Army. There was a lot of shouting, threatening, and blaming, but there wasn't much teaching. The only one of the 1,500 of us who had experience babysitting the mobile refrigerators disguised as APCs was a sour warrant officer sent unwillingly from Alaska to Bamberg, Germany specifically to marry us to the machines. Something in our military subculture disinclined our leadership to listen to him, a mere warrant officer. When it was decided by some cretin at higher headquarters to run the engines once before and once after midnight, the warrant pointed out that some gizmo would go bonkers from carbon accumulation if the M-113 was cranked up so frequently. He was ignored. The machines were cranked up, the gizmo went bonkers; since there was a shortage of gizmos in theater, we had to park the machines for weeks to wait for gizmos. During the height of the Cold War, we introduced new weapons systems and ignored experts in their employment and maintenance.

Since the infantry was not accustomed to maintaining sensitive machines, one wonders why we did not turn to our brothers in armor or ordinance for help, but then one wonders why we didn't turn to our friends in artillery for help with the giant 4.2-inch mortar platoon of the combat support company. (Few infantrymen could put mortar fire on the target. They were a menace to us all.) Tactically, it seemed that we weren't quite sure if the M-113 was a truck or a tank. The building of The Wall in 1961 turned the Cold War up a notch and loosened purse strings for military procurement, but there was much bumbling and stumbling in the integration of the new gear into the hyperconservative post–Korean War U.S. Army that attached more importance at the troop level to painting rocks white, shiny boots, and short haircuts. Stupidity, blended with supreme confidence, produced arrogance. Conscription was the substitute for leadership. Bad leaders had an almost limitless supply of manpower, suggesting to me that what was free was not valued. And form defeated substance, to our later discomfort.

The Colonel Blimps and the junior officers of the 60s exhibited the same distance civil society manifested between the values of parents and their children. From the perspective of one who was a sergeant in Korea and a lieutenant in Germany in the early 1960s, the Army we took to Vietnam was a well-tanned body that concealed a cancer. The cancer was centralization that crowded out individual initiative. Sergeants were pushed aside as junior officers took up their tasks. And the junior officers were bullied by the mindless residue personified by the post-Korea reduction in force. The sickness would be exposed. Meanwhile, incompetence and mental rigidity in training killed soldiers who didn't need to die.

31

Doesn't Anybody Know How to Play This Game?

At the age of thirty, with a false career start behind me, I had serious doubts about my decision to return to the Army. Had I romanticized the camaraderie in Korea? Had I been mesmerized by John Kennedy's inaugural address? Had I been bored as a high school teacher and simply ready for a change? Maybe Lydia, my wife of five years, had it right: the itch was impatience, something that could be scratched in law school or in chasing a Ph.D. in preparation for university teaching and writing. Perhaps a career as a Foreign Service Officer would fill my insistent but indeterminate yearning for noble service, a yearning frustrated by the boobs of Bamberg. What was certain was the yawning chasm between Kennedy's clear summons to nobility on that blustery January day in Washington in 1961 and the mind-numbing reality of the infantry battle group in Germany. One wondered if the initial assignment was bad luck, a tour in a particularly fouled-up outfit. But, perhaps the whole Army had gone to hell.

By 1963 anomalies had piled up in sufficient number to raise doubts about continuing the soldier's trade. I analyzed the situation, precisely the process that had disturbed what passed for my adult leadership: fat and inflexible majors. One set of anomalies was the consequence of modernization. The other was philosophical.

The mechanization of the infantry produced a kind of no-man's-land between the old and the new. The sergeant in a rifle platoon in Korea in 1953 measured defensive frontages in hundreds of yards. The lieutenant in a mechanized rifle platoon in Germany in 1962 measured defensive frontages in kilometers. The sergeant had served in the foot infantry, but as a lieutenant he was prepared to learn new tricks. The problem was that his superiors were still wrestling with the new tricks themselves. They hadn't decided if the M-113 Armored Personnel Carrier was a truck or a tank. Of course, it was neither, but it was new to both the rookies and old soldiers of the 3d Infantry Division. Unfortunately, neither the rookies nor the old guys knew how to fight or to optimize the operation of the APC.

The wide platoon defensive front, measured in kilometers, not yards, normally meant that the enemy in Germany had several high-speed approaches available to him for his tank and mechanized infantry attack. The solution from the defender's position was both simple and insoluble: he required antitank weapons capable of defeating enemy armor or mechanized infantry on several avenues of approach. The antitank systems available then in the U.S. Army were dated and, had they existed in sufficient numbers, were barely adequate. The problem was that a platoon had one 3.5-inch rocket launcher of Korean War vintage, a slight improvement on the World War II "bazooka" of popular memory. So, the diligent platoon leader asked his company commander for the company's two jeep-mounted 106 mm recoilless rifles to cover enemy avenues of approach into his platoon sector. Alas, the request was routinely denied. Two, sometimes three, platoon leaders were begging for the only two gun jeeps the company commander had. Further, for their own survival in taking on enemy armor, the gun-mounted jeeps were employed in pairs. This was necessary because, upon firing, the 106 revealed its position with a very visible back-blast. So the 106 squad leader would fire, then relocate as his partner fired, both scooting to avoid deadly enemy counterfire. The 106 was very accurate, but that damned back-blast invited almost immediate retribution.

The gun-jeep problem was addressed later by putting lethal antitank weapons into the hands of individual GIs, but in 1962, I was castigated for telling duly constituted military authority the obvious: the 106s stored in warehouses needed to be issued on the basis of four or six per rifle company until a better solution was found.

Similarly, the two machine guns and one 3.5-inch rocket launcher in a rifle platoon were inadequate for the battles we were told we would fight. It was clear to me that each of the three rifle squads of the rifle platoon required a machine gun and an antitank weapon. My rants on these themes were quelled by my commanders and their little helpers called "the staff." I was labeled a troublemaker. Lieutenants, like small children, were to be seen, not heard. Not for the last time in my career, I was a pest.

There were other issues that might be called philosophical. I requested ammunition for the M-14 rifles carried by my soldiers, because it seemed reasonable for them to regularly qualify in their primary business: they were called riflemen. Their job was to shoot straight. And several of my NCOs had run rifle ranges and taught marksmanship recently. Request denied. Marksmanship was the concern of others. The Battle Group's ammo was shot up by a rifle team being prepared for the highly publicized international Le Clerc NATO competition. Another strike on the troublemaker. Platoon leaders were told that they were responsible for everything their men did or failed to do, but initiative was crushed by a highly centralized system whose most obvious characteristic was plodding orthodoxy.

That same system decided that an officers' bowling competition, by company, was just the ticket to bolster officers' morale. Not necessarily a bad idea, except that it was mandatory. Officers would leave their troops in the field to go bowling. One trip in an open jeep watching my soldiers being left in the boondocks as I joined the company officers for beer and bowling in a comfortable setting was enough for me. Soldiers in freezing woods and fields—officers in a bowling alley. As one would later ask, what was wrong with this picture? My refusal to bowl, my third or fourth strike, resulted in my transfer to—God help us all—headquarters company. The least technical of men became the Communications Platoon Leader.

Recalling my 1963 career reassessment suggests the question posed by baseball manager Casey Stengel as he observed the ineptness of his recently founded New York Mets: Doesn't anybody here know how to play this game?

Thank God there was a professional team down the road. After an interlude with the Transportation Corps—which I thoroughly enjoyed—I arranged to be traded.

I suppose it is possible to exaggerate the differences between my Bamberg misadventures and my later experiences in Bad Toelz with the 10th Special Forces Group. I just don't know how. The Special Forces command climate was optimal: receptive to initiative from below. The NCOs were extraordinarily skilled, ready to tutor the new officer eager to learn. Sergeant Samson did just that in demolition skills, as Sergeant Hardin did likewise in communications skills. I was the XO, the number two man in Detachment A-4 of A Company, and a very happy soldier. I thought I was being used intelligently. The physical beauty of Bad Toelz and the majesty of the Alps enhanced the assignment, approximating heaven on earth.

And we had our own saint.

32

Vater Unser

Our Priest wasn't *the* priest. *The* priest was 10th Special Forces Group Chaplain and a Master Parachutist, but we had to dress him for every jump. He was alive because fellow jumpers looked out for him. A major, he supported his widowed mother who lived with him. He was, in fact, a mamma's boy. The Group Chaplain was not a bad man. He was an ordinary man with ordinary concerns: do the job according to his lights, conform, get promoted, enjoy status in an elite organization.

Neither was Our Priest another 10th Group Chaplain, young and energetic, who often tagged along when an A Team set out on a mountain walk, and was quite capable of bantering with the roughnecks and happy to join in a poker game. That priest-captain was an Irishman proud of his excellent homilies, or is that redundant? One day after Mass he asked a senior sergeant what he thought of the homily. The sergeant paused, furrowed his brow, and pronounced on the subject: "It was verbose, as usual, unfocused, and too clever. I want you to be clear, concise, and complete. If you were an NCO I'd insist that you attend a course in MOI [Methods of Instruction] or reduce you one grade. But, since you're a priest and an officer, I suppose we'll have to endure your drivel until you're reassigned." The padre fumed. The sergeant was pleased in taking the padre down a notch. Note that this exchange was between two Irishmen, Father Murphy and Sergeant Brennan.

No, Our Priest marched to the beat of a drum unheard by the rest of us. He was the Post Chaplain, meaning that he was assigned to Bad Toelz on the basis of troop population other than 10th Group. He was a captain on the wrong side of 50 when most of us captains had not yet turned 30, and he spoke with a heavy Hungarian accent. Even in Army greens, he had that disheveled Eastern European look. He was socialized neither to the United States nor to the Army; to many in the homogenized and competitive army of 1964, he was different, a ludicrous figure, a loser. But he had an ace in the hole. He was a saint.

Our Priest would knock on the door, ask to watch and bless our sleeping baby, gaze lovingly, pray quietly, and join us for a chat and a tall Bavarian beer as dinner was prepared. It was not entirely accidental that his visits came at dinnertime. One suspects that it was also not planned. At the end of the day he was hungry, so he sought congenial company wherever he found himself, the sight of a child, and a square meal.

He was not a fat man, but he was bulky and awkward. One suspects that in his boyhood and in seminary he was the last one chosen for a pick-up football (soccer) game. He demonstrated his physical clumsiness by breaking a friend's chair, part of a brand new and expensive Danish dining room set, before all the labels were scraped off. Jim and Mary, our friends and victims of Vater Unser, were very angry, but, they grumpily concluded, that's Our Priest.

In the early 1960s, some of the residual rules of post–World War II occupation persisted in administrative barriers to marriages between soldiers and European women. The process was slowed by forms to be filled out, interviews, background investigations, and counseling by commanders and men of the cloth. Maddening administrivia, it was hoped, would cool ardor. Since most American troops in Europe were in Germany, the deliberate obstacles discouraged the marriage of GIs and German women but did not stop them. Many an aging matron married to an old soldier retains just the slightest German accent.

Some twenty years after the war, the social climate had shifted. The so-called *Wirtschaftswunder* (the economic "miracle" of German economic recovery) narrowed differences in standard of living between Germany and the United States, reducing the economic motivation for a German woman to marry an American soldier as a meal ticket. Additionally, a considerable segment of 10th SF consisted of European men attracted to the U.S. Army by the Lodge Act that rewarded five years of honorable service with U.S. citizenship. Among them were Czechs, Poles, Slovaks, Serbs, Croats, Ukrainians, Russians, Lithuanians, Germans, and others. Those men were more at home in Bad Toelz than in Fayetteville, North Carolina. Many of them married German women.

Vietnam service and other "needs of the Service" frequently interrupted "normal" tours. Marriage plans could founder between the rocks of sudden reassignment and the high seas of the deliberately slow process of marriage approval. Our Priest fixed all that.

Blissfully unconcerned with the bureaucratic ballet, he went to the heart of the matter. He determined the seriousness of purpose of the consenting adults, introduced couples to German priests, and man and wife emerged from a German church. The marriage was legal, recognized by American officialdom, and, as they say, they lived happily ever after.

Twenty years had passed—with tours in Vietnam, California, Germany again, Vietnam again, Washington, Virginia, Germany again, West Point, the Army War College in Carlisle, Pa.—between Bad Toelz days and yet another tour in Germany. My wife went to Lourdes in about 1985, a must for us fish-eaters, joining a pilgrimage of Catholic soldiers and their families from many nations. In the quiet darkness, she wended her way carefully to a shrine for quiet worship. Breaking the silence was the unmistakably accented *basso profundo* of Our Priest as he awkwardly and lovingly guided his flock to the same destination. He didn't know how to whisper. My bride addressed him in the darkness by name with a question mark. He removed the question mark, guilty to the charge of being Our Priest. They agreed to meet the next day.

Although, after so many years and so many souls, he did not recognize her in the light of day, he opened a worn notebook arranged chronologically to find "Michael Gole" and the date and place Our Priest baptized our son.

I heard that as recently as the year 2000, he was still stumbling around in Europe, pitching in when God and man need a hand without paperwork. Presumably he still knocks on the door of households blessed with an infant child and the wafting scent of dinner in the making.

The 10th Group Chaplains will one day be happy in Paradise, but Our Priest will sit directly at the right hand of God. I rely upon his loud accented English to make the case to our Maker for my admission, though my paperwork is not up to military or civil service standards.

Gole, oldest of seven children, demonstrating at age three the petulance of an army colonel, Washington Square in Greenwich Village, New York City. He lived on Barrow, 11th, Jane, Christopher, Charles, and Perry Streets in the Village, before moving to 29th Street, Chelsea.

The author in his First Holy Communion get-up imitating a good boy. Born in St. Vincent's, baptized in Saint Joseph's, he attended St. Veronica's, St Columbo's, St. Mary's and Sts. Joachim and Anne. Then the nuns gave him to the Marianists at Chaminade High School.

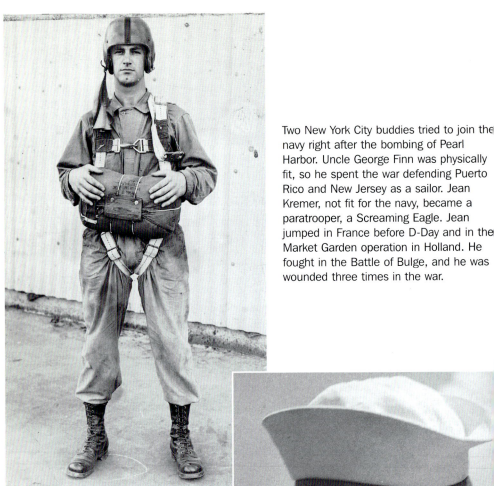

Jean Kremer

Two New York City buddies tried to join the navy right after the bombing of Pearl Harbor. Uncle George Finn was physically fit, so he spent the war defending Puerto Rico and New Jersey as a sailor. Jean Kremer, not fit for the navy, became a paratrooper, a Screaming Eagle. Jean jumped in France before D-Day and in the Market Garden operation in Holland. He fought in the Battle of Bulge, and he was wounded three times in the war.

George Finn

Private Gole, recruit, indestructable and America's secret weapon, in a suntan uniform of 1952. Training at Camp Pickett, Va., included basic training, medical training, and introduction to the Old South. He wanted infantry and to be the Audie Murphy of the Korean War.

ARMED FORCES LIBERTY PASS	SERVICE ARMY	DATE ISSUED 24 Oct 52
LAST NAME—FIRST NAME—MIDDLE INITIAL Gole, Henry G		CARD NO. 85
SERVICE NO. US51177493	GRADE—RATE Pvt	
ORGANIZATION—INSTALLATION—BASE Co A 6th Bn MRTC Cp Pickett, Va		
TIME LIMITS See Reverse Side		
SIGNATURE AND GRADE OF ISSUING OFFICER DANIEL F LAZICKI Capt MSC (Cmdr)		
DD FORM 345 1 Apr 50 GPO 16—62331-1	REPLACES WD AGO FORMS 7 AND 8. NAV PERS FORM 547 AND CG FORMS 2518 AND 2792 WHICH MAY BE USED.	

This first pass allowed the veteran of six weeks to escape the clutches of duly constituted authority for 36 hours. The pass was kept by the first sergeant in a locked drawer in the Orderly Room and given to "good soldiers." There was nothing automatic about it.

At the 25th Division Replacement Company, after a miserable ride north from Pusan in a windowless train, the author got his wish without asking for it. His military occupational specialty, MOS, was changed from medic (1666) to infantry-man (1745). He was now a trigger-puller.

The replacement went from division to regiment to battalion to Charlie Company. Under cover of dark, Buel Nixon, John Plunkett, and the author changed the whitewashed stone "Charlie" sign on the hillside to "Chimpo," Korean or Japanese, they thought, for penis.

Lakeview Manor, home of the author and John Plunkett, his assistant BAR man from Rome, N.Y., and a few rats and mice. Their beds were made of engineer stakes, commo wire, and flattened C-ration boxes, but they were usually on patrol, outposts, or on alert at night.

The Army provided interesting work. Gole with the BAR he carried for five months. It is twice the weight of the M-1 rifle. His platoon sergeant said, "You're a big kid," tossing it to him without consulting the human resources person or his guidance counselor.

The author's normal equipment load for contact patrol activity as BAR man. An assistant gunner usually carried eight extra magazines. Personal pistols, knives, knuckles, and blackjacks were usually brought from home or purchased on the black market or rear areas in Korea. *BAR from the collection of Waldo Ward. Photo courtesy of John Pepper*

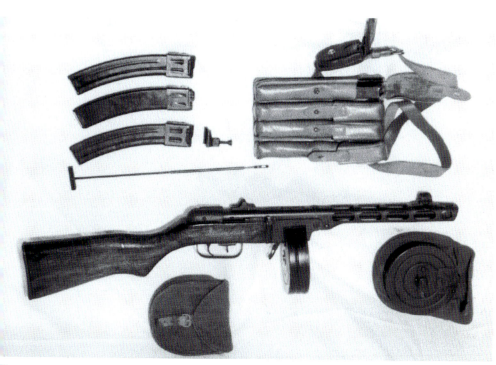

The most common enemy weapon was the Type 50 Chinese submachine gun or "Burp Gun." This was a copy of the Russian PPSh 41. Two types of magazines were used, the 71-round drum or the 35-round box type. The drum magazine seemed most prevalent. A reliable and robust weapon for close quarter fighting; however, it lacked penetrating power. A good choice for an Army that had unlimited manpower. *Burp gun from the collection of Edward Goldman. Photo courtesy of John Pepper*

Kim Yung Hawn, a KATUSAs, Korean Attached to the United States Army, in Gole's squad. During his first night on line, the author "captured" a KATUSA from another squad. They had not been formally introduced. He and Kim looked just like the bad guys.

The author left the Army in 1954, continued his education, and taught at Baldwin Senior High School in New York for three years. In his 1961 Inaugural Address, John F. Kennedy told Gole to ask what he could do for his country. Gole returned to the army at twenty-eight.

Gole, squatting, front row, 4th from right, in Germany, 1965. Edwin McNamara, squatting, front row, 3rd from right, was KIA in 1966 in Vietnam, leaving a widow and four small children. Some died in combat. Others became generals. *Sic transit gloria mundi.*

L to R front: Boggs, Proesser, Young, Bigley, House. *L to R standing:* Hancock, Roderick, Head, Fenlon, Norris, Jenkins, Smith, Cole, Gole, Weakley. From 9 October to 9 November 1966, these SF soldiers led 244 Montagnards on a mobile guerilla mission called BLACKJACK 21.

Montagnards shot water buffaloes and dried the meat by hanging strips in the jungle so that the entire area looked like a Christmas tree. They said, "VC water buffalo" and gave each American a kind of shish kebab of cooked meat and leaves on a bamboo shaft.

L to R: Jim Fenlon, commander of BLACKJACK 21, smirks as Colonel Kelly comments while pinning a medal on the author after they came out of the jungle. Youthful versions of Alvin Young, Billy Boggs, Bill Roderick, Ben Hancock, and Butch House, MD, are also visible.

L to R: Vaclav Hradecky, Major Buttermore, Lieutenant Colonel Stein and the author in Dong Ba Thin in 1967. Escaping Czechoslovakia, refugee Hradecky joined the U.S. Army, retiring a lieutenant colonel. His kids are: a West Point graduate, a Ph.D., a nurse, and a social worker.

L to R: Moye, Storter, Ruff, and Bentley of CCC jumped into Cambodia from the tailgate of a C-130 at 10,000 feet at night on a recon mission. Maintaining visual contact during free-fall and assembly on the ground in a denied area at night is difficult.

L to R, last row: Chuck Behler, Mike Sheppard, and Mike Bentley of RT Montana. Sheppard, ONE-ZERO (Commander), later practiced law. Bentley became a nurse. Behler retired a Sergeant Major. They chose to live on the edge where life and death routinely hold hands.

When conditions prohibited flight over the objective area, recon teams would maintain radio contact with Kontum via this craggy radio relay site in Laos. A few CCC men, rotated on a weekly basis, essentially said to the enemy: "If you want it, come and take it."

Gen. Creighton Abrams, asked Ruff, *(L)* how long he had been there. RT leader Ruff shook the General's hand. Looking him in the eye, he said: "I've been waiting twenty fucking minutes." Ruff retired a sergeant major. SSgt. Don Green *(R)* retired a major.

When landing was not possible, "strings" were dropped through a hole in the jungle. Recon men attached themselves by "D-rings" to the strings. Upper leg circulation cut by straps and sweating troops chilled rapidly at over 100 m.p.h. insured a miserable ride to safety.

A 122 mm rocket's impact point near RT NEVADA's team room, 13 Feb 1971. The method: measure distance to target; place rocket on a couple of boards an angle derived from a firing table; set delayed firing device; leave the launch site before detonation to avoid detection.

CCC was home for 100 Americans and 1,000 mercenaries—Nungs, Vietnamese, and Montagnards—in 1970. A trench with overhead cover and bunkers runs around the perimeter. The small circles are mortar pits. The all-important helicopter pad is not visible in photo.

Czech-born old timer Jan Novy awarded the Purple Heart. The three men with him were KIA. As he left Vietnam he told the author: "Herr Major, die junge Burschen sind gefallen. Der Alter kommt durch." (The young lads fell in combat. The old man survives.)

CCC honors Fritz Krupa, Exploitation Company Commander, KIA. The American facing the empty jump boots is Lieutenant Dobreiner. The American with glasses is German-born Heinz Roesch, who succeeded Fritz as Company Commander and also died in combat.

Nuuanu Pali. Oahu's scenic masterpiece at the head of verdant Nuuanu Valley.

Dear Stammtischbruder! The very, very best regards from a wonderful R&R in Hawaii is sending you your old hard-core buddy, Hauptsturmfuehrer, S/Heinz.

POST CARD

ADDRESS

MAJ. HENRY G. GOLE
%/o BROWN
235 WYNGATE DR.
NO. MASSAPEQUA, N.Y.
11758

The author got this card from Heinz the day after he was informed that Heinz was KIA. It says: "Dear Stammtischbruder, the very, very best regards from a wonderful R&R in Hawaii is sending you your old hard-core buddy, Hauptsturmfuehrer, S/Heinz."

Beautiful wife Lydia and author, with Horst and Poldi Maasen, at the Attaché Ball in Bonn in 1977. The Pentagon, Armed Forces Staff College, and Attaché Course were stops between Vietnam and arrival in Bonn 1973. All about this (3rd) tour in Germany was good.

Ambassador to the Federal Republic of Germany Stoessel and Lydia Gole promoting the author to lieutenant colonel in 1977. The author gets angry when know-nothings criticize the Department of State. Most critics could not qualify to enter the Foreign Service.

Michael Gole, proud career Air Force NCO, and his bride LeAnne, daughter of a career Air Force NCO, are flanked by the groom's parents in 1988. The bride and groom have since given the author and Lydia three (almost) perfect grandchildren.

Col. Don Lunday, old comrade from 10th Special Forces Group in Germany in 1964, retires the author and presents an award in 1988. The author thought himself too sophisticated to react emotionally to ending active duty begun in 1952. He was wrong.

The Special Operations Association opines: "You have never lived until you have almost died. For those who have fought for it, life has a special flavor the protected will never know." The author joins his comrades in believing and endorsing that pronouncement.

33

Ski

ki was never mistaken for Michelangelo's idealized David, the perfect male torso, nor for the handsome and well-groomed Cary Grant. In fact, the stumpy figure God gave him had the look of a body that had fallen into a cement mixer and emerged with some rocks randomly attached to it. But he knew a hell of a lot about a hell of a lot of things, including Europe. Languages were something he acquired with the ease of a dog gathering fleas. His language and survival skills were enhanced by being born in the former Yugoslavia and being kicked around by masters of abuse before joining the U.S. Army and becoming a Special Forces soldier. His native wit and good humor matched his many skills, most of them invisible until required, as evidenced by his readiness to tell those he trusted stories in which he was invariably the butt of the joke. His Hamburg story, told over a beer, is such a tale.

We were reunited in Monterey, California, at the Defense Language Institute where Ski sampled the wares of several departments before being discovered as competent in one language after another. He joined me in the German Department, where I was wrestling with the mysteries of the language of Luther, Goethe, and Grass as Ski relaxed in his competence. The subject, as we imbibed on a Friday afternoon, was accents, how useful they are, how difficult to lose, and what a curse the wrong accent can be.

Ski had enjoyed the delights of Hamburg, that old Hanseatic city of waterfront activity, magnificent brick architecture, fashionable shops, and marvelous churches. To be honest, his focus had been pleasures of the flesh and grape, after which he stumbled in the wee hours in some confusion to his big American automobile parked somewhere in the neighborhood.

Finding said vehicle was a small problem, as was his attempt to put a large key into a door lock that had shrunk significantly in his absence. A bigger problem for Ski was found in the persons of the two Hamburg cops observing an obvious attempt by a suspicious-looking dwarf to break into an American luxury car. Those cops knew the lowlifes attracted to sin city and were prepared, particularly in the hours before dawn.

They approached the car thief to ask what he thought he was doing. Ski's slurred response in fluent bad German—Ski's languages were all fluent and bad—was improbable. Accustomed to manufactured tales, the officers of the law asked what Ski did for a living. When he responded that he was an American soldier, the cops continued their interrogation in English, where-upon Ski's heavily accented English betrayed him. His military ID card was presumed to be as false as his English, resulting in Ski finding himself spread-eagled on the hood of his elegant car as his body was prodded, then deposited in a foul-smelling drunk tank in the local jailhouse.

In due course, calls to the American Consulate in Hamburg and to mili-tary authority revealed that the odd character was in fact both an American soldier and the owner of said automobile.

The moral of the story is clear. Make every effort to speak your newly acquired language without a foreign accent.

Witty and self-deprecating, Ski was also a tough, no-nonsense sergeant. As a bachelor, he lived in barracks. In 1967–68 there were generally two cate-gories of soldier-students at the school: old sweats like Ski and Gole, and bright lads from the colleges who preferred a four-year enlistment in intelli-gence work and staying alive to taking their chances as infantrymen in Viet-nam. They tested and defied the military system and so-called leaders, and routinely put sand into the gears of the Green Machine. With the military pecking order in disrepair, the leaders turned to Ski.

Ski was a pragmatic fixer of problems, but, he reminded military author-ity, he was a student, and not in the chain of command. When more-or-less grown men pleaded with him, he made a deal: he'd fix the problem his way, no questions. The deal done, Ski fixed the problem.

When a second young recalcitrant showed up severely and mysteriously bruised, good order and discipline were restored in the barracks. This con-version of those whose inclination to revolution was exceeded only by con-cern for self-preservation and distaste of injury was effected by a many-sided sergeant, whose explanations in accented English were augmented by hands-on instruction.

My German teachers were first-rate. They were also German and status-conscious. Ski may have modified their sense of propriety just a tad.

A distinguished speaker was to address a foreign policy association in a forum open to the public. My German teachers informed me of the event and proposed we assemble in the bar of the elegant venue for prelecture drinks. I mentioned the plan to Ski, who had both interest and some experi-ence in the theme of the evening. We agreed to meet for that drink before the lecture.

As my wife and I enjoyed our drinks with the faculty, I mentioned that

Ski would join us. Nothing negative was said, but I noted slightly raised eyebrows among the Germans, mostly former officers, and their ladies.

Ski arrived with a most attractive lady, which made for an incongruous pair, not quite beauty and the beast, but you get the idea. The shock effect was not muted by Ski's introduction of the lady as Frau Doktor, a medical doctor as it turned out.

Conversation anticipating the address by our speaker slid from English to German, natural enough to students and their faculty. Someone apologized in English to Ski's lady. She responded in perfect German, her native language.

My teachers no doubt advanced their liberal arts education as they digested the anomalies of the evening. They probably concluded that appearances can deceive, that Ski was a man of many parts.

But I already knew that.

34

The American on the Moon

I n July of 1969, I had been back in Germany for a couple of weeks. I knew I could expect about a year there before returning to Vietnam.

Professional soldiers had seen the shift in public attitude from tepid support to general opposition to the war in Vietnam and observed that German attitudes were becoming less kindly disposed to the U.S. Army. Since the Tet Offensive of 1968 and President Johnson's decision not to run for reelection, the American people and their government had polarized over Vietnam policy. The demons that plagued Johnson and MacNamara would also haunt Nixon and Kissinger as they tried to figure how to get off the tiger's back without ending up in his stomach. At the personal level, in my travels in the United States, I saw the admiring glances at my Green Beret become charges of "baby killer," often spat out by pulchritudinous young things with nice asses. Too bad. I preferred being insulted by acne-faced punks.

German attitudes regarding America and Americans were too complex to describe in a phrase, but generally among older Germans the prevailing attitude was gratitude for the Marshall Plan, CARE packages, the Berlin Airlift, and moral support after World War II, when it seemed the only friend of the political pariah was an Onkel in Amerika. I recall a crude example from Berlin in 1963: a street cleaner saw me in uniform, set aside his broom, doffed his cap, and said, "Danke!"

Just because. Because I was an American.

German youth in the 1960s were generally antiwar, antimilitary, and antiauthority. The anti-Bundeswehr feeling was probably the consequence of German youth's opposition to the American War in Vietnam. This was manifest—among other ways—in the large numbers of young German men who simply refused to serve in the military, preferring an alternative service that their government wisely provided. The young, because they felt no personal guilt for the sins of their fathers, were also tired of the passive way that Bonn followed Washington. German youth—is this surprising to

Americans?—took economic well-being for granted, while the older generation took great pride in the rise from the ashes that was the German "Economic Miracle" of the middle 1950s, that wasn't a miracle at all. It was the product of hard work by Germans and enlightened American economic and foreign policy.

This was the backdrop as I pulled into an Esso station in Bonn, Germany, to tank up before conducting some business at the American Embassy. I was listening on my car radio to breathless reporting of the first moon landing. At that very moment, men, American men, were poised to step on the moon. The gas station attendant pulled himself away from the TV set to respond to a customer: me. Delighted to note the license plates stamped "USA," he took me by the elbow and marched me to the TV set, saying:

"Come! Come! Your fellow Americans have landed! They are about to step on the moon!"

His voice and body English signaled a state of euphoria. His colleague looked away from the TV screen only when he realized that the establishment was graced by the presence of a real, live American. He beamed at me as though I were personally responsible for the unfolding miracle, an event filled with both great promise and great danger, hope and fear inextricably bound together as we watched our species realizing the dream of millennia. Arriving customers expected no service. They joined us, clapping me on the back, admiring the technology, the boldness, the men, the United States, me! It was a rare moment. Several German strangers and I shared the experience. Their joy was real, congratulations offered to me were genuine, my satisfaction was profound as my fellow Americans presented a gift to mankind for which my German companions thanked me, the house American. I liked it a lot. I was as proud as a peacock.

Six months later I was returning to Germany from Switzerland via Zurich on one of man's greatest inventions, a Swiss train. Luxuriating in a first-class compartment, certainly superior to Cleopatra's barge and Air Force One, I noted that it was time for lunch in the only place superior to my compartment, the Speissewagen, the dining car. I sat at a vacant table and resumed my reading. Before long I was joined by a stranger, the norm in European eating places, and I nodded welcome to my new companion as he nodded to me. I returned to my book until the waiter came to our table to take our orders for drinks. I ordered a beer, my companion did likewise. We exchanged greetings and he, noticing my book title, asked in German:

"Are you English?"

"No. I'm an American."

He knew the book, whose title I do not recall, and we discussed literature. I learned that he was a lawyer at home in Zurich and clearly a broadly educated man conversant in many subjects. We ordered our food and continued the conversation which I found stimulating. He was a charming, interesting person. Observing my attire, he exclaimed:

"Aha, you look like you are returning from skiing!"

"I am. It was wonderful. Switzerland is filled with good places to ski, and the Swiss know how to make a visitor comfortable."

"Thank you. I'm pleased that you enjoyed my country."

After a pause:

"Tell me, who will win the downhill in the Olympics?"

He was referring to the upcoming Winter Games of 1972. While living in Europe, I kept track of soccer year-round and skiing in the winter, since most of my European friends tracked those sports the way my American friends followed baseball and football at home.

"Oh, I think the French women are strong. And the Austrian men. What do you think?"

"You are modest. The Americans will win."

"But we have never won the downhill events. Why do you say that? Is this more Swiss courtesy for the visitor?"

"No, no, my friend. My colleague was recently in Colorado and saw your boys training. You Americans will win!"

"Tell me why you say that. It would please me very much to see America win the downhill, but that's unlikely."

He leaned forward and said with great intensity:

"Do you know how they train those American boys?"

"No," I confessed.

"They point the skis straight down the hill, and they go," he said as he pantomimed digging ski poles into snow and the energetic blast off from the starting gate.

"The Americans have decided to win, so they will win."

"Well, it's one thing to want to win and another to win."

"Ah, but it is more than 'wanting.' You have 'decided.' Whatever America wants to do, she does! Your President John Kennedy said to your scientists: 'Put an American on the moon in this decade.' And they did. You have decided to win the downhill in the next Winter Games, so you will. America can do whatever America wants to do. It is only a matter of deciding."

"John Kennedy is no longer President," I said, thinking of his beleaguered opponent of 1960, who now sat in the Oval Office.

"Yes, but whoever sits there is our President, too."

This from a Swiss at the height of the acrimony surrounding the Vietnam War!

When the train pulled into Zurich, the lawyer gave me his card and invited me to visit him, a very un-European burst of spontaneity from a man of his professional standing. Apparently he enjoyed our chat, but not as much as I did. I was very proud to be an American, even when we were being kicked around because of our Vietnam policy. Few Americans realize the enormous reservoir of respect and admiration we enjoy in every corner of the world, even when we trip from time to time. Perhaps we are forgiven because we try to do the right thing. More than once I have been treated like an eminence for simply being an American, a condition to which I was born and for which I often thank God.

35

I'll Never Remember You

Since the 1990s, the disintegration of Yugoslavia has often provided front-page stories. Journalistic accounts from that part of the world take me back to a memorable visit there and, perhaps inevitably, jogs my memory of tales heard over fifty years ago.

As a romantic and a soldier conveniently stationed in Germany, I realized a long-cherished dream in May of 1970 when I visited the land of my father's birth. Despite his absolute conviction that he was born an Austrian, the country he left in 1923 was Yugoslavia. He was an ethnic German in Slovenia, the northwest corner of Yugoslavia. Since he was born in 1909 and never returned to Europe, the intelligence my father passed on to the son born in 1933 was an ode to a Balkan urn: the world of his village was frozen eternally in the memory of the country boy who left the village to raise seven New Yorkers.

That memory was not initially helpful to the pilgrim son in 1970 in a practical way. German place names provided by the father had to be repeated like a mantra until someone, usually a person over sixty who could speak German, would connect the old German name to the Slavic name in place since circa 1919. Through trial and error, using my German and English and my hosts' Serbo-Croatian, I found a town now called Semich, where, according to my father, there was a railroad station. It was, in fact, a tin roof mounted on two-by-fours next to the track. But there I found a Gasthaus whose proprietor would be the source of current intelligence.

My host, on the downhill side of his sixties, arched his eyebrows only a tad as I ordered in German. It was clear that visitors did not run with the bulls through the streets of Semich, nor did I note gaggles of tourists assembled near bridges, towers, arches, cathedrals, or statues, nor any tossing coins in a fountain, none of which were in evidence in any event. As a matter of fact, I soon sensed that my visit might have been the most interesting event in the history of Semich since Marshall Tito—whose picture was prominently displayed in the public room—once flew over the town at thirty thousand feet.

When my beer was brought by my host, I expressed my desire to remain under his roof for a few days. That was promptly arranged at the not unreasonable rate of ten Dinar per night. My razor-sharp mathematics instantly made that out to be about a dollar a night; my graduate school economics made that out to be almost as good a deal as the price of the beer.

In the best European tradition, I asked to see the room offered for the princely sum, and my new friend led the way up one flight of stairs. The room was as neat as it was simple. The most striking features were the view from the single window and—believe it or not—the floor, in that order.

Since the Gasthaus stood in a vineyard on the side of a hill, I looked down, into a valley from which a large onion-domed church sprang out of the surrounding village; the dome, a hundred yards distant, reached my eye level. The road below my window pushed away from the hill allowing a view of the vines to the left. To the right was the impressive railroad station, where not a creature stirred. The view from my window was enough to inspire a romantic poet, or at least it seemed so to the son prepared to see his father's birthplace through rose-colored glasses.

As if to prove that man occupies a position somewhere between angels and animals—his head in the clouds and his feet in the mud—my eyes dropped to the floor. It was extraordinarily clean, but what caught my attention was the varied width of the boards and the irregular spaces between them. The child of 1933 (and veteran observer of the homogenization of truth, beauty, and floorboards in the America of the 1950s) was charmed to discover that standardization had not ruled out the possibility of surprises in Semich. Clearly, too much can be made of irregular floorboards, but they symbolized somehow the opposite of button-down collars, ticky-tack houses, and plastic cups. Perhaps I was prepared to see only the positive aspects of the Heimat.

The room was country-perfect. It even had electric lights, and the hike to the toilet required only a few minutes, if I didn't take a break en route. The unavailability of hot water did not phase this pilgrim!

My host and I retreated to the public room where we sealed our arrangement with a slivovitz, a potent local brew. In a conspiratorial manner, my new friend said that we could talk at length after his regulars departed. I think he was reserved about protracted conversation in German. True to his word, he rejoined me when the last of them was gone and asked how he might help me. I must have appeared to be a man with a mission.

The list of essential elements of information was short: how could I find Mitterdorf, the village of my father, and how could I find his house? I bought the slivovitz, and he talked. His recital was equally brief and expert. The village could be found five kilometers down the dirt road at the end of town. Herr Jaglich, a man of some eighty years, knew everyone and everything about the village: Go there. Ask the first person you see for Herr Jaglich. We practiced pronunciation, sipping slivovitz. YAK LITCH. Accent on first syllable.

More slivovitz, more talk of me, of him, of Tito, of Yugoslavia, Deutschland, and Amerika. One thing was clear: we were splendid fellows. Less clear after our thirst quenching was the exact location of my splendid room and the less splendid but more necessary toilet. Under the motto "all's well that ends well," I crashed and burned, apparently without disgracing the home side.

On the morrow, I rolled out of my crisp sheets, too briefly enjoyed, between four and five in the morning. My uninitiated North American friends need to know that late spring and early summer mornings in Middle Europe—due to latitudes, longitudes, and phenomena too complex for the besotted cognoscenti to explain to simple laymen—happen early, very early, ready or not. Before five in the morning, my onion-domed church was bathed in a soft pink pastel that matched my vineyards and my railroad station. The hike to the toilet accomplished, I was ready to join the Semich chapter of the human race, to the extent that one is ready for anything at five in the a.m.

To my great credit, I recognized my friend and host without benefit of introduction. He asked, in his apparently usual conspiratorial manner, what I'd like for breakfast and, for the first time in my Yugo-adventure, my European savoir-faire let me down with a resounding thud. I ordered "Kaffee und Brot," an early morning incantation that in Germany produced a glutton's delight of various fresh breads, the world's best butter, jellies too delicious to describe, coffee beyond compare, cream, and sugar. But, alas, black coffee, processed to fuel the engine of an army truck, and bread baked the day before yesterday, were plopped on the table before me. I had asked for Kaffee und Brot, and that is what I got—unadorned.

True enough, when I ordered my breakfast, my host did ask if I wanted a slivovitz. In declining, I found myself a minority of one. As guests popped in, each drank an eye-opener and cast that eye about the room searching for the American whose presence was signaled by the distinctive U.S. Forces license plate on the shiny car parked in front of their favorite Gasthaus. Some were curious enough to pop a second white lightening before shuffling off to work. At seven o'clock, I departed for my father's village.

The road was primitive. I dodged large potholes and larger boulders, but the improved dirt road was clearly ancient and quite smooth if one was attentive to the boulders and potholes. After some ten minutes, a small house appeared straight ahead, and the road made a sharp turn to the left as four houses came into view on the left side of the road. A man was pushing a lawn mower under the supervision of an angelic little girl four or five years old.

I stopped the car and approached the man on foot asking in German where I might find Herr Jaglich, repeating the name as I had practiced it. The man smiled and spoke to the girl. She took my hand, leading me to the back door of a neighboring house into which we marched together unannounced. A woman of fifty years looked up as we entered, and again I asked for Herr Jaglich, her father, I learned. She motioned me to follow her into the backyard as she spoke to the little angel.

We stopped on a bank looking down at an old man wearing a net over his head as he tended his bees. He looked up. I said in German: My name is Heinrich Gole; my father was born here and left in 1923. Without skipping a beat, the old man said in German: "My dear God! We sent away a boy, and he sends back a man!" He scrambled up the bank moist-eyed, embraced me, and with great animation told me what a rascal my father was, as though we were discussing the happy events of last weekend.

The improbably lithe eighty-year-old vigorously marched me into his house where he motioned me to sit at the kitchen table as he mused over the half-century as the current events of yesterday. He poured two glasses of slivovitz. The little girl and the fifty-year-old daughter vanished, never to be seen again, to the chagrin of feminists everywhere. He broke and salted the bread. We ate and drank as he welcomed me to the village of my father. I thought I was playing a scene from the Bible and half expected a director to shout, "Print it!" so perfect was our rendition of an ancient rite of welcome. But I was comfortable in the time warp. Even though I felt I was playing out some role as both participant and observer, I was as serene as I have ever been in my life.

My host literally rolled up his sleeves as he asked me how much time I had and just what I wanted to do.

In the next several days, we did what sons in the birthplaces of their fathers have always done. We visited, like stations of the cross, a church, a most modest house, a school, a cemetery, paths in the woods, before finding a place to drink beer and discuss what we had seen. In due course, Herr Jaglich turned me over to a cousin old enough to be my father, a man therefore able to speak German. His name was, improbably, Pepe. I thought a Pepe wore a sombrero, rifle ammo crossed on his chest, and a bushy mustache over gleaming teeth while shouting, "Viva Zapata!" This Pepe was a plainspoken guy whose last name was Golle. That figured. My father's two brothers and a sister who preceded him to Amerika dropped an "l" from the name. Americans said Gole or Golle the same way. Drop the "l." I come from clever peasant stock.

As we wandered in 1970, we frequently came upon the ruins of houses and entire villages not far from my father's village, usually razed and overgrown with vegetation. Each time, I asked Pepe what had happened. The variety of responses affected me deeply, for the responses surprise even a relatively well-traveled professional soldier of middle years with some experience in human foolishness. Italian infantry; German artillery; the RAF bombing at night; American daylight bombing; Tito's troops; Mihailovich forces. That's the way it goes in the old neighborhood. There are lots of equal opportunity misanthropes.

The matter-of-fact manner in which Pepe reported what had happened where once families had lived was striking. That encouraged me to press on with my questioning about his own adventures before, during, and after World War II. My father had never returned to Yugoslavia, told people that he had been born in Austria, and told me that Pepe owned the house where my father was born because Pepe was a staunch Communist and a Tito partisan. Pepe's version, not surprisingly, was different and is generally confirmed by the history of the late 1930s and the war years.

The region in which I wandered had been granted to Mussolini by Hitler. The inhabitants were regarded as being "true to Germany," that is, they had been loyal to old Vienna for about 800 years. They were unhappily and unwillingly joined to the newly created Yugoslavia in 1919 when the victorious powers of the Great War of 1914–1918 dismembered the Austro-Hungarian Empire in the name of Wilsonian self-determination of nations. Hitler, in his deal with Mussolini, took people like Pepe to his bosom. Pepe was relocated to a German-dominated area in which he was given a horse, a house, and land, presumably the property of some other poor soul who was similarly relocated—or worse. He was fully prepared to live happily thereafter.

But a funny thing happened on Hitler's road to world conquest and a thousand-year Reich. Easy victories became hard victories and then turned to defeat. Because Hitler had to scrape the bottom of the barrel, Pepe found himself drafted into the Wehrmacht. Then one night Tito's partisans visited him with an offer he could not refuse: he would join the partisans or they would have to kill him. In this way are staunch Communists converted to the one true faith. It was farewell to horse, house, land, and wife for some time, but Pepe is a survivor. At the end of the war, he was on the right side as Tito did in Mihailovich, and Pepe was re-resettled to become the proud possessor of the house in which my father was born. As far as I could see it, his ideology consisted of making it through one day at a time.

The post–Cold War period seems to have made the eastern part of Europe free for the old tribalisms to emerge. They are characterized by the bloodiest kinds of religiously inspired conflict. That's the way it was for Pepe. Curiously, the worldwide competition between the United States and the Soviet Union put a lid on that kind of behavior, at least in Europe. With that rumination, my odyssey turns to its sweet conclusion and words I shall take to my grave.

I left for Germany via Austria, but still in Yugoslavia, I picked up two hitchhikers, young men who looked like students. They addressed me in

Serbo-Croatian without effect. I tried German with the same result. One said, word by word, "Do-you-speak-English?" I responded in the affirmative, in the same word-by-word manner, adding that I was an American. That pleased them. I was the first American either had ever met, something I heard in almost every conversation in Slovenia. Despite the widely held notion that Americans were disliked during the war in Vietnam, I experienced the opposite, particularly in Slovenia, where I basked in the glow of my American halo. On one excursion with Pepe, a woman flagged me down by jumping in front of my car as I attempted to drive past her house on a country road. She stopped me and ran into the house to return with a photo album into which she excitedly pointed to pictures while repeating "Shee-ka-go, Shee-ka-go!" and indicating my license plates to say "USA, USA!" as in oo-es-ah! These incantations were interrupted only as she hugged me like a long-lost son. My achievement was that I was wise enough to be born an American.

Rural Slovenes, even university students, were apparently oblivious to anti-Americanism during my idyllic visit in the late spring of 1970 before I returned to Vietnam for a second tour there. The engineering students in my car, as we proceeded in the direction of a border crossing point into Austria some two hours distant, were most kindly disposed to all things American and voraciously curious about me and my country. Seldom have I felt so good about being alive. My happy visit to my father's village, the prospect of a leisurely drive back to southern Germany via Austria in the perfect spring weather, and the excellent company combined to produce a state of intoxication. One cannot be sure of such things, but I had the distinct impression that the young men felt just as I did as we conducted our tour of the world's horizon.

As we approached Bled, their hometown on the Austrian frontier, I am convinced that my feeling of regret that our serendipitous time together was coming to an end was shared by my passengers. I said in the very deliberate and formal style of English that we had adopted to accommodate their less-than-perfect mastery of the language, "I want you to be my guests for a glass of beer in the beautiful sunshine before we part."

Conversation continued, but it took a sad turn as the time for good-bye neared. We dropped off one of the lads in front of an apartment building in the small city and bade farewell. The second young man said that such a magnificent automobile should not be driven on the poor road to his village. I told him that it is for such roads that magnificent cars are built.

When we stopped in front of his house in the village, he faced me from the front passenger's seat, shook my hand, and with tears running down his face he said:

"I'll never remember you."

It was not the time for an English lesson. I said:

"I'll never remember you."

I drove away.

I don't know their names, but I'll never forget them.

Herr Jaglich, the keeper of the Gasthaus, and Pepe are probably dead. The students of 1970 are in their fifties. Their part of the former Yugoslavia escaped much of the violence, but I wonder how they are managing in the renewed tribal warfare in that part of the world. I wonder who lives in the house where my father was born.

36

Kent State

n the good company of Austrians and Americans while visiting Vienna in 1970, we heard that National Guard troops shot and killed Kent State students. I had visited that college briefly in 1955, had spent a year in Vietnam from 1966 to 1967, and was to return for a second tour in a few months. The confluence of those places and events invaded my consciousness that night in Vienna and left me irritated, pensive, and depressed. Vietnam, Vienna, Kent. Goddamn it! We were being stupid again.

Between tours in Vietnam, we professional soldiers could not fail to see the popular indifference or tacit support of the war in 1966 degenerate into the widespread American opposition by 1970, or sooner. Passing through airports in uniform early on, one sensed support and respect. Late in the war, barely concealed animosity, even hate, was evident. Friends and relatives at home asked soldiers what it was all about and where it would end, and we pretended to know. Mature Europeans kindly disposed toward America politely avoided the subject, presumably to spare my feelings, but the general opposition to the war, particularly by young Europeans, was in the air. It surfaced as an anti-Bundeswehr movement in Germany, where conscientious objection to military service was widespread. All armies were in disfavor in 1970—if one discounted Jane Fonda's endorsement of the People's Army of Vietnam gun crews in North Vietnam.

A group of us had just returned from the American Embassy in Vienna for a nightcap in the quarters of our American host, a military attaché. We were, as Fate would have it, discussing Austrian youth, since the purpose of the social event at the Embassy we had just attended was to give future leaders access to American officials. Our host noted the time aloud, about midnight as I recall, as he turned on his radio for a news wrap-up.

We were stunned at the news from Ohio. I remember precisely what I thought as I recalled my visit to idyllic Kent State, a picture-postcard campus:

"God help us all! American draft dodgers have shot American war protesters on an American college campus. What next?"

I returned to Vietnam to rejoin skilled and dedicated American soldiers doing their best in an extremely hazardous mission. They knew what they were doing; my government did not. Not long thereafter, my country deserted our allies, deciding in 1973 to do what young Turk journalists had been defamed for advising in 1963 and 1964. I think my faith in my government hit rock-bottom that night in Vienna. The country deserved better than what passed for political leadership from both major parties.

37

Uncle Walter, My Boy, and Vietnam

No one knows with any degree of precision what went on in the heads of our children as we regular soldiers served repeated tours in Vietnam while our kids heard whatever kids hear at school, at play, and on TV. My seven-year-old boy called Cronkite "Uncle Walter." He wasn't alone. Cronkite was the trusted uncle to Americans during the war in Vietnam. He's probably a decent fellow, and I bear him no personal malice, but his signature sign-off, "And that's the way it is," never failed to anger me. I have been known to shout back at the screen, "That's *not* the way it is."

The nightly exit line was portentous and deceptive. It was portentous because it suggested that we had just heard all that really mattered in the world, and we had gotten it as unprocessed truth from the avuncular Cronkite. It was deceptive for more complicated reasons.

The film we saw on TV as "today's news" was, in fact, at least 48 hours old. Film shot in the boondocks was physically transported to Saigon by helicopter or surface transportation and then on to New York by commercial airliners, in those days before real-time direct transmission via satellites was possible. So, the viewer saw video at least two days old that was married to audio stories hot off the wires—AP, UP, Reuters—or to voice communication between editors in New York and reporters in Saigon. That edited product was represented as truth, without the kind of caution that was beginning to appear on cigarette packages. We did not see, for example, "WARNING: the pictures you're watching have nothing to do with the words you're hearing." Or, "The viewer should know that the shooting you are watching is some neat footage from an event that took place two days ago in Dak To, and the news story you are hearing describes an event that took place in My Tho four hours ago." Not saying that was a lie.

My boy had images and words in his head that were his reality. Many of them came from the millionaire anchor man alleged to be the most trusted man in America, who said, "That's the way it is." So, that's the way it was.

137

Combat footage, fresh combat footage, was deemed necessary for an audience whose young was raised on Howdy Doody, an audience conditioned to Uncle Miltie, Ed Sullivan, and Sid Caesar. Show biz and war biz became news biz, and those who brought it to us were trusted. And rewarded.

I got some unsolicited advice from my boy on the day I was to leave him and his mother for another year in Vietnam. It was far more than unsolicited; it was painful because it revealed the depth of his fear for me, a fear I had stupidly missed until that day.

My first tour saw him age from three to four, and I wasn't sure just what sugar plums were in his head as we faced another year of separation and he would advance from seven to eight. During the first tour, I'm told, he pointed to all aircraft he spotted in the sky, saying "Daddy"; when last seen, his father was climbing the steps to enter an airplane. My boy was already a veteran of the war in Vietnam. What was in his seven-year-old head?

I found out.

Just a few hours before my departure, he took my hand and said, "Dad, come with me." He led me to a patch of woods near the attached house in Stewart Field, a subpost of the Military Academy at West Point where he and his mother, joined by my widowed mother-in-law, would stay while I was gone. He told me where to sit. Then he demonstrated, climbing a tree, that I shouldn't climb trees: the "bad guys" would see and shoot me. Next he took up a firing position on the ground, cautioning me to stay low so that enemy bullets would sail harmlessly overhead. Then, crouching, he coached me on how to move through the jungles of the housing area, home to "waiting wives" and their rug rats for a year while Daddy was away. He was dead serious and showed considerable nervousness as he conducted my training.

His intent was clear. He was coaching me in techniques designed to keep me alive, an objective that made good sense to me and clearly mattered to him. The techniques came from TV, and even a seven-year-old knew that Uncle Walter was unimpeachable. His pronouncements had the authority of absolute truth. To be fair to my son and to Uncle Walter, I knew that the boy augmented his TV war-fighting insights with some advanced GI Joe fantasies as he dressed and equipped Joe, the paratrooper, diver, pilot, and master of all military skills. Even before the fighting in Vietnam, boys had "played guns," but GI Joe made it real. Until then, dolls had been "for girls." Somehow the guns made it OK for boys to have dolls.

But there was more than childish play in my training that day. The seven-year-old's concern for his father's welfare moved me, reminding me that my demise had implications beyond a noble death on the field of honor: a fine end for me, but the beginning of serious problems for my wife and son. Certainly my boy's take on the war and what it meant came closer to the truth than the veteran journalist's. The boy didn't garble pictures and words. He went to the heart of the matter.

I'm not sure what Uncle Walter wanted: Justice? Truth? Reputation? Perhaps he was conflicted, as we all were, but I know what my boy wanted.

My son wanted his father.

Part IV

Vietnam: The Men

. . . in which the narrator serves in the 5th Special Forces Group for a year and then another year in Kontum in Command & Control Center (CCC), Studies & Observation Group (SOG), with noble men he cannot forget.

The Zeitgeist and My Little World

The first knock-down-drag-out battle between the varsity teams of the U.S. Army and the Peoples' Army of Vietnam was fought in November 1965 in the Ia Drang Valley. Perversely, both sides drew lessons from that battle that promised ultimate victory. The United States concluded that the experiment with vertical envelopment using helicopters was validated. The enemy concluded that he could neutralize both American mobility and firepower by choosing when to fight and by fighting "belt buckle to belt buckle." The Americans could not use superior artillery and aerial firepower if friend and foe were entangled in very close combat.

Earlier, in January 1963, American journalists present at the battle of Ap Bac had learned a different lesson not welcomed then by American leaders in Saigon, nor by many old soldiers much later. Despite the latest in American arms and equipment, including the M-113 Armored Personnel Carrier, and support from artillery, helicopters, and fighter bombers, the Army of the Republic of Vietnam, ARVN, was unable to defeat lightly armed guerrillas, even in the set-piece battle they sought and got at Ap Bac. What pundits call the moral dimension of war eluded the bean counters. Our Vietnamese were not as prepared to fight and die as the other Vietnamese. Evidence to the contrary failed to convince senior American officials that little brown men running around the jungle with their asses hanging out of black pajamas were determined to fight and win, or die in the attempt.

At the theater level, introduction of regular U.S. forces inclined Americans to say to our allies: Step aside. The first team is here to clean up this mess.

American search-and-destroy operations employed routinely came up empty-handed as GIs stepped on mines and punji stakes, collapsed from heat exhaustion under equipment loads more suited to mules than men, or suffered losses to enemy snipers and hit-and-run methods. Battle was usually the result of the enemy's decision to engage on terms favorable to him.

At the policy level, muddled decisions by civilian political authority, including the President and the Secretary of Defense, reigned. They sent tens of thousands of Americans to die—and cause the loss of millions of Asians—when, by their own accounts, they did not believe we could win the war. Senior officers later told of considering resignation, but they didn't resign, despite an inability to find out precisely what their political masters expected from the use of force. Instead of having the decency to blow out their brains, they wrote memoirs.

I, along with most of the professional soldiers I knew, was eager to contain the "Red Hordes" who were once again threatening Manhattan and Queens. It wasn't much of a war, we admitted, but it was the only one we had. I wanted to "kill a Communist for Christ."

38

Lee, the Sergeant Major, and Bobby Boyd

The return to Nha Trang from Saigon in the summer of 1966 was delayed at least a day, because an aircraft was not available to get us there. This was hardly a cause of despair. The safe house was a pleasant place, and I was on an emotional roller coaster, welcoming the stand-down in sin city.

I had testified that day at a court-martial on behalf of a man called Lee, a good soldier I knew from the 10th and 5th Special Forces Groups. He had shot another trooper as their Delta recon team was poised in what we called "isolation." They were locked and loaded, ready to be inserted into their target area within hours. Mars and Venus collided and changed plans, personal and military. An incident, an affair of the heart in Germany, was revealed in a tent in Vietnam to warriors as the team planned and awaited planned violence. Unknowingly, the man who was shot boasted of an affair and showed a picture of the object of his affection and conquest to his fellows. Alas, the picture revealed the wife of one of his listeners. Said listener did what struck him as being the only reasonable thing: he grabbed his Swedish-K, flipped it to "go-go" (full automatic), and fired it—with two notable results. The tent was cleared in what was later estimated to be world record time; the lover, however, was perforated by a few rounds in his legs.

Appearing in Saigon willingly as a character witness for the shooter at his request, I assumed that he was going to jail, probably for a long time. One does not lightly damage government property in my Army. My best hope was that my testimony would influence the board not to throw away the key to the slammer.

The trial was only an hour old when I was called to the stand, puzzled. Experience with military justice as defense counsel, trial counsel (prosecutor in civil courts), and a member of the board (jury in civil courts) in "Special" courts was minor league stuff compared to what Lee faced in a "General" court. Best estimates had been for a trial of a day or two to establish guilt or innocence, and then perhaps a day for hearing evidence in extenuation and mitigation before sentencing.

143

I testified for Lee, making clear that he was an extraordinary soldier. Later I learned that plea bargaining, to which I was not a party, resulted in no jail time for my friend. I never knew the particulars, but we celebrated his liberty at the safe house. Better that Lee resume mayhem in the bush than rot in prison.

One of the other character witnesses in Saigon from the boondocks was the Sergeant Major in whose company both the shooter and I had served in Germany. He was tall, lean, gray of hair and mustache, dignified, and a veteran of World War II and Korea. His name was Lynch. He had just learned that his son, a PFC with the 101st Airborne, was KIA, Killed In Action. Reflecting on what that meant to the father, the old soldier who had survived combat in three wars, was painful for all of us as we identified with our comrade. Powerful stuff. Good news for Lee. He beat the rap. Bad news for Sergeant Major Lynch. He lost his son.

That was the backdrop to the delay in Saigon. Jim, with whom I was serving for the third time, was also in Saigon to testify for Lee. He and I decided that we would visit Mama Bic's Bar, a Special Forces hangout on Tu Do, the main drag in Saigon, not far from the presidential palace. But there was a problem. Anticipating an abstemious stay in sin city to help Justice balance her scales, we had just a few bucks between us. But Mars smiles on happy warriors. There, in all his manly and munificent magnificence, was Sgt. Bobby Boyd, another of the old guys from Germany, freshly arrived from IV Corps and on his way to R&R with beaucoup dollars. Learning of our quandary and sympathetic to our tactical requirement for a leaflet drop, Bobby threw a stack of bills into the air, and all of us at the bar celebrating Lee's freedom watched the wondrous sight as hundreds of dollars of Monopoly Money MPCs—Military Payment Certificates—fluttered to the floor. Grinning with his toothpaste-ad white teeth enhanced by his sun-bleached blonde hair and red-bronze skin, Bobby said magnanimously: "Take what you need!"

We did; we played; we returned to Nha Trang; we sent our thanks and repayment to Bobby before he left Saigon.

Bobby went on R&R and returned to IV Corps where he was soon to die bravely in a machine gun duel with the enemy in that goofy sampan war in the canals and paddies of the soggy delta. The guys in the team said Bobby really gave it hell, up front as usual. More bad news for us.

In a few days in Saigon early in my Vietnam tour, I had seen Justice by Kafka, the Sergeant Major's loss by Shakespeare, and Bobby's antic life and death by Groucho Marx. These events were among the many threads woven into a fabric of giddiness and sadness characterized by some as surreal and by others, more banal, as Disneyland East. No wonder. The backdrop was exotic. The men were admirable. The story line was uneven.

Well, good for Lee! He beat the rap. He walked. That's why I went to Saigon. For Lee. His simple faith, his trust in the Group's loyalty to those loyal to it just knocked my socks off. He validated my decision to serve. The guy he shot apparently allowed Lee to beat the rap by saying, in the best Frankie and Johnny tradition, "I done him wrong." And the Sergeant Major lost his son. And Bobby—with his generosity and courage so natural. How can a man not love those guys? Can words bring an interested reader to this love? Dunno.

39

BLACKJACK 21: A Long Walk In 1966

The reason for this reflection on a minor military operation that took place long ago is the surprisingly long and sympathetic obituary that appeared in the *New York Times* on 4 January 1998, announcing the death of my old Special Forces boss, Col. Francis J. (Splash) Kelly, on 26 December 1997. Dead colonels usually escape the notice of the *Times*.

The obituary reference to the Mobile Guerrilla Force stimulated a flood of remembrances of things past, a self-indulgence to be sure, but some of the memories regarding the people and operational techniques might be useful to current practitioners of the trade. The best memories—as usual—are of the brave men: the Americans, the Montagnards, and the enemy. So, this is a recollection of good men and an exciting mission, the reflective and anecdotal after-action report behind the "just-the-facts, ma'am" official report.

Clearly, while he commanded the 1st Special Forces Group on Okinawa before assuming command of the 5th Group in Vietnam in June 1966, Kelly had thought through what he intended to accomplish in the year he could expect to command in Vietnam. Compared to his peers, who probably would arrive at their brigades, regiments, and groups without detailed knowledge of their new combat commands, Kelly had a big advantage. Close cooperation between the two SF groups, the constant flow of men back and forth, the special warfare logistics base on Okinawa, and the wisdom of sending the commander of the 1st Group in Okinawa to command the 5th in Vietnam, conspired to ensure that Kelly had intimate knowledge of what was happening in Vietnam and in his future command. He also knew what he wanted: SF troops in the jungle gathering intelligence, disrupting enemy operations, and killing the enemy. That's why he moved so quickly.

The 5th Special Forces Group Commander exercised direct control of all SF operating in Vietnam, most of them in camps established on infiltration routes from Laos and Cambodia beginning in 1964. These were the A Team camps of song (the maudlin tunes of SF medic Barry Sadler), film (the awful

John Wayne film), and memory. (Special Forces and A Team sites were probably synonymous to non-SF people.) The camps were manned by a nominal dozen U.S. Special Forces men (usually seven or eight at any moment, for one reason or another), a comparable number of Vietnamese Special Forces called LLDB (usually unhappy to find themselves in dangerous and Godforsaken places and too often in a state of permanent confrontation with the Americans), and several hundred irregulars, mercenaries called CIDG (for Civilian Irregular Defense Group), many of whom in the Central Highlands had been loincloth–clad, crossbow–armed, seminomads just a year or two earlier when Special Forces troops found, recruited, trained, armed, equipped, fed, paid, and led them. The families of the CIDG in the camps often numbered several hundred women and children living in primitive conditions with rats, various creeping and crawling critters, and red dust or red mud, depending on the season.

The operational concept was to interrupt enemy infiltration into Vietnam and to attract the indigenous population to a secure place. The A Team sites were intended to expand their influence until they created a safe haven for the friendlies and a barrier to the enemy. Results were mixed. To this day there are those who would argue the merits of the scheme as an economy-of-force measure that was very cost effective. That is, lots of bad guys were tied down by relatively few U.S. soldiers and their inexpensive hirelings. Others argue that border camps weren't a bad idea before the build-up of conventional U.S. Forces, but by 1966 they were a waste of elite soldiers.

Kelly wanted his people active in the jungle, preferably in the enemy rear, not static targets awaiting plucking at the initiative of the enemy. In the summer of 1966, he established teams named for Greek letters, adding Sigma and Omega to the already-functioning Project Delta that had established itself as an elite reconnaissance force skilled at finding the enemy and using air assets to destroy him. (One suspects that he chafed at being responsible for the administrative support of the Special Forces troops of SOG, the Studies and Observation Group that conducted operations "over the fence" in Cambodia and Laos, without having operational control of them. SOG was controlled from its headquarters in Saigon, conducting the kinds of missions that fitted Kelly's notion of what special operations were all about.) In August 1966 he established an ad hoc Mobile Force that he carved out of his resources.

Initially the force was called Task Force 777, later renamed BLACKJACK 21. The "2" was for the II Corps area that included the Central Highlands, home to several Montagnard tribes. The "1" meant it was the first of its kind in II Corps—and in Vietnam. The formal mission was:

> To infiltrate into the area of operations and conduct border surveillance, interdict infiltration routes, and conduct guerrilla type operations against known VC installations. Infiltration, reconnaissance, operations, and exfiltration will be executed clandestinely.

In his best New Yorkese, Kelly's guidance was cryptic: "Go out-guerrilla the guerrilla." He and his operations officer, Major (later Lieutenant General) Howie Stone carefully spelled out the meaning of the last word in the formal statement: we would walk into the AO near the Cambodian border, we would have no helicopter medical evacuations, and we would walk out. Since we would care for and carry our sick and wounded, a medical doctor was assigned to the modified A Team of fifteen men. I believe my feeling was shared by the other Americans: the prospect of being wounded without the prospect of prompt medical evacuation from a denied area known for its skilled enemy troops and multitudinous diseases was the most daunting aspect of the mission. Every man knew the deal. Each team member was a volunteer.

Kelly gave the mission to Capt. James A. Fenlon, Infantry. Jim was working in the Group operations section as an assistant S-3 after having commanded an A Team in IV Corps for about six months before the summer of 1966. Kelly liked Jim's blend of assertiveness, enthusiasm, and his relevant recent experience. Jim had been preparing for just this kind of mission for seven years since his graduation from the University of Dayton, his commissioning in the Regular Army, and his completion of Airborne, Ranger, and Special Forces courses. Even in bull sessions in Germany, he was particularly attracted to combat in the jungle.

Jim was permitted to pick his people, but that authority was later modified, sometimes capriciously. He asked if I would join him as his deputy, and I immediately assented, pleased at the prospect of escaping the staff job in Nha Trang where I had worked since June 1966. Jim knew that I had been an enlisted infantryman in the Korean War, and we had become friends while serving together in the same rifle company in Bamberg, Germany. We spent a lot of time together socially and professionally there and later when we were in the 10th Special Forces Group in Bad Toelz, Germany. Later, while I attended my career course, Jim trained at Fort Bragg, completed an intelligence course at Fort Holabird, and went to Vietnam where he commanded his A Team. We corresponded regularly and were pleased to be reunited in the summer of 1966 in the Group Headquarters in Nha Trang.

In early September 1966, the two of us began planning on the basis of: (1) the mission stated; (2) a stay-time of about a month; (3) a probable AO near the Cambodian border west of Pleiku; and (4) a friendly force to consist of SF leaders and Montagnards from the II Corps Mike Force, a Special Forces quick-reaction force located in Pleiku.

As we roughed out what we were about, we took two immediate steps: we asked the Group S-2 for all intelligence available bearing on the AO, and we selected our people from the best men we knew in-country, our kind of guys. I do not recall a single man about whom Jim and I disagreed. One of us said, "Commo," and the other asked, "Are Bigley [Harold J.] and Boggs

[William D.] in-country?" One of us said, "Medics," and the other said, "Are Alvin Young and Ben Hancock in Vietnam?" One of us said, "Bill Roderick," and the other said, "Yeah, Bill is back." Bill was a confident demolitions man with a previous tour in the Central Highlands. He could do anything. With Jim and me, that made seven people. The other eight men were not chosen by us.

Colonel Kelly assigned his Group Surgeon, Capt. Craig Llewellen, to the team, and Craig did all of the premission training with us. He was an impressive guy, a medical doctor who could have commanded an A Team or a rifle company. (I have seen him dance a professional hoofer into the ground, grab a sax from a musician to outplay the pro, and sit next to a piano player to outplay that unhappy wretch, all of this in the five minutes after the hoofer had pulled the "Rube" from an audience to embarrass him in the spotlight.) Tough, skilled in many ways, personable, self-effacing—when not challenged—and popular with the troops, he had already shown personal courage in an encounter we had had with the enemy in the boondocks in the preparation phase of the operation. But, for reasons not explained to us, at the last moment Craig was taken from us, I believe against his will, and Captain Butch [Homer G.] House, M.D., was assigned. That made eight men.

Butch was a stranger to us with little field experience and not much time in-country or in Special Forces. He was assigned as the C Team surgeon in Pleiku. It seemed to me at the time, and upon reflection, that he made the trip from recruit to veteran field soldier the hard way. It was unfair to him, but by the end of the mission he was fully integrated into the team. Being a skilled surgeon, a highly intelligent man, and a world-class wrestler helped. He just had to learn to be a grunt by putting his right foot after his left a few million times without too much analysis or introspection. I don't think he had a clear appreciation of what he had allowed to happen to him. Considering the announced denial of medevacs, we were dubious about the seemingly arbitrary last-minute assignment of a "new guy" to the key position, but Kelly did not invite us to vote on the matter. Fortunately, Butch worked out like a champ. But the switch comes under my heading of capricious.

Another capricious act by Kelly was the assignment of Sgt. Maj. David Weakley to the team. As I understand it, Weakley let Kelly know that Weakley, close to rotation home, regretted that his senior rank had denied him the nitty-gritty of soldiering in combat. Weakley—like Sgt. Maj. John Pioletti, 5th Group Sergeant Major and several times 10th Special Forces Group Sergeant Major in Germany—wanted to go to the boondocks to close with and destroy the enemy without consideration for his elevated status in the U.S. Army. He wanted to take his chances the way a conscript buck-ass-private goes to war, or the way his juniors had gone to the woods while he was safe in the rear. Professional soldiers and hopeless romantics understand that. My issue—I think the team's issue—was not the nobility of the Sergeant Major's quest, nor the generosity of our colonel's impulse. Our question was basic: could he cut the mustard? Some senior people suffer the willing spirit–weak flesh malady, or the atrophy of the animal skills required in close combat; they are simply past it, over the hill. But I am pleased to report that the Sergeant Major proved himself a superb combat leader. He was a valuable asset in many ways, but most particularly in quietly cementing two disparate groups whose friction threatened the success of the mission from the beginning. A slight digression into the important issue of morale, confidence, and discipline is in order.

The II Corps Mike Force was an elite organization. It was the quick-reaction reserve of the Special Forces C Team Commander, the force that would go to the rescue of an A Team camp in danger of being overrun, or die in the attempt. It was also the element available to exploit a target of opportunity—instantly. In addition to three light infantry companies, the Mike Force also had a small reconnaissance platoon called Eagle Flight that conducted recon, ambushes, the rescue of downed pilots, and whatever task needed doing quickly.

Many of the Americans and "Yards" (Montagnards) of the Mike Force had cut their teeth in combat in A Teams on the infiltration routes and graduated to the Mike Force. Many had multiple tours in Vietnam or repeated extensions of the normal one-year tour. They were handpicked men, brave and skilled—and they were warlords.

Their Montagnard mercenaries were also selected by Special Forces soldiers from A Team sites for demonstrated courage, loyalty, and skills. Like most elite forces around the world, the Yards and Americans of the Mike Force lived better than most troops, but they were expected to accept hazardous missions without blinking and to die without much fuss. That was the deal.

First Lieutenant Gilbert K. Jenkins looked, talked, and wended his way through the boondocks like a mountain man from the film *Deliverance*. He was a former NCO in the 10th and knew and was known by Fenlon's handpicked guys, all veterans of the 10th. More significantly, he loved his Yards and they loved him. When he snapped his fingers, his people jumped. Anyone messing with his Yards would deal with Jenkins the way a Little League coach had to deal with the players' moms. He did not welcome the strangers from out of town who: (1) were placed over him, robbing him of his autonomy; (2) didn't know the AO the way he did; and (3) would probably get him killed on a suicide mission dictated by headquarters commandos who didn't know a foxhole from an anal orifice. Jenkins was the original unhappy camper.

SFC Richard T. Norris was the Company Commander of the company earmarked for the mission. Supreme joy and confidence are not the words to characterize his reaction to the new state of affairs as not one, but two, captains—strangers of unknown experience and merit—injected themselves into what had been a perfectly satisfactory command arrangement. One suspects that as a boy he was not inclined to take candy from the nice man in the car.

SFC Robert F. Head was a platoon leader in the company commanded by Norris. Among his less-endearing qualities was a way of saying "sir" as an obscenity while staring in a manner that could only be read as insolence. He also had testes the size of watermelons, a gyroscope instead of a heart, and initiative in close combat that made him a gifted small unit tactician. Sullen and resentful, he also proved to be totally dedicated to the success of the mission. He was a risk taker who never paused at the doorway to danger, but he didn't care for SOBs from out of town.

Jenkins, Norris, and Head were unhappy at the prospect of putting their asses and their Yards on the line with strangers calling the shots, a perfectly appropriate response. Jim and I talked it over, and he chose not to address possible mission-endangering attitudes for several reasons. First, we would have felt the same way, had the situation been reversed. Second, sooner or later, professional soldiers would recognize a simple fact: Kelly was the Group Commander; he had sent us to do a job. Third, as we went about the preparation phase, we expected the Mike Force men to decide for themselves the competence of the new leadership. Fourth, Jenkins, Norris, and Head were in consonance with the C Team Commander, his staff, and the Mike Force Commander, none of whom understood why Kelly departed from the usual way of doing business, which would have been to give the mission to the C Team Commander who would have given it to the Mike Force CO. (Clyde Sincere, winner of the DSC for extraordinary courage in combat, the Mike Force commander at the time, my former neighbor in the 10th, and a man I'm proud to call friend, has a long memory. As recently as June 1997, Clyde told me once again that he didn't understand why Kelly hadn't given him the mission. That does not, however, prevent us from hugging when we meet, giving updates on our kids, and buying one another drinks at reunions.)

This digression points to a potentially fatal schism that was bridged by time, shared danger, mutual respect, professionalism, and success, but I think Sergeant Major Weakley's personal intercession held the disparate factions together until those other factors did their work. The Sergeant Major and the three leaders from the Mike Force made us twelve.

I don't know how or why we got SFC Wayne L. Smith, but I'm glad we did. He showed up one day from an A team site with his Montagnard interpreter, Charlie. Smitty was the prototypical strong, bronzed, silent man. My most vivid memories find him listening intently to a plan or order and nodding once. That meant, "It will be done." And it was. I don't remember him ever discussing anything. He would respond with absolute clarity if asked a question, but mostly he listened, nodded once, and executed. He served as a platoon leader on the operation. I also recall that for the last couple of weeks in the boondocks he was half naked. We each carried just one change of clothing, a black pajama shirt and one pair of black pajama pants, in our rucksacks, and we wore jungle fatigues. Early on, Smitty's fatigues were ripped to shreds, and his flimsy black PJs soon exposed his butt. He never complained about that or anything else as he cheerfully did whatever needed doing.

He treated Charlie like a son, and I was told that he somehow later got Charlie to the United States when that was almost an impossibility. Charlie was about sixteen, had been with Special Forces for three years, and spoke English, Vietnamese, and French, in addition to his Montagnard dialect. Smitty said that Charlie goes where Smitty goes. That was that. We had thirteen Americans.

The last two Special Forces soldiers were both medics, SFC John M. Prosser and SFC George D. Cole. I do not know how they came to be assigned, but both worked out well, both were quiet, unassuming men, and both served as assistant platoon leaders and medics.

To recapitulate, Fenlon was task force commander, Gole was deputy, House was surgeon, and Weakley was the operations and intel sergeant. Norris was company commander. Roderick, Head, and Smith were platoon leaders. Hancock, Prosser, and Cole were platoon medics and doubled as assistant platoon leaders. Jenkins was recon platoon leader, and Young was medic and ran the point as the recon platoon lead almost all of the time. Bigley and Boggs were our commo men. Except for talking to airplane drivers by voice on FM radio, external commo to 5th Special Forces Group was shortwave, and internal commo was voice FM radio (PRC-25). BLACK-JACK 21 was directly under Group control, not under the C Team in Pleiku.

You can consult learned anthropological sources for scholarly insights into the Montagnard culture, but for operational purposes, note the following. The Yards had the muscular definition and size of lightweight to welterweight fighters, and I don't recall ever seeing a fat one. They were closer in color to the average American black than to the Vietnamese, had pug noses compared to the longer, thinner noses of the Vietnamese, and were generally shorter and stockier than Vietnamese men, whose bone structure was light, almost delicate, on the order of a slim Caucasian woman. Americans familiar with the Yards could distinguish them from the Vietnamese at a glance. Not so apparent was the fact that our Yards were 100% malarial and 100% tubercular, meaning that we often had several experiencing the characteristic high fever and general debilitation of malaria, and, at night in the jungle, respiratory irritation caused them to bark like dogs.

The Yards were jungle-dwelling hunters and slash-and-burn farmers. They would clear a patch in the jungle, drag a stick or wooden plow

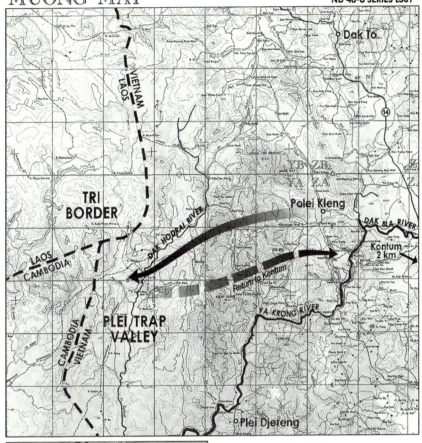

Scale 1:250,000

1. Blackjack 21 began infiltration by foot from Polei Kleng in early October 1966, conducted raids and ambushes in Dak Hodrai area and returned to Kontum 7 November.

2. Recon teams from Kontum (MACVSOG, CCC) launched into Laos via Dak To.

Map, courtesy of U.S. Army Military History Institute. Graphic adaptations by Jim Kistler, USAWC, Visual Information Division.

through it, farm until the soil was exhausted, and then move on to a new patch of jungle to be cleared by slashing and burning. In the distant past, they had been driven to the highlands by a Chinese migration from the north that occupied the coastal and lowland regions of what is now Vietnam. The Yard attitude toward the Vietnamese ranged from dislike to hate. The Vietnamese treated the Yards like something less than human, a lord-serf style familiar the world over. The more sophisticated Yards had national aspirations, and it was alleged that the leadership of FULRO, a French acronym for the Yard organization, was in Pleiku, mostly in the Mike Force. Tensions flared between Yards and the Vietnamese, sometimes visibly in uprisings and actual firefights, always quietly simmering and resulting in "accidental" deaths on both sides.

The American Special Forces soldier loved the Yards. In addition to a winning innocence and child-like sweetness, the Yard was tough, brave, and loyal. The fact that he treated his Special Forces leaders like royalty was a nice bonus. Illustrations abound, but one is engraved in my memory. As I began my second tour in Vietnam in 1970, I explored the 5th Group headquarters in Nha Trang, including the once-familiar Mike Force area there, while awaiting assignment. The commander, a fellow major, saw me wandering in his domain. We introduced ourselves, and he showed me around. He was particularly proud of his Montagnard hospital. As we entered, a bedridden legless Montagnard popped up on his stumps, located about half way between his hips and where his knees used to be, and saluted while smiling and saying, "Good morning, sir!" The commander chatted with him as I managed to suppress tears, wondering what would become of the legless man when U.S. forces left Vietnam. The picture in my head was of filthy invalids crawling and begging in Asian city streets.

Our BLACKJACK 21 policy was no nonessential talking on a rest break, so Roderick pointed to Cole, a medic, and then to Jimmy, a Yard interpreter. Cole looked a question mark at Roderick who whispered harshly, "Look in his eyes. Glazed. Take his temperature." Cole did that. Jimmy had a temperature of 105 degrees, and there were no medevacs. His condition deteriorated rapidly, and he became delirious. We constructed a litter and carried Jimmy for a couple of days. Then he walked with the aid of a stick with a wet rag around his head while we carried his equipment. Then he walked with just his weapon for a couple of days. Then, after a week, he walked with his rucksack and the rest of his gear. He was one tough little son of a bitch.

(Four years later as I surrendered my medical records to the little dispensary in a special operations camp in Kontum, there was Jimmy to accept them. We embraced and he said, "Captain now major." I said, "And Jimmy now medic." He laughed saying, "No more patrol!")

On another day we stopped for a rest break. Tired and soaked with sweat, I pulled out my wine-red pack of Ruby Queen cigarettes. Two remained. I caught the eye of the Yard who carried my radio. (It was not an accident that he was tall. So was the Yard who walked behind me. No point in making it easy for an enemy sniper to pick out the American.) He spoke not a word of English, but the glance we exchanged said it all. He smoked as heavily as I did, and he wasn't lighting up. I extended my arm toward him; he took a cigarette and smiled a thank you, knowing that we were smoking the last of my cigarettes. For the rest of the operation, on rest breaks he took my canteens before my butt hit the ground and without a word filled mine and his with water.

On one of the shakedown operations before we went for the long walk, we stopped in the jungle on a particularly sultry midday for *pak* time, the *siesta* of that part of the world. The task force described a wagon wheel, as in any good western film, with the command group in the center. Hammock slung, I was doing some very serious relaxing when my dream was shattered by the sound of automatic fire and lots of it. After the initial shock and estimate of the situation, it was clear that the Yards, anticipating our return to Pleiku the next day, had killed several water buffalo. Severely reprimanded, the Yard leadership announced that they had killed "VC buffalo." In an hour, the jungle was red with meat hung to dry from every limb within reach. In two hours, each American was eating a delicious kabob of meat and jungle veggies, the Yard peace offering for an unusual breach of discipline. We chalked it up to playfulness and their common sense call: many miles from any human settlement, whose property were the now wild beasts? Each Yard brought a couple of kilos of meat wrapped in leaves to his extended family.

Despite their splendid fieldcraft, marksmanship was not among the many qualities of the Yard. One suspects that their initial training was hasty, and their firefight experiences in the jungle exploded at very close range, where the inclination was to rely upon "go-go" rather than carefully aimed shots. Arming them with the U.S. weapons family of World War II, the M-1 rifle and BAR—both big for Asian people—gave way to providing smaller fully automatic weapons, mostly the M-2 carbine but also the .45 caliber M-3 grease gun and the Thompson submachine gun (also caliber .45). As we trained our Yards on ranges with newer weapons—the LAW (Light Anti-Tank Weapon), M-60 machine gun, M-79 grenade launcher, and M-16s—we discovered it was almost impossible to break bad habits. They loved to pump out rounds more than they liked to hit targets. In the field we learned that fire discipline was foreign to our wonderful Yards. Once, a single, armed enemy trail watcher was engaged by a platoon. It sounded like World War III as every Yard who saw the enemy had to fire every round in his weapon until the dead enemy was little more than a grease spot on a river bank. Corrections elicited smiles and affirmative nods, but we continued to see more volume of fire than accuracy.

The fieldcraft was what one would expect of primitive jungle dwellers. One day as we got close to an enemy we hoped to find blissfully unaware of our proximity and strength, we ascended for an entire day in a rocky, narrow stream almost entirely covered by the branches of giant trees. As we stepped from stone to stone, the Yard in front of me snapped off a stick, tied a length of suspension line thread to it, fashioned a hook from the safety pins that came with ammunition bandoleers, and rolled a small ball of rice that he tamped around the hook. Amused at the sight of a combat-loaded and armed soldier fishing from a moving column, and condescending in my paternal recognition of the child's innocent optimism, I became a believer as he pulled up a small trout. His sign language asked me to fill a plastic rice bag with water. I complied. He put the fish in the bag; I tied the bag to the back of his rucksack. For the rest of the day I watched a swimming fish at my eye level as I climbed that mountain.

On another occasion, the Yards killed and shared with me a creature whose description has earned me the polite disbelief of friends and strangers around the world. I remember the night well, because it was the only time we dug foxholes, a prudent measure after a day of high adventure on 5 November 1966, when the enemy almost bagged us. As I dozed off, I saw what I believed to be a monkey scurrying in the tree directly above me. Interesting, but not the first monkey I saw on that walk. Then I heard a dog barking. That was unusual in the jungle, and it seemed the monkey was barking. I slept.

The next day the Yards showed me a lizard-like creature they had caught on a long pole with a noose attached. The lizard's body was chunky, about eighteen inches long, with a tail about the same length, and claws at the end of frog-like appendages. They insisted that this was the barking, tree-scampering beast of the previous evening. Later they gave me meat from this strange creature. Yes, it tasted like chicken.

(I was beginning to doubt my own recollection when Bill Roderick and I returned to Vietnam in 1993 and saw the critter in a hotel game room in Pleiku containing stuffed samples of the local wild life. At least Bill and I can continue to believe one another about God's little joke. We also heard tigers at night and saw elephant dung on trails, but the lizard tale should do for now.)

After yet another tough day of putting one foot after the other and during our meal of yummy cold wet rice, Butch House asked me if I smelled ammonia earlier as we had spent several hours climbing a mountain that turned strong young legs to jelly. I had. Butch said that the smell came from burning muscle tissue. We had burned off all fat. Now we were digging into our capital. In that connection, the difference between the Yards and the Americans was very evident. We Americans were in good health and chock full of a long list of immunizations and malaria pills. Despite the loss of a lot of weight (I started the operation at 180 pounds and weighed in at 143 when we got back to Pleiku, a weight loss typical of our team), the Americans could have continued the mission well beyond thirty days, with some loss of efficiency and with more frequent rest breaks. I don't think the Yards could have continued much longer, because they lived quite literally from hand to mouth. No capital. We joked about what seemed a reflex: Yard's ass hits ground, Yard's hand reaches for rice. There seemed to be a crossover after a couple of weeks as the Americans walked themselves into ever-better shape as the Yards walked themselves into exhaustion.

The most innovative techniques we used at the time were our response to the question: how could we subsist for about a month deep in the enemy's rear while remaining undetected—and without becoming packhorses? To conduct raids and ambushes in the enemy's backyard, we needed to rely upon surprise. A combination of stealth and mobility was our ace in the hole, not organic firepower; we relied upon fire support from the sky when we engaged strong enemy forces. We had to be light to be mobile.

Resupply was by A1E aircraft flying out of Pleiku. Face-to-face coordination between the team and pilots who invested themselves in the wild project was probably the key to the success of a nonstandard (if not crazy) idea. The A1Es bombed us with napalm containers, but the containers were filled with items we prepacked or stored in Pleiku. A flight of birds would drop bombs—or make passes as though dropping bombs—one terrain feature from us. Meanwhile, a flight would bomb us with our resupply in the napalm containers. We experimented with conventional parachute drops and with ponchos serving as parachutes, but we settled on simply taking cover by hugging a tree as the containers were dropped near us, without parachutes, from an altitude just above tree-top, usually about 150 to 200 feet.

We also experimented with various means of vectoring the aircraft and settled on a simple and effective system. Jim Fenlon became very good at bombing us with manna from heaven. Our CW message from the previous day indicated where we were and the time we wanted to hear birds overhead (usually about thirty minutes before daylight so that the drop would be in darkness and the location of the bundles would be in first light). When Jim heard the birds, he guided them by voice. Then he blinked a flashlight once to provide the pilot a target for his final approach. The drop was executed on Jim's voice command. Then we filed by as each soldier was given two sandbags that had been tied together in Pleiku. They were plopped over his rucksack. Each sandbag contained a combination of rations, bug juice (insect repellent), batteries, and C-4 (a plastic explosive) we had packed in Pleiku. Later in the day we could redistribute items, as required. We took five resupply drops during the operation, recovering 86 of 88 bundles. We were satisfied with the results, but, needless to say, Mother Nature and the human condition intervened.

Despite the promise of a dry season at the time and place of BLACKJACK 21, on one occasion we were weathered in and without food for five days (and on another we were without food for four days). I have a distinct memory of Bill Roderick, unshaven, gaunt, and smiling as he approached me out of the ground fog and light steady rain that reduced visibility to a few meters. I was tucked into a hammock under a poncho feeling sorry for myself. I was hungry, had been out of cigarettes for days, had a low-grade fever, and had drunk all of my "GI gin" cough medicine when I recognized what a wonderful gift Bill was preparing to share with me. At the bottom of his rucksack he had found a soggy, bent, long, Pall Mall cigarette. The near-zero visibility enabled us to build a small fire by which we ceremoniously dried and rolled the Pall Mall. As we passed the cigarette back and forth, we puffed and exchanged a kind of litany:

Home, he said.

Hearth, I said.

Food, he said.

Sex, I said.

Warmth, he said.

Rest, I said.

Clearly that cigarette was endowed with more magic than Aladdin's lamp.

At the moment I go to my Maker, I suspect several images will flash into my consciousness as I fade. One of them will be puffing on that butt with Bill in the fog and rain.

One of the resupply drops recalls two bittersweet memories. We had recovered all bundles at first light, slung the goodies-laden sandbags on their rucksacks as the troops filed by, booby-trapped the deliberately ill-concealed napalm containers, and moved for about an hour when we formed a perimeter to redistribute our new treasure. In the course of sorting out food and ammo, we enjoyed a surprise—minor in the course of human events but so important to combat troops in a dicey situation. The supply people had included a bottle of booze and a large can of fruit juice in one of the bundles. Hungry, filthy, and smiling, we passed the bottle and juice can around as we toasted a reserve officer from Pennsylvania named Hess. He had volunteered for Vietnam and was in the Special Forces S-4 (supply) shop in Pleiku. It was he who helped us with the rigging of the napalm canisters and the resupply concept, and it was he who provided the happy surprise. That's the sweet.

The bitter happened on the very day that we returned to Nha Trang from Pleiku at the end of the mission. As we were in flight, Hess was in a chopper with Clyde Sincere. Clyde was returning to his Mike Force in the boondocks, when the chopper was hit by automatic weapons fire as it prepared to land. In his absence the bad guys had gained control of the landing zone.

The pilot said, "I don't have full power. We gotta lighten the load!" Clyde looked around to discover that he and the pilot were the only ones not dead or badly hit. He did the only reasonable thing: he took two M-16s and charged an NVA company as the chopper limped off. Clyde was wounded and won the Distinguished Service Cross. Hess was killed.

Not once during the operation did I ever see or hear that the men I've named hesitated when directed, daily, to do hard or dangerous tasks. More often than not, one of them initiated prudent actions without direction. (The reader needs to know that your reporter does not bask in the afterglow of a one-time adventure nor in the coziness of old age. He saw other brave men in combat in C Company, 27th Infantry Regiment [Wolfhounds] as a BAR man during the unpleasantness in Korea in 1953 and in 1970 when he enjoyed the company of the always-outnumbered recon men of MACV-SOG, who routinely challenged the best light infantry in the world on infiltration routes in Laos and Cambodia.) Perhaps the BLACKJACK debriefing by a psychiatrist in Nha Trang testifies to the "chemistry" that made the team special. After he had had at us for a couple of hours, he made motions suggesting that we were done. Yours truly then asked a simple question, to which our shrink gave a simple response more loaded with wisdom than I suspected at the time.

I asked: "What is the most interesting aspect of our operation to you, professionally?"

His response: "That the informal chain of command was congruent with the formal chain of command."

I asked if that was unusual, and he indicated that it was.

Upon reflection, I think that means that each of us was prepared to accept—I think the current jargon of touchy-feely is "internalize"—our role. That is, every man on BLACKJACK 21 believed that he could command the whole deal, but each was prepared to suspend that impulse and to accept the formal arrangement of rank and his place in the chain of command. I think that experience, skill, training, and demonstrated competence combined with a sense of purpose were very important, but the icing on the cake was confidence and affection that resulted in cohesion. All of these elements added up to a simple and fortuitous fact: I had the privilege of serving with pros. I don't think many of us would have survived 5 November 1966 if each of us had waited for instructions before acting.

Starting at midnight, we had made a single rope crossing of the fifty-meter-wide and swift-flowing Dak Hadrai River. By first light of 4 November, all 272 of us were on the far side, from which we had heard the sounds of hunting and general horseplay, indicating the success of our long walk: we were now one hill mass from Cambodia, and the enemy was happily oblivious to our presence. We established hasty ambushes and killed two men moving south on a high-speed trail and captured some one hundred potato-masher–type hand grenades packed in banana leaves in sealed metal containers. Then we occupied a company-sized bivouac area and sat, like Goldilocks awaiting the return of the three bears.

The squad-size stay-behind ambush led by Head was called back to the main body and ran into an ambush by some twenty to thirty enemy that killed two of his Yards with automatic weapons at a range of ten meters. Meanwhile, the main body had another contact with men in NVA uniforms, killing one and surprising the usual tenants of the bivouac area as they came home.

The plot thickened. Head was pinned down several hundred meters from us, and we had our own problems—the sound of digging and movement indicated that we were up against good NVA troops now deliberately pressing our main body against the Dak Hadrai River. Jim Fenlon organized a platoon to relieve Head, but Head, sensing an enemy build-up, used his initiative to break contact by personally throwing three fragmentation grenades at the light machine gun and firing several automatic bursts from his M-16. The first of Head's people I saw returning to us was smiling as he pointed to his rucksack leaking crumbs from bullet holes. The fact that we were all together again simplified our lives. Our task now was focused: kill the enemy and get the force out of there.

Jim calmly contacted the II Corps FAC (Forward Air Controller) for BLACKJACK, who was always out of sight but within voice radio range, and I moved to the riverbank to select a crossing site. The story is told sequentially, but the events were overlapping or simultaneous.

The FAC produced constant tactical air support by diverting Air Force and Navy birds from routine scheduled missions and by putting high explosives and napalm on an enemy some fifty to one hundred meters from us. This was possible because the FAC was a brave man who sat in a cone of enemy fire as he put his marking rounds on our tormentors. (Later, in Kontum, I met the man. He was a rosy-cheeked Santa Claus, a grandfather and veteran pilot of World War II, not the white-scarfed, steely-eyed stud I expected.) Jim controlled the strikes from the ground.

Bill Roderick, with a telescope on his M-16, and Ben Hancock, who had spotted the NVA some two hundred meters away, were belly-deep in the river killing NVA troops attempting to cross the river upstream at a point where there was a sand bar in mid-stream. The enemy only needed to get one sharpshooter to the other side, and we would have been a replay of Thermopylae as we attempted to cross the river on a single rope. Ignoring my shouts to get out of the river—I was concerned that, if hit, they would be swept downstream before anyone could react—Bill and Ben continued to kill the would-be flankers.

Head appeared, assessed the situation, assumed that I was at the prospective crossing site, and, as I recall without a word, tied off one end of a 120-foot length of nylon climbing rope, swam to the other side, tied off our crossing rope, drew it taut, and returned. He just did what needed doing at a narrow place.

Billy Boggs and Harold Bigley, our commo men who never missed a scheduled transmit or receive during the mission—despite frequently unfavorable weather and the press of time caused by the tactical situation—looked like altar boys on a picnic as they watched the entire scene with almost amused detachment. They plunged in when needed, but they scrupulously abstained from meddling in the chain of command.

[An important note here is that my failure to mention what the others were up to is not to damn with faint praise. I have described what I saw where my piece of the action took place.]

Upon returning to Nha Trang to be debriefed, to help Jim with his after-action report, and to fatten up, the team was sent to the winds. Jim Fenlon and Dave Weakley went home. Jim later served in Okinawa, in an infantry unit on a second tour in Vietnam, in Alaska, and as a Soviet specialist. I lost track of Weakley, Smitty, Cole, and Prosser. Just recently I heard that Smitty died in retirement. Weakley made a second career with a civilian agency. Jenkins, Norris, and Head went on at least one more BLACKJACK mission. Jenkins died in 2003. Norris lost a leg along the way. I understand that Butch House is a distinguished hand surgeon. Billy Boggs ran recon in Laos for MACVSOG and retired a sergeant major. Roderick, Young, and Hancock went to Project Delta. Roderick was wounded on a recon but survived to become a very prosperous builder in Los Angeles. Young retired a sergeant major and does security work in Texas. Ben Hancock also retired a sergeant major, surviving numerous machine gun wounds in one leg and various exotic diseases. He was always getting banged up. Even in peace in the 10th Group in Germany, he managed to snap both legs in a climbing accident.

A couple of years ago in Las Vegas, several of us broke away from the annual Special Operations Association Reunion to assemble for a BLACKJACK 21 dinner: Roderick, Young, Boggs, Hancock, and Gole, all 10th Group men before Vietnam. Three of us had wives in tow. At the end of that evening in the privacy of our hotel room, my wife told me that it was difficult for her to believe that these nice men had experienced such dreadful things. She found it particularly necessary to confirm that Ben Hancock, whom she found so sweet and gentle and interesting on the theme of environmental protection, was a sergeant major and that he was a part of that craziness. She is right, of course. Ben is an improbable character. But then they were an improbable and unforgettable lot. I always knew that, but I didn't write it until I saw the Kelly obit in the *Times*.

40

Bill Holt

olt was a new guy. So was I. He was the junior of the two medics in our team, A-4, 10th Special Forces Group, and I was the team XO. I had served as an enlisted soldier for two years and as an officer for about three when I joined the Group in Bad Toelz. Holt arrived a Specialist 5, so I assumed he possessed basic soldier skills. I was wrong.

Before we went to the field for the first time, I had formed impressions of my teammates. I was particularly impressed by Sergeant Sampson, the senior demolitionist, and Sergeant Hardin, the senior communications man, both of whom had tutored me one-on-one in their skills. They were both first-rate teachers, both had finely tuned senses of humor, and both were rascals. Properly deferential in teaching me the ABCs of disciplines in which they were masters, their humor and patience came through as I learned how to encrypt messages in the one-time pad and the difference between wood-cutting and steel-cutting formulas. In addition to their specialties, they were superb all-around soldiers. I enjoyed their company in garrison and even more in the boondocks. Part of their charm was their dislike of bullshit. Their anarchic tendencies were well concealed, but I spotted them and liked them all the more for the secret sins we shared.

Team Sergeant Kulbeck was a highly intelligent and tough taskmaster with long service in the 82d Airborne Division behind him. I admired the man, but the rascals of A-4 resented his authoritarian approach to leadership, a residue, no doubt, of his experience as a platoon sergeant and first sergeant of the teenaged wild men of the All American Division. Captain Ask, our team leader, was not a fire-eater. He was a methodical, considerate, and decent man always willing to tap the experience of his people and to give credit to others. I remember all members of the team very well. Those described stood out, but I particularly remember Holt.

Every spare moment he had was spent with his nose in his Merck Manual, the medic's bible. I also recall his frequent questioning of Sergeant Muhlhausen, our senior medic, a very bright and technically competent guy.

Holt was a gentle, open, naïve man in his early twenties when we were together in A-4 early in 1964. He and the assistant demo man were the team's youngest. Most of us were in our thirties. Foul language abounded, but he didn't use it. I don't recall if he drank alcohol, but if he did, it was certainly in moderation. We shared crap details, and he never griped. He was too good to be true. However, our first shared experience in the boondocks revealed his Achilles heel.

One night on a tall mountain in deep snow I had crawled into my sleeping bag as Holt assumed radio watch near me at a trail entering what passed for our command post. He conducted initial commo checks with listening posts we had established on the trail up the mountain. They would detect anyone sufficiently rabid to climb the mountain hip-deep in snow in the middle of the night. Immediately apparent was his total ignorance of military radio procedure. I hissed, "Holt! Get over here!"

In brief, he hadn't the foggiest notion. I discovered that the conscientious junior medic had spent almost all of his time in the Army since basic training learning medicine. The fact was that his promotions had been pegged to the successful completion of several excellent and demanding technical courses. He had very little training in weapons, and almost none in demolitions, communications, intelligence, and operations. That night we broadened his liberal arts education, starting with voice radio procedure. Later it dawned on me that his cross-training, formal and mostly informal, would be the product of his peacetime soldiering in 10th Group, his first assignment to an operational detachment. And, of course, his positive attitude ensured his professional development.

When Lang Vei fell about four years later, I learned that a couple of the Special Forces soldiers got out. The A Team there had been in a vulnerable position from the beginning. The camp was close to the Laotian border and close to North Vietnam. It was ready for plucking when the enemy decided to pay the price.

When it came, the North Vietnamese assault was supported by PT-76s, light tanks. The team fought on the outer perimeter, pulled back to an inner perimeter and fought some more, pulled back to the command bunker and fought some more. Several Americans were dead, and the rest were wounded. One of the PT-76s actually rolled over the bunker. That's when Holt, the team's senior medic grabbed a LAW, a light antitank weapon, and went out to kill the tank. The guys who got out said he was never seen again.

I see him. He has his nose in a Merck Manual. He learned voice radio procedure, weapons, and a lot of stuff. He didn't have to learn attitude or courage.

41

Mr. Fritz

met Heinz in Bad Toelz earlier and in a different incarnation, but he told me this tale in 1971, when we were together in Kontum, before he was wounded for the third time. He would be hit a fourth time.

On a previous tour in Vietnam as a lieutenant, Heinz had worked for an organization whose purpose was to penetrate and eliminate the enemy's infrastructure. Many of the Americans involved in these necessarily covert operations were military, but for the duration of his attachment to this outfit, no rank was mentioned. Heinz, Prussian born, had been a sergeant in the 10th Special Forces, gone to Officer Candidate School, served in an A Team and in the IV Corps Mike Force, a kind of Terry and the Pirates band of mercenaries, before he joined the spook outfit. No one hearing his German accent would ask why his code name was Mr. Fritz, and no one who knew him well doubted that his work was the source of personal pride and pleasure.

Heinz, as Mr. Fritz, was given intelligence indicating that local Viet Cong in the vicinity of Dalat would pass papers and cash to a North Vietnamese group in transit to an unknown place farther south. Chances were that such a transaction would involve middle- or high-ranking officials whose elimination would hurt the enemy. The source was well placed and usually reliable, the target was important, and the night and location were known to him. Heinz decided to go for it.

The people working for him were a rather bloodthirsty lot with whose skills he was thoroughly familiar, allowing him to tailor his force to the task. One could never be sure about such matters, but it was likely that a group of two or three VC would conduct the hand-off to four or five NVA political types. So he selected seven of his best fighters, insuring that an M-60 machine gun, command-detonated Claymore mines, and weapons capable of firing both bullets and 40mm grenades were part of his package.

Concern for broadcasting his intent obviated visiting the scene on the ground, but he arranged to overfly it in a low and slow bird with the Forward Air Controller who normally worked the area. They found the location of the prospective transfer of papers and funds, but in a single pass they could not actually see the convergence of trails under the dense canopy of the jungle. However, glimpses of trail traces feeding into the area of interest indicated that the convergence was there. Further, Heinz noticed an open area close to the trail junction hidden by the forest. A plan was taking form.

Upon landing at home base, Heinz joined the pilot for a cup of coffee while they did a map recapitulation of the mission they had just flown. When Heinz traced his finger over the objective area, the pilot said that the clearing Heinz had seen was an artillery registration point. Heinz hadn't expected Fate to smile on him so broadly. Pressed for confirmation, the pilot took Heinz to the Fire Direction Control tent and introduced him to the people there as Mr. Fritz. Indeed, it was so. The clearing in question was a valid registration point that had been fired and confirmed.

Heinz outlined his scheme in detail to the artillerymen, who were delighted at the prospect of firing a mission at an observed enemy. Most of their missions were so-called H&I fires, that is, Harassment and Interdiction: unobserved fire at points where an enemy might be found, such as a road or trail junction, bridge, or river fording point. In fact, it was routine. Worse. The soldiers at the guns called it jungle-busting; they suspected that H&I was generally ineffective. On the other hand, hearing the words, "Fire mission. Troops in the open," from an American voice in the jungle was almost as exciting as Romeo hearing the word "Juliet." Artillerymen loved shooting at observed targets.

Heinz worked out concentrations and call signs with his new friends. He was Mr. Fritz; they were Zeus Thunder. As a former mortar man, he appreciated what indirect fire can do. He selected first the concentration on the trail junction. Then he selected a wall of fire between the likely location of the enemy and his route of withdrawal. Then he selected his initial destination, should he be required to break contact and run like hell, calling it a rally point. It would be useful to pop a marking round there to guide him through thick forest and what promised to be a starless night. Heinz felt good. It might be a dry hole, but if things got sticky out there, it was reassuring to know that a firing battery was eager to shoot for him. Normally he operated out of range of friendly artillery or in urban areas where it could not be used for fear of killing innocents.

He felt even better when he discovered just how much of the deadly fires could be brought to bear on his potential target. The trail junction he planned to stake out was within the effective range of four firebases, each of which had a mix of four or five 105mm and 155mm tubes. The bases were established both to cover an area of operations and to be mutually supporting in the event that the enemy took a notion to overrun a base. The 105s were doubly effective weapons because they could fire indirect support for friendlies out in the boondocks, and they could also be fully depressed to fire evil beehive rounds into assaulting enemy troops. The latter defensive fires would spoil the entire day of the bravest attackers as swarms of steel arrows literally dismembered human beings. The closer the enemy came to his objective, the firebase, the denser the wall of steel, and the more likely that enemy troops would became greasy rugs on a jungle floor.

Heinz rejoiced in the knowledge that four bases could fire in his support. He was further impressed as the artillery officer said to his senior sergeant, who had been monitoring every word as he studied a map: "Encrypt that and send it to firebases Alpha, Delta, and Fox. Give 'em a 'standby.'"

This was said in an almost offhand way, suggesting to Heinz that these guys knew what they were doing. He savored the warm fuzzies pervading his body, his acknowledgment of competence.

Upon his return to his troops, he explained the mission, assigning specific tasks for actions on the objective and for a thorough search of bodies and rucksacks after the execution of the ambush. Killing wasn't enough; they were also in the intelligence business. Compensating for possible misunderstanding due to language differences forced Heinz to walk his mercenaries through every step of the actions expected. In a perverse way, that insured that his Nungs, Montagnard, and Vietnamese were better prepared than U.S. troops might be. Nothing was assumed. They rehearsed deliberately. Then they rested.

Heinz moved his people through thick jungle slowly while it was still light. Stealth was more important than speed. Then he waited for dark and put the team in position, as rehearsed. It was a starless night. They waited.

He and his killers heard the familiar muffled clinkety-clank of troop movement in the jungle in the middle of the dark night. They had done this before. Heinz smiled as he anticipated the enemy's shock at the brevity and violence of the ambush he would trigger personally. Then the smile faded. The characteristic sounds of combat troops on the move continued without pause. Heinz prayed the only way he knew: "Holy shit!" There were too many for him to initiate contact. He'd kill a few, but the best light infantry in the world would then assault into his ambush site in a disciplined and determined manner until his team was overrun. Not for the first time, the infantryman said, "Thank God for artillery!"

"Zeus Thunder, Mr. Fritz," he whispered into his voice radio.

"This is Zeus Thunder, over."

Heinz breathed a sigh of relief. Of course he expected them to be there. Where else would they be? Nevertheless, alone in the middle of the jungle with his thugs, it was reassuring to hear that American voice.

"Fire mission. Three hundred troops in the open. Fire Fritz concentration one." Best to overestimate the number of enemy. The guys back at the guns would salivate as the target description was shouted for all to hear.

"I say back for possible correction. Fire mission. Three hundred troops in the open. Fire Fritz concentration one."

"Roger. Do it."

In less than a minute Fritz heard: "On the way. Wait. You adjust."

Again in less than a minute the rushing sound of incoming was heard, and Heinz really said a prayer to guide the 155 and 105mm projectiles away from him and onto the enemy troops.

His prayer was answered. Four firebases poured explosion after explosion almost simultaneously on the target. At the first pause, Heinz spoke:

"Fire for effect. On target. Keep it coming."

"On the way. Four rounds per tube. Wait."

During the short pause, terrible cries and groans were heard, but soon they were silenced by new and almost continuous explosions. On the order of 60 to 70 rounds landed on the target. Shrieks of pain were heard during the second interruption of fires.

"Repeat," said Heinz, and another 60 to 70 rounds exploded on target.

At this point in his story, Heinz got to his feet as he continued the tale, pacing and waving his arms. His severe overbite became even more pronounced as he stared into my eyes.

"Herr Major! There were so many of them! I did no damage assessment while it was still dark. If only five percent were still combat effective, they could kick my ass. I waited, listening to moans and a little movement. In an hour it was first light. Still I waited.

"Herr Major! In the first sunlight . . . *es war die am schoenste Sache die ich je gesehen habe! Der Dschungel war rot mit Blut.* It was the most beautiful thing I have ever seen. The chungle was red with blood! Then I did a recon and body search. I counted over a hundred recognizable bodies. I think the body parts added up to another hundred, but some parts looked like chopped meat. In the branches, on the leaves, mixed with earth on the torn up ground. "It was the most beautiful thing I have ever seen."

Heinz did neat work. Like most craftsmen, he took pride in his work and was pleased to share this description of one of his several masterpieces with me.

42

Mad Dog

We all had code names. Fritz chose Mad Dog as his. He was probably unaware that a legendary Special Forces soldier was known by that name, but that was typical of Fritz. He was ahistorical and probably not conscious of very much beyond the immediate. That does not mean that he was stupid. His concern for the mission and his personal reputation simply filled him with the now, leaving little room for anything else. His teachers probably found him to be an impulsive or hyperactive little boy.

He cultivated his reputation as a wild man. How else would one explain his conduct in an elegant hotel or in the field?

He had the good or bad luck to go on his R&R at the same time as his commander, an older man, old enough to be Mad Dog's father. That coincidence was not irremediable: Formosa is a big island.

Mad Dog's recollection of the highlights of a week of hedonism focused on the professionalism of a pair of beautiful, tall, Chinese prostitutes who were twins and worked together—literally. By day they showed him many new and exotic sights that delighted him, and by night they taught him new and exotic feats of near-gymnastic eroticism. That was the highlight of his R&R, according to Mad Dog's debriefing to his friends at home base.

But a third person from Kontum observed an event starring Mad Dog, an event that an ordinary man might regard as noteworthy when reviewing with his friends in Kontum the highlights of the week on Formosa. Mad Dog failed to mention it.

Note that our protagonist's commander viewed his holiday week more as a traditional middle-class vacation than an exercise in intoxication and intercourse. After many years in the Far East, he had friends on the island, enjoyed touring, and welcomed gentlemanly dining. One evening he was enjoying good company and fine food in an elegant restaurant when Mad Dog learned of his location and decided to honor his commander with a visit.

Mad Dog entered the restaurant on a motorcycle with his twin hookers sharing the back of the bike. He roared into the dining room, screeched to a halt after colliding with two tables, and dismounted, somehow without injuring his pulchritudinous passengers. Executing a baseball-style slide that terminated with him clearly safe at his commander's feet, he snapped to attention and saluted as he enunciated badly the Special Forces motto: *De oppresso liber*. Honors concluded, he slid back to his motorcycle, mounted, and departed, upsetting two more tables before bouncing down the entrance steps with the twin beauties fastened to him.

The commander's reaction, then and later upon the return flight to Vietnam, is not recorded. It is likely that, except for embarrassment diluted by some amusement, there was no reaction. The commander was a wise man. He may have noted that Mad Dog's act was insane, but it was also over, done, finished. Certainly the events in Laos just days before the R&R flitted through the commander's mind as a mitigating circumstance.

The Studies and Observation Group Headquarters in Saigon wanted a North Vietnamese Army prisoner of war from a specific uncongenial place in Laos. Said place being in the area of operations of CCC, Command and Control Center in Kontum, CCC got the mission: snatch a prisoner. Upon learning of the mission, Mad Dog announced that he and his faithful team would be pleased to enter the tightly secured area filled with enemy hunter-killer teams specifically tasked and trained to hunt down and destroy teams like Mad Dog's. He would grab a prisoner and return him to Kontum. Then he did it.

A true believer in the Fort Benning approach to problem solving—KISS: Keep It Simple, Stupid—Mad Dog laid out his solution. He would take six men: himself, another American, and four Montagnards. They would rappel down ropes not far from a road under the jungle known to be capable of truck traffic, stake out and shoot up a convoy, snatch a truck driver, dash to a landing zone, and return to Kontum.

He selected an ambush site on a turn of the road, killed the occupants of the first and the third trucks, grabbed the driver of the second truck, put a sandbag over his head, bound his hands behind his back, put a rope around his neck that Mad Dog held, and ran like hell to a preselected helicopter landing zone. The bird returned to Kontum after refueling at Dak To. Saigon got the POW, and Mad Dog solidified his reputation as a brave wild man. Commanders remember such details.

Mad Dog was killed by a bullet no one heard fired. He was sitting in the door of a helicopter en route to what turned out to be a "dry hole," a place devoid of enemy, and toppled out, already dead from a head wound. Some little person in the boondocks fired a one-in-a-million shot that killed a brave man. I think he was twenty-three.

43

Heinz

einz arrived in Kontum as a captain in late 1970 for his third tour in Vietnam, joining me in CCC, MACVSOG. We conducted operations, mostly reconnaissance missions, in Laos and Cambodia. Initially assigned to Recon Company, he assumed command of Exploitation Company when Fritz Krupa, AKA Mad Dog, was killed.

I was with Heinz in our aid station when he was patched up after being wounded for the third time, and Robbie, his first sergeant, was wounded for the tenth time. Those two had served together in the IV Corps Mike Force, a quick-reaction unit in the south of the country, in a previous incarnation filled with wild adventures in which they outdid one another in tactical skill, courage, and stamina. The oft-perforated pair made no secret of the joy they derived from close combat and their pride in their professional skills. Our civilization would probably be pleased to ignore or deny it, but some men like to fight, to put it all on the line in the deadliest game men play.

Heinz and I had a close professional relationship, but we got to know one another well on a personal basis via our *Stammtisch* that met once each week in Kontum, when the members were at homebase. The tradition of the Stammtisch in Germany finds birds of a feather assembling at a particular table in a particular Gasthaus at a particular time on a particular day. Often in a small village, very old men who went to school together sixty years in the past and served in the army together fifty years in the past meet weekly until all are dead. Sometimes it ended that way for considerably younger men in Kontum.

There were usually four or five of the six or seven Stammtisch brothers available and present on the appointed evening. The others might be shivering somewhere in Laos as we relaxed in our simulation of Gemuetlichkeit, but they were always with us in spirit. I was the only member of the group not born in Germany, but I had the subscription to *Der Spiegel*, the German newsweekly, the German music, and a desire to be an attaché in Germany or Austria one day. I was a major and the senior man, which mattered in the military pecking order, but that was irrelevant to the Stammtisch. We gathered weekly because we enjoyed each other's company and, I suppose, because our temporary focus on things German took us away from the frequently ugly reality of the here and now.

The others brought their native language and good things to drink. The German hospital ship *Helgoland* off Da Nang was staffed by German nationals pleased to give delicious beer and Weinbrand to the German-speaking Special Forces soldiers who visited them. We, in turn, were pleased to share our riches with Doc Smith's German male and female nurses, dedicated souls supported at subsistence level by Caritas, a Catholic charitable organization. Doc Smith was an American doctor, a mature woman and a saint who treated sick and wounded people without regard to their politics. Clearly, the Stammtisch was an anomaly in the primitive and bellicose setting of a special operations camp, an odd combination of the gentlemanly and the barbaric, German and American, violent and merciful. That's why it meant so much to us.

Upon completion of my second tour in Vietnam, I was assigned to the Pentagon in August 1971. In September I received a letter from my former commander in Kontum, LTC Galan (Mike) Radke. He said he knew of our close relationship and regretted to inform me that Heinz had died in combat on 10 September, shortly after returning from his R&R spent in Hawaii with his wife. His fourth Purple Heart was his last. The war lover was dead.

The day after I got the letter from Radke, I got a postcard from Heinz in Hawaii postmarked PM 8 Sep 71. It said:

Dear Stammtischbrudder! The very best regards from a wonderful R&R in Hawaii is sending you your old hard-core buddy,

Hauptsturmfuehrer,
Heinz

44

Fat Albert: One-Zero

The One-Zero was the star of the SOG recon show. The reconnaissance team was called RT, RTs were named for states, the RT leader was called the One-Zero, and all Americans had code names. Fat Albert was the One-Zero for RT Alabama. He was one of the best leaders in Kontum in 1970, another way to say that he was an extraordinarily skilled and brave man.

To "run recon"—where the men of CCC in Kontum did their job for SOG in Saigon—required a high level of soldier skills and motivation. In fact, it required balls just slightly larger than watermelons. The men who went into Laos in small teams were well-trained Special Forces soldiers who took further special instruction in Vietnam in techniques proven useful in combat operations. We called it the One-Zero School. Students actually went into "Indian country" and worked against pop-up targets who shot back.

Fit, skilled, and highly motivated, the recon man's first assignment in a team was as the number three American. The leader was One-Zero, next was the One-One, and next was the One-Two. The RT is the only military unit I know of where a junior soldier routinely led senior men. Recon men, regardless of rank, began as the One-Two. Advancement to One-One and to ultimately leading a team required the recommendation of the One-Zero. It wasn't at all unusual for a Staff Sergeant to decide when a Master Sergeant or Captain was ready to lead an RT.

SOG had been sending teams into Cambodia and Laos under military control since 1964. At first the American-led teams simply outclassed the enemy, but by 1970 he had developed effective countermeasures, two of which deserve special mention: hunter-killer teams and communication. Highly trained North Vietnamese light infantry hunted down the recon teams. They were very good. They were alerted by a means of communication that began with a single soldier whose mission it was to observe several clearings in the jungle that represented potential landing zones for American helicopters. He also watched trails. When a helicopter appeared to touch down, the observer, typically armed with a German Mauser '98 rifle, an American M-1 rifle or carbine, or an old French weapon, signaled by firing his weapon or by banging on metal or bamboo. The primitive signals were relayed until they reached a radio, by means of which the hunter-killer teams were sent to pursue the American teams on the ground in Laos. Then it was our first team versus their first team in a winner-take-all contest. The loser died.

Fat Albert had two Americans and a dozen Montagnard mercenaries assigned to his team. Most of the teams had three Americans and twelve Asians. The indigenous team members could be Chinese, Vietnamese, Cambodian, or Montagnard. The One-Zero decided who would go on a specific mission. For pure recon emphasizing stealth, the team leader might take two Americans and two to four Asians. For a prisoner snatch requiring firepower, he might take three Americans and nine indigenous. The larger the team, the more difficult emergency extraction might be in an area characterized by dense foliage and clearings often large enough for only one chopper. Indeed, often there was just a hole in the jungle canopy large enough to drop ropes. The various One-Zeros inclined to go light or heavy, but the mission ultimately determined the number of men and the types of weapons and equipment for the job at hand.

Fat Albert took his One-One and four Montagnards on his last mission, a recon patrol into a notoriously dangerous area of Laos, a place where teams could expect contact. The enemy went to extraordinary lengths to hide something in the area.

The RT found a well-concealed high-speed road—connecting turnaround points, trailer transfer points, supply points, and hospitals—and watched enemy traffic to ascertain density and use. The information was new and had to be gotten to Saigon where plans could be made to interrupt enemy traffic on the so-called Ho Chi Minh Trail. Long voice communication by tactical FM radio invited enemy detection and the loss of surprise. The One-Zero and One-One each made extensive notes and shared them.

On the third day on the ground, the team bumped into two enemy soldiers in a meeting engagement at twilight that surprised friend and foe alike. Not quite alike. Fat Albert's point man, his senior Montagnard, got the drop on the enemy, killing both with short bursts from his CAR-15. The RT then moved from the scene of the contact for about an hour in the darkening jungle before setting up for the night. The six men sat back-to-back in a circle with Claymore mines in front of them, providing 360-degree coverage around their version of a circled wagon train. The Claymores fired evil pellets parallel to the ground with devastating effect, rather like giant shotguns. Six giant shotguns. The mines were connected to a device in Fat Albert's hands, enabling him to activate all of the Claymores simultaneously. The team drill called for immediate movement after the activation of the mines, while the enemy was confused, in shock, and dying. The idea was to break contact with the hunters.

The night passed without incident, but before first light, as the team prepared to leave its overnight position, the RT members heard the thrashing of enemy troops hunting for them. After moving for some thirty minutes, it was clear that the enemy was hot on their tail. The disregard of noise discipline in aggressive pursuit announced that the hunter-killers were confident that they outnumbered and outgunned their prey. Fat Albert made a quick decision. He directed his One-One to take three Montagnards on a designated azimuth to a preselected landing zone for extraction. He and his point man would delay the enemy and then link up with the others for extraction. The One-One was told to move for ten minutes and wait. That's what he did. As he moved, he spoke to the out-of-sight but ever-present fixed wing aircraft that coordinated insertion and extraction of teams and served as the RT's contact with the rest of the world. The familiar voice of a fellow sergeant from Kontum guided the One-One along the azimuth to the extraction site. After ten minutes, he paused and waited for Fat Albert.

He and the three Yards heard the brief firefight, recognizing the weapons engaged. Straining his eyes along his back trail, the One-One saw movement after some fifteen minutes. Anxiety became relief as he recognized Albert, but relief became concern as he made out the American carrying the Montagnard, piggyback. Albert lowered the Yard to the ground. The wounded Yard took up a firing position with his weapon oriented in the direction from which he had just come. Albert, clearly visible through a break in the jungle at a distance of some thirty meters, faced the main body of his team—all four of them. The pantomime that followed had been rehearsed countless times in the training areas around Kontum and on previous operations. The One-Zero extended his arm, palm facing his assistant. That meant pay attention to me. He pointed in the direction the main body had been moving and pumped his right fist up and down. That meant go in that direction, double time.

Despite the clarity of the dumb-show, despite the discipline of the team, and despite the unquestioned authority of the One-Zero, the One-One found himself motioning: come to me, come to me.

Albert froze, extended his palm to his assistant, pointed in the desired direction of march, and vigorously pumped his fist up and down.

The One-One moved as ordered.

Within five minutes the One-One heard ominous sounds. There was another violent firefight on the backtrail where Fat Albert would delay the enemy hunters. AK-47s had initiated the fight, a bad sign. CAR-15s responded, but many AKs drowned out all other sounds. Then the One-One and his three Montagnards heard two single shots. They continued on the prescribed azimuth. After talking to the man in the aircraft who would cho-reograph the aerial circus that would get the team out of the jungle and back to the safety of Kontum, the One-One found himself in an opening in the jungle from which he could see the sky. He put a bright ground panel on the jungle floor to identify himself. The pilot said:

"I got orange."

The One-One answered:

"Roger. Orange."

In a corner of his mind he tucked away the sounds of two distinct single shots and what that meant. For now he was too busy to mull it over.

With positive identification the airborne controller—called Covey—organized fire support for the men on the ground and organized to get them out. Without positive identification, the jungle was a green blanket through which stick figures could not be sorted out. Friend and enemy, if seen at all, were blurs of black and green with similar rucksacks and indistinguishable weapons. And with one exception, all were small brown men.

As the extraction bird maneuvered to drop ropes to the team through the hole in the jungle canopy, the conductor of the aerial circus worked his magic. Once he had visual contact with the team—that orange ground panel—he put Army helicopter gunships on the backtrail of the team to keep the enemy off the team with an effective device the recon men called "nails," small dart-like projectiles fired from rockets that did awful things to human bodies. Then the conductor of death used napalm and high-explo-sive bombs on the enemy. He alternated various types of aircraft, depending upon their available stay-time—a factor of the rate at which they burned fuel and their distance from home base. The propeller-driven A1Es could remain overhead for several hours, so Covey worked them on targets until the jets, the fast-movers, arrived. Since the fast-movers had limited time on target because of fuel consumption rates, Covey used them before he would lose them, stacking the A1Es upstairs as the fast-movers expended their bombs and rockets. The A1Es were the ground soldier's best friend. They could loiter for hours, fly low and slow, and carry everything but the kitchen sink. The helicopter gunships had to be used quickly, since the flight from Vietnam consumed most of their fuel.

While working the birds providing fire support, Covey also guided the extraction chopper in a stunt much trickier than it appeared. First, the extraction bird found the hole in the jungle canopy. Then it hovered over the opening under full power while a crewman dropped two ropes to the RT. The ropes twirled from the backlash of the straining blades, threatening to become fouled in trees. If that happened, the ropes would be cut to save the aircraft. In fact, even with soldiers in tow, the ropes would be cut if they became wrapped in the foliage. Trial and error got the ropes into the hands of the men on the ground. They hooked into the loops in the ropes, securing themselves by means of D-rings attached to their load-bearing equipment. Two men found the two loops per rope. The One-One was the last of four men to hook up. He saluted the chopper, the signal to pull the men out of the jungle. During the twenty-minute flight to Vietnam, bad things happened. The sweating men on the strings would get icy cold from the high-speed dash to safety in Vietnam; legs would be painfully numbed as the big leg arteries were squeezed by the leg straps attached to the load-bearing equipment. But they were safe, if being suspended on the outside of an aircraft charging just above the hostile forces at well over a hundred miles per hour is safe.

As the chill set in and his legs numbed, the One-One took a deep breath, rejoicing that he had gotten his three charges out. Then he thought of Fat Albert, and he cried.

45

RT Cookie

our men would jump into Cambodia from the tailgate of a C-130 at 10,000 feet. Jim Storter, a captain, former sergeant, and now reconnaissance company commander, led the team. The NCOs going with him were: Ruff, a no-nonsense reconnaissance team leader; Bentley, the junior man and an experienced combat recon trooper; and Moye, a cool veteran recon man who knew how to make men smile. They had all been in Vietnam for years, some for as long as four or five years. They knew one another well. One or another might have spent all of his Vietnam years in SOG, pulling missions in Laos, Cambodia, or in the DMZ separating north from south Vietnam, but most had done other Special Forces tasks in Vietnam before joining SOG.

The big problem with all combat jumps is assembly on the ground. Linking up with three other men on the ground at night—a day drop was out of the question—is tough. For one thing, the ground belongs to the enemy. Discretion in revealing one's whereabouts is mandatory. To find the others, without being found by those who would kill you, was the first object of the exercise. Then the assembled team could go about the business of snatching a prisoner, tapping a commo line, watching a trail, or whatever the headquarters in Saigon wanted this time.

Exiting in a free fall at 10,000 feet over Cambodian jungle reduces the probability of detection by the enemy, but it also compounds the assembly problem. A static line combat drop at 500 to 700 feet, as for example behind the Normandy beaches in 1944, could result in considerable jumper dispersion, even if pilots put jumpers on the right drop zone. A high-altitude, low-opening stunt at more than ten times the 1944 altitude, could put jumpers to hell and back all over southeast Asia if the jumpers didn't remain close to one another in the long fall. In the dark. In a denied area. Loaded with weapons, ammo, grenades, water, rice, radio, survival kit, and whatever special equipment was required for the job at hand. To land close enough to find one another in the boonies of Cambodia takes training.

Maintaining visual contact with fellow jumpers in the air while falling into a denied area requires concentration, skill, discipline, a couple of technical devices, and great personal courage. It is exciting stuff for the jumpers and those who care about them.

The mission was on for oh-dark-hundred. Although it was out of our hands at CCC and up to the Air Force and our four guys, we were with them in spirit. An hour before oh-dark-hundred found a dozen men at the launch site in the TOC, the bunker housing the Tactical Operations Center. They monitored the now-quiet radio frequency linking us to the C-130 and the airfield. Among the intent listeners were the launch officer and his NCO assistant, the CCC commander, the XO, the ops officer and his NCO assistant, the recon company commander and first sergeant, and some special friends of the jumpers. I was the operations officer.

As H-hour approached, more men drifted into the TOC until they spilled into the larger room next to the launch site. The commander took note of the growing crowd, but he said nothing. It was evident that most of the Americans in camp wanted to hold out a hand to the four jumpers. Just before contact was made with the airfield, notifying us of take-off, there was a stir in the TOC. RT Cookie had arrived.

The recon teams took their names from states. Joe Walker was California, Mike Shepherd was Montana, and so forth. The team logos, with state name and some ferocious caricatures of skulls, fangs, wild beasts, swords, blood, or other suggestions of mayhem, were on the breast pockets of team members, U.S. and indigenous. All of this was quite unofficial. Cookie, in wit flowing from modesty, for he didn't run recon, had designed a team logo consisting of a crossed fork and spoon superimposed on a stitched stack of pancakes. His faithful indigenous minions proudly displayed their logos as they served food in the mess hall and as they moved about the camp. The recon men liked that. The superb food Cookie prepared and presented in no way diminished his status with the troops, nor did his presence on the chopper pad as they returned from hours or days of sheer terror "over the fence." His questions were: what and when do you want to eat?

Allowing the commander to greet the returning team first, then to be greeted by their friends—in reunions always drenched in emotion—Cookie discreetly approached the team with cold beverages of their known preference. Just before the intel types took the team away for a demanding debriefing that could last for hours, Cookie took their orders for the meal to follow the shower after the debrief. We treated returning teams as royalty, because in our subculture they were royalty.

No one ever said the words, but all of Cookie's actions were a salute to very brave men who had cheated death again. We all knew it and loved Cookie for it.

Unexpected and uninvited, the mess sergeant was there, dispensing coffee and freshly baked cookies to the other unexpected and uninvited now listening in silence to the rushing sound of the radio. A break in the rushing sound: take-off. After half an hour of coffee and cookies, at about three in the morning, we got "bingo." They had exited the bird. Another half-hour and radio relay, a light aircraft near but not over the jumpers, reported that Jim Storter came up on the radio. He had linked up with one other jumper. Within another half-hour we got the word: link-up complete; continuing the mission. The wave of relaxation was palpable. Voices were raised, and men started to move, most of them to bed. The time was still oh-dark-hundred. Our guys were in Cambodia with their asses hanging out, but they were on the ground, together.

Profane roughnecks had sweated out the team's infiltration, and, with Cookie's coffee and snacks, we saluted the jumpers without saying the words.

46

Two POWs

The first North Vietnamese POW I interrogated was on 5 November 1966. He was fatally wounded. He had been hit three times with rounds from the high velocity M-16 rifle: in his chest, in his abdomen, and in his upper leg. The young man of nineteen or twenty was strangely serene and smiled at me from his supine position as I addressed him. There was no indication of pain. He was in shock. Perhaps death would come without pain.

We had succeeded in penetrating an enemy base camp complex undetected, after thirty days of walking to a place in Vietnam that was very close to both Cambodia and Laos. Five minutes earlier, some of our people, not yet set up in deliberate ambush positions, got the drop on this man in the uniform of North Vietnam as he and two companions pushed loaded bicycles south on the Ho Chi Minh Trail. Another enemy soldier had been wounded, but his brave companion immediately returned fire with an AK-47 before supporting the wounded man as both disappeared into some very thick jungle.

The fellow on the ground had been made as comfortable as possible, given the austere circumstances under triple-canopy jungle in the middle of nowhere. I examined two tin boxes of wooden-handled grenades packed in banana leaves. They looked like a slightly smaller version of the German World War II potato-masher type I had seen in films as a kid, and the kind I had seen in Korea a dozen years earlier. I think they were made in China. They had a very high failure rate. The canteen he carried bore scratches in the soft metal, probably his name.

A Montagnard, who spoke Vietnamese and English, in addition to his native dialect, acted as interpreter. I gave the wounded man a cigarette, an unfiltered and stumpy Ruby Queen that came out of a maroon package. I didn't have the mentholated cigarettes preferred in that part of the world. War is hell.

I lit the cigarette, noticing that he could still use his hands. His serenity was eerie, considering the three holes that would kill him and the large strangers into whose hands he had fallen. Asked where he got the grenades, he told me. Asked where he was bringing them, he told me. Asked how many soldiers were in his destination camp, which was only a couple of kilometers from where we were, he told me: one hundred. Adding up what he said and the circumstantial evidence, it seemed that an enemy company was resting, training, and refitting in a bivouac area along the trail. It was supplied by traffic on the trail that wended its way south through Laos and into Cambodia and Vietnam. The enemy company would reenter the fray when directed to do so.

I learned that the young man had been in the army less than a year, that he was from the vicinity of Hanoi, and that he had a nice smile. He died. We occupied the enemy bivouac area and, like Goldilocks, waited for the return of the three bears. That's another story.

The second North Vietnamese POW I interrogated was in the summer of 1970 in the latrine of the Tactical Operation Center in Kontum. We wanted to keep him in a secure place, but we didn't want him to see the charts, code words, and maps that were plastered all over the TOC. So there he was, in the latrine. He was brought in blindfolded and with his hands tied behind his back. This prisoner was also a new soldier. He was a conscript fresh out of basic training, a former university student on his way to the war in the south as an engineer private, when he was snatched by one of our teams sent into Laos for that very purpose.

Since I had already spoken to the American team that had snatched him, I knew the conditions of his capture and was concerned about his readiness to be cooperative. He had to be terrified, given the unrelieved shocks and hard knocks he had experienced in the previous three hours. A group of big-nosed round-eyes had popped out of the woods, killed all of the men around him in an extremely violent few seconds, grabbed him and tied his hands behind his back, dropped a sandbag hood over his head, put a rope around his neck, dragged him running through the jungle, and tossed him into a helicopter for his first ride in an aircraft. All of this without having checked his luggage with the friendly clerk.

Upon arrival at our chopper landing pad, he was unceremoniously lifted from the chopper like a sack, still blindfolded and bound, moved by jeep to find himself sitting on a concrete floor surrounded by large, hairy men, who, he had been told by his superiors, would torture him until he died. This was enough to spoil the day of any red-blooded American boy—or a Vietnamese university student who, all things considered, probably would rather be chasing girls around Hanoi. If he wasn't numb with fear, if his trousers weren't soiled and wet, this POW was a better man than I.

He was.

Instead of a stunned prisoner, I saw a slight youngster who looked like Charlie Chan's number one son. Grinning as he smoked and joshed, as though with fraternity brothers, he was surrounded by several American soldiers who were also smiling broadly as they chatted with their new friend through an interpreter. Next to our enemy was a mess hall tray that the Godless Communist had wiped clean. The hand without the cigarette held a cold Coke. It was apparent that our prisoner was being treated as a pet by the baby-killing Special Forces soldiers. I watched for a few minutes, thinking—may God be my witness—that our style was not that of the interrogator in *Darkness At Noon* nor that of our colleagues in the Hanoi Hilton where Americans were routinely beaten and tortured. Perhaps a hard-core regular might have clammed up or lashed out at his captors, but it was apparent that our celebrity-of-the-moment was a lad pleasantly surprised by the good treatment. That suited me.

I followed a checklist we had developed for the purpose, and as Damon Runyon would put it, "He sang like a boid." The kid was a rookie, but he was bright and provided useful information on both the use and maintenance of the trail: he was a pick-and-shovel laborer, fixing the trail as he moved south. We confirmed the locations of various concentrations of enemy troops along the trail and learned of others, mostly logistics troops at turnaround points, field hospitals, resupply points, and rest areas; and we improved our trace of the various kinds of trails that comprised the Ho Chi Minh Trail. In fact, the "Trail" was a bowl of spaghetti with foot paths crossing bicycle paths and both crossing and intersecting roads, some suitable for small vehicles, others improved dirt roads suitable for big trucks and high speed. Their variety gave the enemy logistics planners options. Most of the trail was hidden by vegetation, and the enemy was expert at camouflage where nature failed him, for example, tying treetops together with vines to conceal trails from overflying aircraft. We valued information about the trails for our SOG exploitation by raids and ambushes, but even more for exploitation by friendly air or possible major ground operations by conventional friendly forces.

We learned what they thought about us as well, and it made us feel good. The enemy on the trail feared us, requiring political commissars to work overtime allaying soldier fears and that universal military phenomenon, the shithouse rumor. Actual enemy losses contributed to rumor and fear and conspired with the general acceptance of animism, to our advantage. Somehow our operation got tangled up in the spirit world, crazy talk to most westerners but serious business to many non-Christians in Asia. Our heavy use of helicopters, speedy communications, accurate and visible aircraft fire support from special birds at night, and the B-52 strikes without warning added up to a kind of magic, especially to rookie enemy soldiers.

The sudden appearance and conduct of our SOG men was intimidating. Suited up in black or black-forest green uniforms with load-bearing equipment in place, black spray paint finished the uniform and equipment camouflage job from neck to puttees and boots. Then faces and necks were blackened. Hands were blackened or gloves were worn. Heads were adorned by bandannas and various covers of choice. Finally evil-looking weapons completed the menacing image the enemy would usually first see as his senses were being bombarded by the shock of violent automatic fire from close range, often accompanied by the shrieking of comrades reduced to chop meat by claymore mines or other fiendish devices. The suddenness of ominous flash and bang frequently caused the evacuation of bowels. There were several names used by the enemy to describe our teams, all of them suggestive of magical qualities.

The interview—even filtered through a less-than-expert interpreter and a less-than-expert interrogator—revealed the usual suspicion of regular soldiers by conscripts and universal GI wisdom.

"How were you taken prisoner?"

"Bad luck. There was sudden shooting and the black soldiers caught me."

"Why bad luck?"

"Every time we moved, I was in middle. I never want be first or last. Up north and on trail. Always be in middle. This time sergeant said work over. We go to rest place to eat and sleep. I just start walking on trail. I thought this a safe place. Then the black soldiers come. They take me because I am in front. Bad luck."

"What happened to your friends?"

"Dead. Black men shoot others. Then we run away in jungle to airplane."

"You have good luck. The others are dead. You are here eating and smoking. No more war for you."

He thought that over and smiled.

"Maybe good luck."

"Did you know we were in your area?"

"Yes, but lieutenant and sergeants lie. We heard helicopter the day before capture. Leaders say not to worry. Black soldiers go away. But they not go away. Leaders always lie.

"They say no danger. There is danger. They say we walk not far. We walk far. They say easy work. Then we do long hard work. Always they lie. In training they lie. On trail they lie."

He smiled philosophically.

"Army always lie."

One suspects that the comments of this young man in 1970 or 1971 about his army would differ in no significant way from the freely expressed opinions of U.S. Army conscripts whose views of "lifers" seems close to my POW's views of his army and his leadership.

The first POW died deep in the jungle on 5 November 1966. I sincerely hope that the second POW survived all of the foolishness, completed his education, and enjoys good health to accompany his good humor as he prepared for his fifty-fifth birthday dinner with his children and grandchildren.

47

Patients & Medicines: Snuffy

FOUO" was typed next to Snuffy's name as I read the sick list; the list indicated in which hospitals around Vietnam 5th Special Forces men could be found and the reason for hospitalization. FOUO meant fever of unknown origin. (It also meant "For Official Use Only" in a different context. Love those acronyms!) In Vietnam, it suggested malaria of one kind or another. There were several flavors, only two of which were prevented by "the big pill" and "the little pill" we routinely popped. But it could be one of several exotic tropical diseases, or something as prosaic as flu or a bad cold. That he was in a convalescent hospital meant that, however uncomfortable he might be, medical authority expected him to be back for duty soon. Being very sick or badly wounded was a ticket to Japan or to the United States. He was nearby. I got a bottle of booze as a part of my Florence Nightingale kit and visited the old soldier.

Snuffy Conroy was already one of the oldest men in 10th Special Forces Group when I had met him several years earlier in A Company. He was the Team Sergeant for A-1 and I was a lieutenant in A-4. One of a diminishing group of World War II vets still running around in the woods, Snuffy had served in the 101st Airborne Division in The Big War and in the 187th Airborne Regimental Combat Team in Korea, making several combat jumps along the way. We younger guys, officers or sergeants, admired our big brothers who had jumped into Normandy, Munsan-ni, and other inhospitable climes. In addition to being a real hero, he was personable, generous, and always prepared to help a rookie. And he had a vast array of skills. He was a good mountaineer, skier, swimmer, and sound in all the fundamentals of soldiering, leading, and teaching. Mutual friends had told me that his recent recon missions into Laos were so bold and fruitful that General Westmoreland, with whom Snuffy had served earlier, personally debriefed him. Snuffy was known for getting close to the enemy with a motion picture camera. One of his team told me that the clicking of the camera so near bad guys sounded like the ringing of Big Ben at noon in London, or the boom of cannons in the 1812 Overture, but Snuffy treated such derring-do as a Sunday walk in the Bavarian woods. He was short, stocky, ruddy, usually wore a grin, and, of course, he used snuff.

I found him sitting on a cot in a hot, airless squad tent in the tent city that was the hospital just outside of Nha Trang, a short distance from the 5th SF Group Headquarters. He wore no grin until he recognized who approached him. Then he put one on. Sweaty, pale, and obviously feeling rotten, he cheered at the sight of a familiar face and the prospect of some company. As a veteran of being sick in a lot of different places, I was reminded that being sick in the tropics is worse than being sick anywhere else. Nha Trang is a tropical paradise. FOUO does not belong in Paradise. Period.

We did the where's-so-and-so, sharing stories of what our mutual friends were up to, and he appreciated the bottle I brought for medicinal purposes. I joined him in nipping from the bottle so he wouldn't be lonely—and to hold off illness and evil spirits. Most of our buddies from the 10th Group in Germany could be found in 5th Group in 1966 or in clandestine operations, where they wanted to be, but some served in the 101st and in "leg" infantry companies, mostly young officers from the 10th who were needed to command rifle companies. Some SF officers were diverted from SF and sent to infantry divisions to organize and train their reconnaissance companies. Commanding a rifle company in combat, aside from being an important and responsible job, was regarded as just the right thing for a young officer to do. Serving in SF had sex appeal among the American public but was regarded as a sideshow by Army officialdom. The mainstream Army demonstrated little enthusiasm for hanging out with mercenaries, irregulars, and thugs far from the flagpole and even farther from the amenities provided by our logistics system in great abundance. Institutional wisdom said that one SF tour for an officer was OK; more than one was career suicide. It was different for senior sergeants who could and did remain in Special Forces. Some, like Snuffy, did recon into Laos and Cambodia for Studies and Observation Group, a secret outfit whose ground elements consisted mostly of SF soldiers. We chatted about the guys, the Army in general, the course of the war, and other topics. I remember my effort to get Snuffy out of harm's way.

"Snuffy, isn't it time to turn recon over to the kids?"

The sweaty old man on the cot fully understood what I was doing. Three wars as a combat trooper sufficed. Go to the well too often and you sooner or later fall in. I wanted to keep him alive.

"Well, yeah. Maybe just a few more."

He was killed two weeks later, practicing his craft his way.

48

Bro John

Sometime in the fall of 1970 I walked into the TOC, the Tactical Operations Center of CCC, where I concerned myself with operations and intelligence gathering. A sergeant said:

"Message for you, sir, from Major Lair, 173d. The major said call him soonest."

I thanked the sergeant and called Don Lair, AKA "Buck," with whom I had studied history at Stanford University a year earlier. The Naval Reserve Officer Training Course building had been burned down by war protesters before we arrived, and the Stanford Research Institute was wrecked while we were there. The Students for a Democratic Society, Black Panthers, and Black Student Union were busy at the time. We went to Vietnam to escape hazardous duty.

A voice answered: "173d Airborne Brigade, S-3, Air. Sergeant So-and So, sir!"

"Major Gole, CCC. May I speak to Major Lair?"

"Sir, he stepped out, but I have a message for you. He had me write it out. Message follows: 'He's OK. We know he's OK. Specialist John Gole was wounded yesterday and is in Cam Ranh in the 10th Convalescence Hospital.'"

My brother, one of six Gole boys, was in a rifle squad of the 173d. This was the second time he was hit.

"How do you know he's OK?"

"Major Lair called the company. They said it wasn't serious. Plus the hospital they sent him to is for short stays and return to duty. The Major wanted to be sure that you know it is not serious."

"Thank you and thank Major Lair for me. How is it that the S-3, Air shop knew my brother was hit?"

"Major Lair saw a list of casualties. He said the name was unusual, and he thought of you. He said you mentioned you had a brother in the 173d. He knew you'd want to be notified."

"Well, thank you and thank him. Out."

I told my commander what happened. He told me to get out of there and see that the kid was in one piece.

Two years earlier, when John was seventeen, I picked up the phone in my quarters at Fort Ord in California to be greeted by my father calling from New York. Unusual. Normally I initiated calls, and my mother spent more time on the line than my father. After spare amenities, the conversation went like this:

"John's driving me crazy!"

"What now?"

"He wants to joint the Marines. I told him to finish high school first, but he just mopes around. So I signed the papers."

"What papers?"

"The enlistment papers. I tell you, he's driving me crazy!"

"You signed? Are you watching TV? They're stacking young marines like cordwood at Khe Sanh. He isn't even physically mature yet. Do you want to sign his death certificate?"

"What the hell am I supposed to do?"

"I'll tell you what to do. You put mom on, and you tear up the enlistment papers you signed."

My mother got on the phone and asked:

"What did you tell your father?"

"What's he doing?"

"He's tearing up those papers."

"That's what I told him to do. John's really driving dad nuts, isn't he?"

"Yes. We don't know what to do with him."

I paused. My poor wife was about to be inconvenienced by my crazy family. Not for the first time. Her growing up was as modest as mine, but her family was straight ahead, no surprises. One and one was always two. My family was unpredictable. Sometimes one and one was three. Or eleven. Or zero. The best advice she ever got was from the priest who told her not to marry me. I was a puzzle to her. My family was entirely mysterious. But I saw a solution to the John problem.

"Mom, tell me how you react to this plan. I pay for his flight out here. He lives with us. Either he goes to school or gets a job. Once he's eighteen he can do what he wants. He might change his mind. It's worth a try. Wadda ya think?"

Pause.

"Tell your father. Let me think."

My father got on the line, and I repeated the proposal.

There was no pause.

"Yes. I don't know what else to do. I'm outta ideas. The change may be good. Yes. Thanks. Let's do it. Here's Mom."

"Mom? You heard? What do you say?"

"Yes. I'm afraid your father is going to have a heart attack or kill John." Hmm. Best to keep both alive.

We took care of the administrivia and John arrived in San Francisco. He was a tall, scrawny, insolent twit without the foggiest appreciation of life beyond eating, sleeping, and wanting to be a marine. He was a . . . a . . . a seventeen-year-old. And it was 1968. But, as they say in Boy's Town, "He ain't heavy. He's my brother."

I made a point to stay off his case for a few days. My inclination was to slap the shit out of him. His insolence surpassed even his great ignorance, but he was just a tad intimidated, perhaps wondering what he had gotten himself into: my clutches (bad) and whatever "California" suggested to his goofy reading of the tea leaves (probably good).

He slept. Give credit where it's due. He was a prodigious sleeper. Olympic! My wife claimed that she could actually see him growing. In due course, I put a can of beer in his hand and explained the Henry Rules. In one week he would decide to go to high school or he would get a job. "Job," I explained, was defined not as pumping gas, drinking beer, and raising hell. I endorsed the school track and shut up. I did my best imitation of a reasonable man. Doubtless he saw just another rule-making authority figure who "didn't understand."

The following week he decided he would go back to New York to finish high school. And did. At nineteen, with some meat on his bones, he went through basic training and jump school, arrived in Vietnam, and got shot. Twice.

After hitching aircraft rides from Kontum to the hospital a couple of hours away, I presented myself to an officious son of a bitch who told me my brother was AWOL, Absent Without Leave! AWOL from a hospital? I asked what condition the kid was in and learned that he was, in fact, OK. They were preparing to release him when he took off. I told the clipboard-toting jerk to check with the 173d, if he wanted to locate John, and I turned to leave.

A scrawny kid in pajamas, witness to this exchange, sidled up to me.

"Sir, are you John's brother?"

"I am. Do you know where he is?"

"Yessir. He said he was going to the Special Forces in Nha Trang to see you."

"Thanks. That's the headquarters. He won't find me there. Tell me what kind of shape he's in."

"He's fine, sir. He asked to be released. When they didn't release him he said, 'Screw the REMFs. I'm gonna visit my brother.' An' he took off."

I took my cue and took off. Eventually I ran down my brother.

John lived happily ever after as a New York City firefighter—until he was seriously injured at a fire. I think John was pleased to get the United States of America and the City of New York in a pissing contest about who had to pay for which parts of his roughed-up body. He took said disabled body, one wife, and two sons to the mental and physical state of Washington to live happily ever after just off the yellow brick road. One considers the possibility that ole snake-bit might keep his mind on the task at hand and both wheels of his high-powered motorcycle on terra firma as he cruises the yellow brick road.

49

Chinese Medicine

The Vietnamese senior officer at CCC was one very sick lieutenant colonel. He was in my domain, the Tactical Operations Center, to look at some maps of Cambodia in connection with a recon mission. As we moved along the wall where the maps were displayed under thick glass, I noticed his swollen lids, glassy eyes, and the constant need of his handkerchief to mop his brow and wipe his nose.

"Sir, you need to go to bed. You look terrible."

"Feel terrible. But tomorrow be OK."

"Really? You have a bad bug. You should rest."

"Tonight, Chinese medicine. Tomorrow number one."

Sure enough! When I saw him the next day, he was fit. Recalling our conversation of the previous day, he said:

"You see! Number one! Chinese medicine."

A few weeks later I wallowed in self-pity with some kind of a bug that produced burning eyes, dripping nose, and the general miseries. Again I cursed the too-muchness of the tropics, where everything is overripe, including sickness. Grippe or flu or whatever-the-hell-it-was should be accompanied by snow or wind or both. Stinking heat, humidity, clothing sticking! It's unnatural. Woe is me.

The Vietnamese commander took one look at me and pronounced firmly:

"Tonight you come my hooch. Chinese medicine. Tomorrow, number one."

I protested weakly, but what the hell! A good Special Forces soldier attaches great value to close rapport with indigenous personnel. Besides, the commander was being kind. I had eaten and drunk mysterious and foul-smelling stuff for the sake of rapport. I had hung out my ass often enough for my Vietnamese brothers. I could humor the believer in magic, claptrap, or Chinese medicine for the greater good of Vietnamese-American relations.

"OK, sir."

"You come my hooch 1900. My houseboy know Chinese medicine."

I did, and the houseboy did.

I was directed to take off my shirt, keep on my T-shirt, and sit in a chair with my head hanging over a big can of boiling water generously laced with various herbs, giving off a strong but not unpleasant scent. The houseboy covered me with a poncho and heavy blanket, tucking the bottoms so that I was sealed in a cocoon, just me and the bubbling can between my knees.

What primitives! The things I do for my country.

The houseboy didn't have much English, but his boss knew the form.

"You stay as long you can."

Soon I was dripping sweat and mucous. Lots of both. My T-shirt and trousers were drenched, and I had about as much as I could take.

As I came up for air, the colonel spoke.

"Now you go your hooch. No shower. Go in bed. Pull blankets up to head. Go sleep. Tomorrow number one."

And so it was. I was fine in the morning after experiencing what was essentially a combination of a vaporizer and steam bath, a treatment that beat the hell out of "take two every four hours and come back in a week." Chinese medicine numbah one!

50

Lope's Got a Gun

I felt the hand firmly shaking my shoulder and heard the familiar quiet but insistent voice at the same time.

"Major. Major, wake up."

I did. The voice belonged to Ken Locke, my partner in crime, a man I held in very high regard. He was the senior NCO, and I was the boss in the intel shop in our SOG camp in Kontum.

"What's up?"

Things often went bump in the night in our line of work. Usually disturbed sleep meant that one of our teams in Laos was in serious trouble. Or that bad guys were skulking in the neighborhood. Or that a bird was down and we had to get the pilot. Or . . . God only knows. It was actually wildly exciting. Too bad stuff didn't happen just between sunrise and, say, nine or ten at night. And too bad that young men got hurt. In Camelot it rains only between midnight and four a.m. Why can't shit happen between nine a.m. and five p.m.?

"Lope. He's got a rifle. Won't let anyone in his hooch. Says he's gonna shoot himself."

I was lacing boots and wide awake. My only natural military talents were that I woke up easy and liked Army chow. Not happy. Easy.

"Why?"

"Dunno. He's been drinking. Some of our guys talked to him from outside his room. He said he'd shoot anybody who comes through the door. They got me an' I went. He told me not to come through the door. Sounds like he means it. I thought maybe he'd listen to you."

"Yeah. Thanks. Maybe. Let's go," sez I, noticing that it was after midnight.

I had to talk a loaded gun away from a soldier once in Germany. Not fun. All things considered, I'd rather be in Philadelphia.

193

The camp was quiet as we moved in the darkness from one side to the other. One sensed presence on the perimeter that was always manned, but most of the men in camp were sleeping in hooches like the one we approached.

A couple of the my S-2 guys stood vigil near a door to a room in the hooch. Ken addressed them.

"Anything new?"

"No. We tried talking to him, but he said, 'Go away! I mean it! I'll shoot if you come in.' So we waited here for you."

"Hmmm," I said in that profound way officers use to show mere mortals and enlisted swine how it's done. What I meant was, oh shit. Now what?

Ah well. Let it begin.

Lope was an old soldier with more than twenty years of service and several years in Vietnam. Maybe discipline would kick in when an eminence addressed him. Like Major Me. And I liked him. I think he liked me. Maybe that counts. Shouldn't shoot friendlies, even majors. Especially a nice guy like me. I had noticed no signs of instability in him, but he had a loaded weapon now. And knew how to use it. And he had been drinking. And he seemed to have a case of the oh-woe-is-me. Life is filled with details not clearly addressed in field manuals. Nor in the Baltimore Catechism. That's why armies have fire-breathing geniuses as officers. Like me.

The prospect of falling on the field of honor did not attract me at that moment; the prospect of being drilled by one of my own guys was singularly unattractive. Ignominious. Irrationally, I wondered what my brothers and the men I grew up would make of that. "Hear about Henry? Too bad. They say he was shot by one of his own men." I was already shot, dead, buried, mourned—and now the bastards made it my fault! Damned ingrates.

"Lope, it's me, Major Gole."

"Go away, sir!"

"Hmmm." This time I meant a profound oh shit. He said "sir." Maybe he would shoot me respectfully.

"I wanna talk to you."

"Go away! I mean it!"

"Nah, I gotta talk to you. We can fix it. I'm coming in slow. Alone. Let's talk."

"I'm telling you, don't come in!"

I chanced a peek through the doorway. His rifle was on his bunk, not in his hands. Good sign. But it was close. He was sitting next to it. And I noted the magazine in the weapon. Now we were looking at one another. That mattered. I don't think he wanted to shoot me. Maybe he couldn't if we had eye contact and I made sense to just one person in the universe: him. Even Bambi had a chance if the hunter looked into those wide and soulful eyes.

"I'm peeking at you," I said stupidly. Even now I can't think of something smart that I coulda, woulda, shoulda said in the circumstances.

I stepped into the doorway. He didn't reach for the weapon. Things were looking up. He was probably temporarily dazzled by my wit. "I'm peeking at you" was a real show-stopper.

I babbled the kind of memorable stuff I share with my black lab dog when no two-legged types are around, and I advanced a step or two. No movement of hand toward the rifle. Maybe I would not die this night. Maybe I could go back to bed. Somehow I was standing right in front of him. I know it wasn't a flying carpet that got me there, and the Holy Ghost was probably busy with His other responsibilities. But there I was.

I sat next to Lope—on the rifle. He started to cry. I put my arm around him and made some more black lab sounds as I eased the rifle further away, mostly because it hurt my butt.

I listened to his recitation of the litany of the world's ills and the basic injustice of the human condition. He had it about right, but I couldn't fix the world. I confessed to that deficiency. He kinda wound down, then he dozed off. What a helluva a guy I am, I noted.

I told my guys to get all the good killing stuff—grenades, rifles, pistols, knives, and assorted fiendish devices—out of the hooch. His roomie flopped out on the other bunk. Another guy would watch from the doorway and be relieved by others until wake-up time. I told them to say nothing about this to him or to anyone else.

I went to bed.

We never referred to the incident again. I think he knows it happened. It did.

51

We Gotta Get Outta This Place

B ob Hope, the great entertainer of American troops from World War II through Vietnam, did not come to Kontum. A lot of entertainers and tourists overlooked us in 1970 and 1971, apparently preferring even Philadelphia, Peoria, and Kalamazoo to Kontum.

Janis Joplin didn't visit either. Too bad. She would have gotten on famously with our guys, and they would have liked her a lot in person. The reckless abandon with which she wailed, shrieked, and banged out "Me and Bobbie McGee" was heard everywhere and always in our camp until it became a kind of anthem. I'm not sure, but I think the line "Freedom's just another word for nothin' left to lose" hit the men of CCC right in their fatalism. She let it all hang out. So did they. She and they held nothing back. She lived for now. So did the SOG men. They also lived for one another.

Every couple of months, talentless entertainers came to CCC, sent by The Big Morale Guy in Saigon who presumably was obligated to do good for the troops, particularly those in places designated "remote," like us'ns in Kontum. He sent us a bunch that sure as hell agitated the audience that night.

The group consisted of four Filipinos, whose distinguishing characteristic was volume. The "lead singer" was an Australian blonde, generously proportioned from her big toe to her northern region. Her third distinguishing characteristic was very white skin, enough to cover the considerable all of her. The prospect of a view of the all of her held the audience summoned by the noise announcing the third-rate event. It was the only show in town, and she was a lotta woman. She did not sing well, but what the hell, she wasn't there to sing well. She was there to be a round-eyed woman with lots of visible skin.

The audience was everyone in camp, the thousand men not on combat operations or away on stand-down. The U.S. and Vietnamese commanders sat together at the place of honor, a table close to the stage. Some sixty American and thirty Vietnamese Special Forces soldiers were also in the tin-roofed amphitheater, gathered at tables in fours and sixes. They and the stage for the entertainers filled much of the room. Completing the scene was the rest of the camp's population, mostly Nungs, Montagnards, and Vietnamese, with a sprinkling of other ethnic types from around southeast Asia, mercenaries all. They filled the back of our rough-framed amphitheater and flowed over to the outside by the hundreds to line the walls of the structure. The timbered bottom of the walls was four to five feet high before becoming screened windows for another three or four feet. The just-over-five-feet mercenaries, some in shadows, some in the fading light from inside, provided an unusual sight from a seat inside. Disembodied heads with bright eyes and sometimes-shining teeth were pressed to the screen all around the hall, framed by the shadows of those behind. Unlettered folk found it spooky. Literate types might have seen an amalgam of Joseph Conrad's shadows on the Congo and Dante's figures on the far side of the Styx. A teenager would call it weird. Hollywood called it *Apocalypse Now*.

The booze flowed. The booze always flowed at CCC. Nowhere was the Old Army motto—work hard, play hard—taken so seriously. Teams performed extremely hazardous and physically demanding missions for which they studied, trained, prepared intensely before executing with one hundred percent of their beings. Then they played with the same intensity. On this night, the men in camp played.

It wasn't the lack of talent that sparked a scary reaction. We didn't expect talent. It was the pockmarked drummer.

Apparently the band-cum-bountiful blonde concluded its gigs for GI audiences around Vietnam with "We Gotta Get Outta This Place." The small, brown, grinning, pockmarked drummer was gleefully banging away, approaching the finale, when he raised one hand forming a V with two fingers. His body language said that this boffo conclusion usually evoked an encouraging reaction from audiences that joined in agreement with the lyric by singing: "We gotta get out of this place." The V, which meant victory when Winston Churchill formed it, had become an antiwar symbol. The booze, throbbing music, and generally bad vibes set the scene. The V flashed by Pock Mark lit an invisible fuse.

As though on cue, the flash of the V during the playing of the familiar tune elicited a roar of "NO! NO! NO!" that became a chant as the American CCC men stood on the tables as though performing a drill. Then the entire room took up the cry in unison: "WAR! WAR! WAR!" The air was heavily laden with pure malevolence as the audience advanced by walking foward on the table tops toward the stage while roaring, "WAR! WAR! WAR!" The drummer, wide-eyed as his head pivoted left to right and back again, taking it all in, seemed to realize that he had provoked the reaction, but he was confused—as I was—by the speed with which this musical high had been transformed to fear approaching terror in the highly charged atmosphere. He didn't know what had happened. Neither did I. He was frightened. So was I. I think in that moment the lives of the band were at risk. This could have meant minor murder and major paperwork.

At the brink of a mass madness, sage Sergeant Moye redirected something well under way. He jumped on the stage, grabbed the microphone, made a brief remark to the audience and turned to the drummer, telling him exactly what to do. Moye started to sing to the tune of "He's Got the Whole World in His Hands." He motioned to Bemis, a recon man of many talents, who jumped up to the stage, took the guitar from a musician paralyzed with fear, and strummed the old church tune "He's Got The Whole World In His Hands" to lyrics known to the CCC men.

> He's got a CAR-15 in his hands.
> He's got a CAR-15 in his hands.
> He's got the whole world in his hands.
> He's got mini-grenades in his hands.
> He's got mini-grenades in his hands.
> He's got the whole world in his hands.

There were several more verses and several more tunes to soothe the savage beasts. Bemis played, Moye acted as master of ceremonies, the band did what it was told, the mood passed, and the band got outta CCC safely. I think Moye saved a drummer's life. Maybe a band's. I think I know what it is to be in a lynch mob.

52

Die Junge Burschen

Jan Novy was going home in the morning, so I joined him for a farewell drink. We'd met first in Germany, in the 10th Group; we bumped into one another several times on a previous tour in Vietnam in 1966; and here we were in Kontum in 1970, he, a senior sergeant headed to 10th Group and retirement in New England, and I, a major in midtour in the special operations camp.

Jan, a dozen years older than I, was already a mature man when he escaped from his native Czechoslovakia in about 1950 to become a Displaced Person in Germany, a DP to those with memories stretching back to the early post–World War II years. His path to Kontum went through a DP camp, the Czech Labor Service in Germany, the U.S. Army in Fort Bragg, the 10th Group in Germany, and the 5th Group in Vietnam.

As the U.S. Army in Germany was reduced to a small constabulary force in the draw-down immediately after the Second World War, non–U.S. Army armed security personnel were hired to guard its various installations and U.S. property. Young homeless males from Middle and Eastern Europe, seeking new lives, represented a cheap source of labor. They needed food, clothing, a roof over their heads, a little training, and a small cash incentive to survive in rubble-strewn and dislocated Europe. The marriage was made in heaven. Destitute, drifting, desperate young men became guards in Czech, Polish, German, and other Labor Service organizations, typically organized in national groups, all of them under the command and control of the U.S. Army. Some spent their working lives in these outfits, retiring in Germany; some found their ways to Canada, Australia, the USA, South America, and only God knows where else. Many found a home in the U.S. Army and became my friends.

Legislation, universally called "the Lodge Act" in Special Forces, granted U.S. citizenship to qualified male DPs in exchange for five years of honorable service in the U.S. Army. Many Labor Service men jumped at the chance to become Americans. Jan, called "Leatherhead" because of his wrinkles and tough hide, was one of the original SF men of the 77th Group and was still serving honorably over twenty years later. Other "Lodge Acts" would retire as sergeants major and as officers after thirty years.

The old man was morose as he prepared to depart Kontum. Instead of joy at surviving another tour in Vietnam, Jan wept for his dead friends. I knew the story, but Jan, slightly buzzed, told me again.

He and three other Special Forces soldiers were driving in a jeep from Kontum to Pleiku—a sometimes hairy, sometimes safe trip, like so much of the Vietnam adventure—when the enemy ambushed them. The other three were killed. When Jan awoke, his watch and wallet were gone. Franklin Miller, later awarded a Medal of Honor for his actions on a recon mission in Laos, had interrupted the enemy search of their kills by assaulting them from his gun jeep that fortuitously came upon the scene during the search. Jan's head, bloody from going through the windshield, was such a mess that the enemy assumed he was dead. Miller's arrival and Jan's bloody appearance saved his life.

As we sipped a cognac in farewell to him that night before his departure, Jan repeated the words: *"die junge Burschen . . . die junge Burschen . . . Herr Major, der Alter kommt wieder durch. Die junge Burschen sind gefallen"*—"the young lads . . . the young lads . . . Major, the old man comes through again. The young lads fell in battle."

I saw der Alter several times in his retirement before he died in New Hampshire much later. I hope he had a happy reunion with the young lads, his American buddies, and with his older friends from Middle Europe. One senses that he had some pleasures along the way, but happiness eluded him. In many ways, he personified a certain Middle European sobriety that borders on permanent sadness.

53

Thank God I Had Yards

t was 1971 and time to go home. I was a tired Major completing a second tour in Vietnam, convinced that I had shared a year with the best combat soldiers in the world and equally convinced that it didn't matter to anyone outside of our fraternity. The American people, press, and Congress just wanted out, and the administration was casting about for an exit "with honor." A whitewash job called Vietnamization would leave the Vietnamese holding the bag as the United States pretended that our allies could win the war that we could not win with 500,000 American troops, a mountain of supplies, more bombs than we dropped on Germany in World War II, and a score of harebrained schemes. My first war as an enlisted soldier in Korea, the earlier tour in Vietnam, two assignments in Germany, various professional courses, and academic degrees provided me with a veneer of realism or professionalism—perhaps it was cynicism—and protected me from depression as my country deserted the Vietnamese.

My two companions from Kontum, however, were unprotected. They were reserve officers, representatives of the best America offers the world. At the height of the war in Vietnam, they graduated from college and joined the Army. After basic training, they attended Officer Candidate School, Ranger School, Airborne School, and a number of courses to qualify for Special Forces. Then they volunteered for Vietnam and spent a year leading Montagnard irregulars and U.S. Special Forces soldiers in hazardous combat operations in Laos and Vietnam. The troops were mercenaries and the chain of command—company commander, platoon leaders, platoon sergeants, and squad leaders—were American soldiers. My two young friends, probably twenty-three or twenty-four, had served honorably and well. I admired them.

Pete Landon had been wounded as a platoon leader on a particularly harrowing mission. [Almost thirty years later, that mission, Operation Tailwind, was falsely reported by *Time* (15 June 1998) and CNN (7 and 14 June 1998). Journalists, some quite famous, were fired or kept off the air as

201

their reporting sins were exposed. Happily, some Special Forces soldiers settled out of court for enough money to pay for the education of their grandchildren.] But in 1971 Pete was healed and ready to go back to join civilians in the Land of the Big PX. So was Jake Dobreiner, a Hollywood-handsome and self-effacing lieutenant.

The three of us learned that we would have a lazy day of doing nothing in the Cam Ranh Bay replacement center before boarding "the Freedom Bird" for the United States on the following morning. That suited us. We dunked our bodies in the South China Sea and rested.

Late in the afternoon, as we strolled about the barbed wire–surrounded compound, one of us spotted a stand selling soft ice cream, the kind that comes out in a swirl. We got on a line behind scruffy American troops also headed for the ice cream dispenser. As we went our way, ice cream cones in hand, one of my companions commented on the deplorable appearance and demeanor of the soldiers. The other responded by saying:

"Thank God I had Yards." [Translation: Thank God my troops were Montagnards and not Americans like these.]

"Yup," assented the other, sucking up his ice cream.

Two young American volunteers were leaving their war, happy to have served with nomadic tribesmen who had just recently stepped from the most primitive circumstances—complete with crossbows, loinclothes, bare-breasted women, and slash-and-burn agriculture—preferring them to American soldiers. The quiet observation, so matter-of-fact and so unselfconscious, impressed me more than a rant of indignation might have.

Discussions in the 1990s of the Vietnam War skate over how rotten our Army was in the 1970s, how confused policymakers were, how disillusioned idealists had become, how disinterested the American public was, and how alienated young blacks were.

Have we forgotten?

That the "man in the street" has forgotten is not surprising. It was a long time ago. But policymakers and professional soldiers need to remind themselves how tenuous is the support of the American people for any war not conducted for a clear purpose and as a great crusade.

54

Billy B's Silver Star

knew Billy Boggs from our service in the 10th Special Forces Group in the early 1960s in Germany. He was quiet and had a reputation among his peers for being a first-rate commo man, cool under stress and a tough soldier. It was natural that Jim Fenlon, who commanded, and I thought of him as we selected the men for a dangerous mission requiring skilled and brave people. In the Special Forces vernacular of those days, we put a bad hurt on the enemy. Billy was solid as a rock and technically expert.

I lost track of Billy B, but in the early 1990s we reestablished contact when he called out of the blue. In later tours in Vietnam, he had served on recon teams with CCN, SOG, a cross-border operation based in Danang with launch sites closer to Laos. That was a coincidence, since I had been engaged in similar operations for another element of SOG.

Billy retired as a sergeant major, but he continued to ply his trade as a civilian, training Saudis for a while. Then he did some teaching of counter-terrorist techniques for South American airlines. It was in discussing another job in South America that we reestablished contact. He called and flattered me by asking if I were interested in getting involved again in wild fun and games. He said he called because I reminded him of himself: the worse things got, the more detached and analytical I became. Coming from a soldier I respect, that was music to my ears. The job didn't pan out: the planners estimated that we'd be killed upon arrival by some very bad people for the right reason or for another reason. But I was pleased to be in contact with Billy B again.

I didn't know of his heroics while on patrol from an A Team camp at about the time I was plotting to kidnap him for BLACKJACK 21, but I wasn't surprised.

His Congressman pinned a Silver Star on Billy's chest in 1999 for valor displayed in 1966. The citation and newspaper accounts get it about right, but I don't think he'll mind if I tell it to you the way old soldiers tell such things to one another.

Billy was recommended for a Distinguished Service Cross, a DSC, an award just below the Medal of Honor in the U.S. Army's pecking order of awards for valor. Chatting with an old comrade a few years ago, the friend mentioned the DSC as though it had been awarded, and Billy said he never got it. Angry, the friend said he had seen the written recommendation in 1966 in Vietnam. Someone had dropped the ball. The friend made it his business to rattle his Congressman's cage. Said Congressman queried Department of Army. Eventually Billy's Congressman got into the act. To summarize, Billy got the Silver Star, downgraded from DSC for reasons unclear. When Billy's active duty Special Forces son-in-law asked for leave from Fort Bragg to attend the ceremony in Townsend, Massachusetts, the Group Commander packed off the sergeant son-in-law and his A Team commander, a captain, to represent the Army at the ceremony. As a radio journalist likes to say, now the story behind the story.

Billy was to take out a patrol from a remote A Team site to a dangerous place with a man new to the team. When told that he was to take a Catholic chaplain and yet another straphanger with him, Billy objected, pointing out that he had been to this place before and knew it to be a hot place with bad guys ready to tangle assholes. It was not the kind of mission for three American novices in the area of operations. Ordered to shut up and do it, Billy shut up and did it.

The walk in the woods was spoiled when the enemy conducted an ambush that seriously wounded the priest. The enemy used the priest as bait, hoping that some dumb American would try to get the wounded man out of harm's way. Noting the seriousness of the priest's wound, Billy was the dumb American who went for the bait. He took the precaution of killing a shit-pot of enemy with hand grenades and his automatic weapons fire. He was pissed at the bad guys, pissed at the cretins who ignored his sound advice, pissed at amateurs, and generally pissed at the world. When he was temporarily finished killing bad guys, he dragged the priest to safety, saw to some heavy-duty first aid, killed some more bad guys, and got the badly wounded man of the cloth medevaced. The man survived, and Billy has had contact with him into the 21st century.

Billy went from that action to BLACKJACK 21 with me and our friends. To demonstrate that old dogs are beyond retraining, he went on the near-suicidal recon missions of CCN into Laos when the Surgeon General should have certified that walking in Laos was definitely harmful to the recon man's health. The obtuse old soldier's saving grace is his affection for his black lab and his readiness to give a parched old veteran a drink when such types visit the Squire of Townsend.

Billy is the right stuff.

Part V

Ripples

. . . in which our narrator grows gray, realizes that he will not die in combat, and ruminates about a half-century, good men, and a nation that remains man's best hope for personal fulfillment.

The Zeitgeist and My Little World

God peeked from behind a fluffy cloud, instead of from his favorite whirlwind, and gave me His take on America's Big Picture on the downward side of the twentieth century. It went like this. The winners of World War II celebrated in an orgy of materialism, spoiling their brats. The brats got caught up in the causes of the 1960s. During and after the contentious Vietnam War, the society became unglued. Blacks pursued their agenda, so everyone else imitated that agenda by discovering their ethnicities. Gays wanted respect. Women wanted equality. It was generally agreed that Western Civilization, cavities, white males, the common cold, and melting pot were unhealthy. "Illegitimacy," "sin," "promiscuity," "shacking up," and "wrong" were stricken from the language, and words like "pissed off" and "asshole" found their way to what passed for polite society. Diversity, single parenting, burning the Stars and Stripes, and killing unborn babies were OK. The military and the police were not. Waitresses addressed mature couples as "you guys," and it was bad form for parents to control unruly children at home or in public. Dot.comers replaced MBAs and lawyers as child millionaires. Government was bad, and politicians scheming for power had to be from the heartland and condemn Washington, D.C. before moving there to stay. Anchovies were left out of Caesar's salad, roadmaps were not free, and people said, "That's OK," when they once said, "You are welcome."

Terrorists flew airplanes into the World Trade Center and the Pentagon. Cops, soldiers, firefighters, blue-collar workers, and the Stars and Stripes were OK again, at least for a while. While no one was watching, sleazy bastards took over corporations and my Church, and nincompoops and spoiled children governed.

My little world continued to be the subculture of the professional soldier. The nature of the work and the cultural opportunities in Washington made bearable the general prison atmosphere of the Pentagon, the dense traffic, and the high cost of living. Four years as an attaché in the American Embassy in Bonn was a delight. The work, Cadets, and colleagues made teaching history for three years at West Point pure fun. While at the Strategic Studies Institute at the U.S. Army War College in Carlisle, Pennsylvania, I wrote to my heart's content and bought a house. Unfortunately, my penultimate tour was miserable. I worked for a three-star martinet who boasted of replacing walls in the Pentagon with glass so that he could watch his officers the way Scrooge watched his clerk in *A Christmas Carol*. He was also proud of firing an old lady who ran the snack bar in his major transportation command in New Jersey. We did not have a loving relationship.

After a happy second tour at the Army War College, I retired in 1988 to earn a doctorate, teach, write, and observe the human comedy from my house in the woods of Pennsylvania. I have time to think.

God help us all.

55

Cool Pops

ichael was ten when we arrived in Bonn in 1973 for what turned out to be a four-year tour at the American Embassy. He had lived in Bamberg, two different apartments in Frankfurt, two in Bad Toelz, and then in Fort Eustis, Williamsburg, Fort Ord, Palo Alto, Garmisch, Stewart Field, Washington, and Norfolk. For two of those years his father was in Vietnam. After his twelve bedrooms in ten years, we were all pleased at the prospect of stability, happy to be in Germany, and delighted with our large ground-floor apartment that afforded us an unobstructed view of the Rhine River some two hundred yards distant. Most of all we were glad at the opportunity to remain together. Mother and son relaxed in the expectation that Dad's assignments to Vietnam were behind us. Problems were few and minor in that idyllic period in Germany, and the job was a joy.

A tiny issue upsetting our calm featured the tall cherry tree that stood in front of our apartment building and the little boys' need—absolute need—to climb the tree to eat the cherries. Michael and his little pals went up, way up, and parental strife ensued as mother exclaimed:

"Oh, look at him!" as she headed for the door.

"Whoa! What are you going to do?" asked the presumptive master of all he surveyed.

"I'm getting him out of that tree!"

"You can't do that."

"He could fall out of the tree!"

"True, but God made cherry trees to feed birds and to be climbed by little boys."

"But he could be seriously hurt!"

"That's also true, but please don't go out there. For a whole bunch of reasons," said the second-in-command, incredulous that his bride didn't understand about boys and trees. She was raised as one of two girls. I was the eldest of seven, six of them boys. Secure in my knowledge of the filthy little beasts that are boys, I had my way. That time. I got the if-looks-could-kill special, but she acquiesced.

And then there was the bicycle. On a Saturday morning some two weeks after our arrival, my bride, that mistress of indirection, invited me to our terrace for a game of Twenty Questions, to which I, in my boyish innocence, responded by presenting myself to the appointed place.

"What do you see?"

After seventeen years of marital bliss, even the most dullard husband recognized the baiting of a trap. Minimizing damage, I confessed to my ignorance, a fair description of my normal state in such situations. She helped me.

"The kids. Kids on bikes. See them? Your kid is not on a bike. His bike is in the storeroom. In pieces."

After a pause to suggest deep thought by the leader of men, I announced:

"I think it's time to assemble Mike's bike," said the dullard, pleased with himself for the original idea.

"Good idea," said de facto authority, nourishing the notion that her mate was capable of obedience, if not creativity.

I dragged the bike to the terrace, found the rusty tools, and was joined by Michael, who had a knowing look on his baby face. "Fix" meant twisting the handle bars out of their parallel alignment with the frame and putting the pedals back on, pedals removed for the trip from Virginia to Germany. Piece of cake! And an opportunity to transmit some useful technical information and skills from father to son.

Alas, the lesson deteriorated in the usual manner as my handyman skills emerged for my son to see. Befuddled and flummoxed and bleeding from my knuckles, I did the only reasonable thing. I cursed the Japanese manufacturers, the American packers, and the German un-packers, that entire unholy alliance of cretins whose purpose it was to reveal my incompetence in the presence of my sole heir, serving his apprenticeship as a cycle repairman at my knee.

At this point Michael intervened.

"Uh, Dad. Go get a cup of coffee."

I did my best Colonel Blimp "harrumph" and exited stage left. Upon my return to the terrace, Michael handed me the tools, mounted the perfectly assembled bicycle, and cast a pitying glance upward at the head of the household, saying:

"Dad, you're sad."

He rode off to join the other kids on their bikes.

He liked to watch me dress in my gala uniform, the one that made me look like a doorman at the Paramount Theater. I demonstrated some impatience. Indeed, perhaps the objective observer might have noticed a semblance of apoplexy and some moderate expletives as I wrestled with the

attaché ropes and the metal decorations that gave the jacket an uncorrect-
able port list.

As a ten-year-old he called that get-up "Daddy's cursing uniform."

There comes a time, a first time, when the son passes the father in some
shared activity. For Michael and me it happened on an Austrian ski slope.
As we zipped along, he was faster, smoother, and, at thirteen, threatening
to be taller than his father. I paused on a hill for a breather and to take in
the panoramic view, a reason for skiing that vies with sneaking peeks at the
fannies of young female skiers. In the temporary absence of young female
skiers, I gazed at the skyline in the distance. Mike pulled to a halt beside me,
pausing the way a coiled spring pauses.

I saw a mountain Gasthaus whose chimney emitted a lazy strip of smoke
and realized that my legs were just a bit trembly. I was ready to sit, eat, and
drink a beer.

"Mike, see that hut putting out the smoke," I said, pointing.

"Yep."

"That's where I'm headed right now."

"Oh, Dad, come on! One more run!"

"I'll be the one behind the bowl of goulash and the beer bottle."

"One more run!"

"You make the run. See ya at the Gasthaus."

He did both.

In fact, I rather enjoyed the prospect of the boy emerging from his all-
elbows-and-knees phase to young manhood. That's why just the two of us
shared this ski expedition in Austria, the guys' thing, while Mom remained
on the home front. She approved.

My reasoning was uncomplicated. An intense assistant army attaché in
Bonn at the time of this trip, I took my job very seriously and loved it.
Michael had been moved about like a steamer trunk, often living with Mom
and Grandma, while I got intense about everything I got my mitts on or
thought about. The final tally of kitchens and apartments was twenty-nine
by the time I retired from the Army. When I was in Vietnam the second time,
Michael and I corresponded regularly, probably establishing a closer bond
between father and seven-year-old son than that of stay-at-home dads and
their kids. But I felt guilty about not being attentive enough to my young
family, leaving the burden to my wife as I dove into jobs, schools, and
adventures. Ski trips for the two of us was my way of playing catch-up with
my boy.

"Mike, you ever been in a sauna?"

"No, Dad."

"You know the deal? Real hot. You sweat a lot in the steam. It's good to
relax your muscles after a day on the slopes. Old guys need it more than
young guys, but it's kinda neat."

"I'd like to try it."

"OK. When we come off the hill we'll do it before dinner. Then we'll really sleep well tonight."

In the late afternoon we made our way to the sauna through a well-appointed complex of showers and cold-water baths right out of a James Bond film. Antiseptic stainless steel and handsome tiles abounded deep in the bowels of our hotel. Into the empty sauna we ambled to take seats side by side on one of the facing benches. Within minutes we dripped sweat in comfortable lethargy, eyes heavy with fatigue and from drowsiness-inducing heat.

Shaken from our reverie, my eyes and Mike's popped open as the door moved. We were joined by another pair of people, one of them, we observed from a distance of two feet, missing that anatomical feature down south that distinguishes buoys and gulls, but graced with a pair of full and rounded appendages up north. North and south were—ummmm—uncovered. Mike glanced in my direction, but I avoided his eyes in an attempt to be the cool dad, looking the way I tried to look when I held a full house as another player holding three-of-a-kind "raised" into my trap. The couple parked their variously configured anatomies directly across from father and son. There wasn't much to look at in the confines of the cabin but one another. She had draped a towel on her lap, but her chest was there in all of its rotund magnificence.

After a not-too-comfortable period in which I played blasé sophisticate and m'boy's unspoken curiosity was palpable, I indicated to Mike that it was time for a shower before dinner. We left, nodding to our companions in sweat. Neither one of us alluded to the novel experience as we showered and made our way to our room. Only once we were there did Mike surface what was on our minds.

"Dad, do men and women always share the sauna?"

The man of the world, Cool Pops smiled.

"Mike, that never happened to me before. Usually men's hours and women's hours are posted. Different hours."

He smiled.

"You mean you were as surprised as me?"

"Yep. Maybe more so. I was the one to suggest the sauna."

"When I looked at you and you looked away, I thought you didn't know what to say or do."

"You got that right."

I think we both recognized that Mike knew a couple of new things about his father: Mike was the better skier, and Cool Pops could be embarrassed and at a loss for words. I value the memory.

Michael had gone from climbing cherry trees with little boys to taking steam baths with naked European women, in just one shared overseas tour. Dad looked to the future with fear and trembling.

56

Welcome to Bonn and Sin Loi

While I was in the American Embassy in Bonn from 1973 to 1977, the Federal Republic of Germany accredited diplomats from the Soviet Union and the People's Republic of China, including military attachés, after a long period of nonrecognition; however, the poor bastard from the Republic of Vietnam found himself a man without a country. I recall the Soviets and Chinese with humor and the Vietnamese with sadness.

Anticipating the prospective arrival of the Russians, I had discussed with the right people on the American and German sides some mutual advantages that might accrue to Uncle Sam and Germany. The nominee for the military attaché post in the German Embassy in Moscow, a brigadier general, had done a course at the American school in Garmisch to tune up his Russian language and to get up to date in Russian affairs before he deployed to the Soviet Union. My involvement in these matters put me in touch with an old acquaintance who commanded the U.S. Army Russian Institute. I called him, Roland by name, to tell him that the Russians were coming to Bonn. He asked me to get the Russians to Garmisch. Since Roland and I had often bantered and made silly jokes, I asked if he were serious. Indeed he was. He wanted to expose his student officers to a real live Soviet.

Roland, who had served in the American Embassy in Moscow, wanted a three-dimensional training aid. Moreover, both of us recognized the far-out possibility that if the Soviets accepted our invitation to the American school, we might have an entree to the Soviet Canada-USA Institute as a quid pro quo. Since we had no particular secrets in Garmisch—after all, Russian language and recognition of Soviet military uniforms and equipment were not spy tradecraft—and we were very curious about the Canada-USA Institute in those days, the small investment in effort could produce a larger benefit to Uncle Sam at low risk. Besides, bamboozling the Russian newcomers promised to be good fun.

Life abounds in ironies, particularly if one is attuned to them with the historian's professional burden of asking, is that true? (That absolutely necessary question angers lay people, but let's save that one for another day.) For reasons unknown to me—and not demanded by others—the official reception welcoming the Russian delegation, a very big deal at that time in the Cold War, was held in the stately old Hotel Dresden on the Rhine in Bad Godesberg. That fact was noteworthy to an attaché trained in German history, but of little interest to others. The place was a notorious Nazi hangout in the bad old days of the Third Reich. It was also the site of one of three international meetings (Berchtesgaden, Bad Godesberg, and Munich) that comprised what was later known as the "Munich sell-out" of the Czechs in September 1938. So, I became a player in the 1970s version of the game played in the 1930s. Who-eee! I liked it.

Feeling like a character in a British 1930s black-and-white film, I took up my ambush position awaiting the Russians in the ballroom used for the reception. In due course, God delivered my targets to me: an army general and an air force colonel. The general really did look like the barrel-shaped and beribboned Russian general of the "Grin and Bear It" panel of the Sunday comics of Cold War days. As they came from the reception line, I was the first to greet them with an explosion of bonhomie exceeding anything they might expect, even upon their return to Mother Russia after crushing their Czech or Polish socialist sisters. The general recoiled after my manly handshake, studied my uniform, and read aloud the insignia that soldiers wear like billboards.

"Uu ess?"

"Yes, U.S. I am Henry Gole, the American."

The three-way conversation was in German with two Russians and an American huddling in some privacy for a few minutes before the others descended upon the new boys in accordance with who-knows-what instructions from their masters.

I quickly established that I was indeed an American, that I welcomed my Russian friends, and that I wanted to take them to the American spy school in Garmisch.

I confess. I knocked them over with a feather. Despite all their briefings, they were still new boys without the kind of support afforded the rest of us upon arrival to embassies long established in the Federal Republic of Germany. For them, all of this was a first since The Great Patriotic War. And here was a crazy greeting them like a long-lost brother and inviting them someplace to do something while they were still pissing vodka from home.

They conversed briefly in Russian. Then the air force colonel, who could have been the real boss or KGB, spoke in English, confirming what I had said in German. I told him he had it right. Further, we would drive to the spy school in a big American car at a time of their convenience.

By now others had congregated to welcome the new boys.

I'd like to think that they spent at least part of the night burning the air with a report and a request for instructions from Moscow, but I don't know that happened. I do know that in the following months the Soviet general hid from me at receptions behind fat ladies, food tables, and decorative trees.

Meeting the Chinese diplomat from the People's Republic at an outdoor reception at the residence of the Canadian attaché was quite a different experience. It was the second time I saw him. His first appearance was at a dinner that did not lend itself to moving about the way one does at a cocktail reception. A German friend of mine, his official host, took him around for brief introductions and a handshake. Later the German told me that the Chinese knew every person in the room by name. He was a bright chap who did his homework. I studied his dossier, and I would learn that he studied mine.

I was under a tree in the appropriate attaché posture, glass in hand, when he approached me. This time I had hung back as the others introduced themselves and chatted him up. The Chinese at the time did not use rank. He was Mister Hsiung. He addressed me in German, in the German manner, as Herr Gole. He was Herr Hsiung. Our chat was pure fun. I think we shared a similar sense of whimsy and honest curiosity. It went just about like this.

"Herr Gole, you have been here over three years."

"Yes. You have been in Pankow for six years."

"Yes. You studied German history at Stanford University."

"Yes. You studied German language and literature at Humbolt University."

"Do you like the Germans?"

"Yes. Do you?"

"Yes. What do you think about two Germanies?"

"Better than 300."

"Herr Gole, you were in Korea in the war."

"Yes. Were you?"

"No. I am too young. When will you go home to America?"

"In one month. When will you go home to China."

"Ha. I do not know. It is too early. What will you do in America?"

"I will teach at West Point. Do you know it?"

"Yes. West Point is very famous."

"What will you do when you go home?"

"I do not know. It is too soon."

He let me know that he knew something about me, a mere lieutenant colonel and a new one at that. I did the same. I think he was as amused at the game as I was. We said our polite good nights.

A few months later, his boss arrived. Apparently the clever and acculturated Hsiung had set things up and greased the skids before the old man arrived in Germany. And he was an old man. He had been on the Long March with Mao, commanded a division in Korea, and was attaché in Hungary before arriving in Bonn.

As luck would have it, I was with the Chinese and the other attachés on a visit to a field exercise when Mao died. When our helicopter touched down, a German officer, recognizing me as the American, told me about Mao and asked if the Chinese knew. I said that they couldn't and aimed my informant at Lieutenant Colonel Joachim von Alvensleben, our chief baby-sitter on this trip. Joachim took them aside and performed his unpleasant duty. In the big helicopter I was directly opposite the Chinese as we departed. I had the distinct impression that the old man was crushed. The young man pretended to be.

When North Vietnamese tanks rolled into Saigon, the attaché representing the Republic of Vietnam was quite literally a man without a country. Most of his immediate family was with him in Germany, but he was cut off and almost certainly ignorant of what was happening to his friends, his extended family, and his country. I'm unaware that the American Embassy was officially instructed to assist him and his colleagues. Perhaps the response from Washington was just sluggish, but there was commiseration at the personal level. The French stood up to be counted officially. Whether as one-upmanship vis-à-vis the United States, because the man had family in France, or out of a sense of responsibility for the former Pearl of the Orient, French behavior was responsive and sympathetic. Ours was not. Sin loi. Sorry about that.

Why is it that the compassionate and decent American people are represented by a government with a bureaucratic face so easily caricatured?

57

Mac and Mack

Mac

I t was 1987 or 1988 when one of my favorite cadets from my teaching days at West Point, by then an infantry company commander and captain headed for Special Forces, called from Fort Campbell to the Army War College with a request. Would I talk to his Executive Officer? That young man was also considering a branch transfer to SF. His name was MacNamara, and he planned a visit to Carlisle, where his mother lived. I assented, and in due course the young man showed up at the U.S. Army War College. I took him to the cafeteria. Soldiers talk best during the day over a cup of coffee and far from telephones.

We had discussed several relevant topics, including the cast on his leg from a parachute jump mishap, and were halfway into the first cup when I asked,

"Why do you want to go to Special Forces?"

"My father was in Special Forces . . . ," he began.

Bam! I interrupted immediately as it struck me.

"Was your father Ed MacNamara? Edwin? KIA in Vietnam."

"Yes, sir."

Several thoughts bumped into one another in the next millisecond. Mac! Why hadn't it dawned on me earlier? Why didn't I connect the young man sitting opposite me with Ed? Too many MacNamaras—as a New Yorker and well-traveled soldier, I knew quite a few. Because I hadn't made any more of the young man's visit than the old guy informally telling the young guy about some aspect of the Army, something I had done often enough over the years. Because my friend asked me to talk to his friend and I responded reflexively, without reflection.

Now, looking at the son, memories of the father flooded over me as pictures flitted through my head from twenty-five years earlier, pictures from when father Mac was XO and I was the operations officer of a B team in A Company, 10th Special Forces Group in Bad Toelz in 1964. The familiar faces of the men of A Company were and are fixed in my mental file because a picture of the whole company has hung above my desk for many years.

215

There he is, right next to me. Behind us are Wenzel Hradecky and Roger Seymour, not far from Mike Spiegelmeier and Jim Guest. Mike got three stars and Jim got two. Roger later commanded the 10th Group. Wenzel is a close friend. And there are Jesse Hancock, Bill Roderick, Bill Holt, Brian Loy. Yeah. Mac and I are side by side in the photo. And Roman Rondiak; Ludwig Faistenhammer, our commander. Jesse Hancock and Holt were also KIA later in Vietnam.

I remembered that Ed MacNamara had five little kids. I was looking at one of them, now in his middle twenties.

In 1966 I had seen Ed's name on a list of incoming people to 5th Group, grabbed a jeep, and met him as he got off the bird in Nha Trang. We smiled greetings, shook hands, tossed his gear in the jeep, and I put him in a cot in a hooch in the Group headquarters complex. I found cold beer, we talked, and I suggested that he relax for a couple of hours before chow while I facilitated his processing at the headquarters. We ate together that evening and talked, mostly about where our mutual friends were and how they fared. He took care of his business the next day, got his assignment, and was ready to depart. Back in the jeep to the aircraft, a handshake and a "Good luck!" and Mac was gone—forever, as it turned out.

Going to a job in SOG, he transferred somewhere along the way from the U.S. bird I put him on to a Vietnamese Air Force H-34 helicopter for the final leg to destination. Notorious among Americans for poor maintenance, the VNAF bird lost the tail rotor at altitude. That meant loss of control resulting in wild oscillation. Those not flung out to die in the fall would burn when the chopper crashed in the jungle. I hadn't thought about any of this for a long time.

Back to the cafeteria at the War College in the late 1980s.

"I knew your father in Germany, and I was with him hours before he died. Tell me how you think he died, and I can confirm or correct."

The young man had the outline of the story essentially right. There was no need to go into gruesome detail. I didn't mention that I drafted the KIA letter from the Group Commander to Mrs. MacNamara, his mother; nor did I mention the protracted correspondence, as she had trouble simply letting go. Some well-meaning male kin of World War II vintage had suggested that there might be a mistake. *Y'know how the army always makes mistakes. There was a case of this guy. . . .* But I tried to imagine being the young mother of five rug rats, assimilating the idea that Daddy was simply gone. Gone. Never to return. He was dead before he sent a letter from Vietnam. It must have been hard to digest. He had just climbed on the commercial bird in the States and a few days later the Army says he's dead. How could that be? It must be a mistake.

Young Mac and I reviewed all that. I would have wanted it that way if I were he. As we spoke, I noticed Don Lunday, another SF colonel, passing through the cafeteria. "Don, come over here and meet Ed Mac's son." He did, and we all talked about 10th Group and 5th Group and the good men. John Waghelstein, another SF colonel hove into view, so he joined us. I think it did the lieutenant some good to meet SF guys who knew his father when the father was a captain; it did me a hell of a lot of good. In due course we parted. The patron saint of old soldiers had done himself proud.

As of 2004, young Mac continues to serve in Special Forces. He is currently commander of the Golden Knights, the Army's demonstration parachute team.

Mack

It had been a very pleasant evening in Bonn. Our German hosts, a retired officer and his wife, had conducted a Weinprobe in the best Rheinland tradition and fed us—several foreign attachés and our wives—a fine regional meal. Cognac in hand, the gathering took the form of several small conversation groups scattered around the large room. I sat on a comfortably warm marble slab covering a radiator, forming a bench in a window, and the lady with me was the wife of a German Luftwaffe officer assigned to the Ministry of Defense. She was a teacher with whom I had chatted often on the official cocktail circuit. I had taught in a high school for three years, so we shared pedagogical, political, and military interests. Conversation was easy.

A few minutes before eleven, the unofficial witching hour in Bonn for thank-you, wonderful-time, good-night, the lady glanced at her watch, saying,

"Well, Herr Gole, it seems to be about that time."

"So it is."

"We have to get home to see to our house guest. Two guests actually, a mother and daughter."

Pause. A sudden flash.

"Oh, you would be interested to know about them. The mother is a beautiful woman, my friend from our school days in Munich, and a widow. Her American husband was killed in Vietnam. The ten-year-old daughter never saw her father."

Joe Mack, I thought. Amazing. This could be the opening scene of a novel or play. The profile fit perfectly. Munich. Beautiful widow. The ten-year-old girl who never saw her father. Joe was killed in 1966. This nice German lady is talking about Joe's widow and kid. Here. In Bonn. Ten years later.

"And the father's name is Joe Mack," I said spontaneously, flatly, with certainty.

Stunned, wide-eyed, and suddenly very intense, she fixed those wide eyes on me, asking:

"Wie ist das denn möglich?"

Clearly shocked and—sorry—looking as though she had seen a ghost, she repeated:

"Wie ist das denn möglich? Wie konnten Sie das wissen?"

How is it possible? How is it possible? How could you have known that?

Realizing then that in my surprise I had shocked her by blurting out Joe's name, innocently and thoroughly rattling my partner in Cognac, I apologized for the ambush before explaining.

When Joe married in the spring of 1965, he commanded Operational Detachment A-1 in Germany and I was the operations officer of B-1, the next higher headquarters over Joe's team. Blonde, lanky, laconic, personable, he was a likable man quietly dedicated to Special Forces. His XO was Roman Rondiak, a friend of mine from infantry days in Bamberg. His Team Sergeant was Snuffy Conroy, a rock-solid combat vet of both the 101st Airborne in World War II and the 187th Regimental Combat Team in Korea. (Snuffy had been tight with then-General Westmoreland from their time together in the one-eight-seven.) These bits and pieces, Joe's bachelor party and wedding, my son's health, and some later events in Vietnam answered the lady's questions, making the story both memorable and improbable.

The bachelor party was in the Ruh' am Bach, a rural Gasthaus on the edge of Bad Toelz and, as its name suggests, an idyllic spot on a stream. Roman was there, as were Jim Fenlon, Ludwig Faistenhammer, and, I think, Clyde Sincere, Michael Spiegelmeier, Jim Guest, Giles Thomas, Joe Vara, and others from A Company. Joe Mack lent himself to the boys'-night-out foolishness by dutifully drinking all drinks proffered and promptly vomiting outside. He returned somewhat sobered and, after splashing some water on his face, asked, "OK. Now can I just enjoy this party?"

That performance suggests the essence of the man. He went along with the ritual you'll-be-sorry bonhomie of his last hours as an unmarried man, and then he did a very good imitation of a reasonable human being.

On the day of Joe's wedding, my son Michael was quite ill. As a matter of fact, the attending doctor was so concerned with my son's sustained high fever that he literally put my boy on ice. We realized that he was close to death. So we didn't attend the big wedding—the bride's father had distinguished himself in politics or by being very rich, I don't recall the reason or details—but I certainly remember the day of the wedding, a big day in Bad Toelz and Flint Kaserne. We were all happy for Joe and his lovely lady.

Joe was a rifle company commander in the 101st when he was killed in Vietnam a year later. The captain sent to assume command of Joe's company was Roman Rondiak, his XO from A-1, that team in Germany. What are the odds?

Snuffy Conroy, the Team Sergeant with Joe and Roman in the 10th in 1964, was running recon with SOG in 1966, in the DMZ and Laos. He had brushed aside my suggestion that recon was young stud's work, saying that the old machine still had a few miles on it. He was killed within a few weeks.

Since the fun and games in the 10th and 5th Special Forces Groups, I've run into Fenlon, Guest, Spiegelmeier, Faistenhammer, and Sincere in Vietnam, Germany, Fort Bragg, Fort Leavenworth, and Las Vegas, and I see Hradecky regularly in New Hampshire. This recital, stream of consciousness, or something like it, was my way of telling the sweet wide-eyed lady in Bonn in 1976 why I remembered Joe, his widow, and his fatherless little girl immediately. They are part of a permanent tangle of bittersweet memories.

Sunflowers

By 1975 I had known the Bundeswehr officer, a brigadier general, for over a year. He was a friend of my boss, the Defense Attaché, and a decorated veteran of combat on the Russian front in World War II. Over drinks I opined that the fighting between Germans and Russians from 1941 to 1945 was the toughest sustained combat in centuries. What had it been like to him as a young infantry officer? He smiled, saying: "Herr Gole, I walked east for two years. Then I walked west for two years."

Right, I thought. The German attacked east from 1941 to 1943. Stalingrad was the high-water mark for the Germans and the turning point of the campaign. Much vicious fighting remained, but from the beginning of 1943 until the end, it was all downhill for the Germans, as they wore down and the Russians got better at the business of war. He said it without bitterness, so I pressed on. "When did you know the war was lost?"

"Hah! Good question. I remember the moment."

He described daily advances of motorized and mechanized forces as Germans bagged prisoners by the tens of thousands and broke Russian resistance again and again, while the main German body followed on foot with horse-drawn wagons. At the end of a long march one day in the summer of 1941, his column circled to form all-around security during hours of darkness before resuming the advance in the morning.

He awoke at first light and climbed a gentle rise alone to get a look about the countryside. The sight convinced him that Germany would lose the war. That got my attention. I asked what he saw. He said that he had seen sunflowers in all directions, *bis zur Ewigkeit*, to eternity. He realized at that moment that there was no way Germany could swallow the vastness of Russia. Despite unrelenting advances and uninterrupted tactical successes, a sophisticated German, accustomed to seeing several villages and a varied landscape from a similar vantage point at home, was simply overwhelmed by the sheer size of the enemy's homeland. Over three years of intense fighting remained, but he knew the task was impossible. The sunflowers told him.

I Have German Friends

nother attaché took a seat next to me in the Luftwaffe aircraft
before we took off, saying in German, "I heard you speak German."
Before responding in that language, confirming he had heard right,
I studied his uniform and noted that he was a lieutenant colonel assigned to
the Netherlands Embassy. He smiled and asked what I thought of the Germans. I said I rather liked them. He said, "Yes, but sooner or later they'll
fall out with weapons prepared to fight another war." We chatted about
Germans as we flew from Bonn/Cologne to north Germany for a demonstration of the Gepard, an antiaircraft weapons system being fielded by our
hosts in 1973. I was the new boy on my first *Attaché Reise* (attaché trip)
with the accredited foreign military attachés. The Dutchman, Kaes, didn't
care for Germans.

Over the following three years we were often together for professional
and social reasons, and we became friends. He was an excellent companion
of sophisticated wit, with a wife as bright and as charming as he. Both were
linguists. He was a gifted engineer. In the course of time he told me what it
was like for him as a boy in a German-occupied country. We were the same
age, so I mentally transported myself to the Netherlands from 1940 to 1945
as an almost eight- to an almost thirteen-year-old. Some of his relatives died
in the war, he actually played a role in servicing the rat line that got downed
American and British aviators to safety, and he never forgave the Germans.

Shortly before Kaes returned home at the end of his tour in Bonn, we
were together at a reception that was a short walking distance from my
apartment. As I walked home after the reception, he slowed his car to offer
me a lift. He knew where I lived, and I said jokingly,

"I think I can make it."

"Yes, I think you can, but I want to talk to you."

"OK, but I drive a hard bargain. You'll have to join me for a Cognac."

We settled into comfortable chairs with our drinks, just the two of us,
and I sensed his need to tell me something that was very important to him.

"You know I'm going home next month."

Since I had already affirmatively responded to the invitation to his "turn-over" reception, I said I knew.

"Do you remember what I told you when we first met on that plane three years ago?"

"I do. You told the new boy, the naïve American, that Germans are incurable warmongers, waiting to fall out with shotguns and hunting rifles so that they could once again dominate old Europe."

He paused before reviewing some ugly wartime experiences. Then he asked me how well I knew a certain German couple. I knew them casually, and they seemed the right sort. Then he leaned forward and said very earnestly:

"Die sind meine Freunden. Nicht bekanten sondern Freunden."

He said it in German, though we had been speaking English. The distinction in German is as important as it is clear: "They are friends. Not acquaintances but friends!"

At this point, he had tears in his eyes as he explained that some of his friends and relatives in the Netherlands would never understand or accept that he could have German friends. He went on to surmise that he would lose some Dutch friends who could never forgive or forget German behavior during the occupation. He wanted me to know. As he departed he said, "Ich habe Deutsche Freunden."

60

Mary Asked

t was Academic Year 1977–1978. She was in the Class of 1980, the first class in the history of the United States Military Academy at West Point to include women. So it was in her second year as a cadet and my first as a teacher in the Department of History when she posed the question in the minutes before formal instruction began.

"Sir, what do you think of women at West Point?"

Ambushed!

Caught in the headlights!

Department of the Army and the Academy were unequivocally clear on the subject. The debate was over. Women were at West Point. They *would* succeed. Officers *would not* make public statements to the contrary.

I had no personal problem with women students. Unlike the graduates of the place, I had done undergraduate and graduate work at coed institutions without thinking about women, except to admire them. But I did have personal reservations about women at West Point—no doubt a product of the bias of an American male born in 1933 with combat tours in two wars behind him. It was my view that the Military Academy existed to produce warriors, and women were barred from, for example, the infantry. A two-tier system seemed to give places to women that might have gone to the men who do the heavy lifting in war.

But it was a done deal. In the best military tradition, there is time for discussion, but once the boss decides, soldiers salute and execute the decision. So, attempting to be loyal to the system I served and honest in my response to a student's question, my response was a limp-wristed:

"Well, Mary, they certainly brighten the gray on gray of this place."

Thank God the PC police didn't hear me stalling with the meaningless drivel of one simply not "with it." I was Colonel Blimp and didn't like it. My comment smacked of the very sexist condescension women were fighting. I could have done better.

Despite institutional protestations to the contrary, like the ripples caused by tossing the pebble in the pond, one couldn't be quite sure for how long and how far the ripple affected the rest of the pond or, in this case, the rest of the soldier's trade. The implications of physical differences had been discussed endlessly, but there were less visible and unpublicized implications. Military jargon two decades later would call this phenomenon "the law of unintended consequences."

Before women had been admitted to the locker room, newly commissioned West Point lieutenants marched off to the Infantry, Artillery, Armor, Engineers, and the Signal Corps. They might, after their apprenticeship, go to the technical branches, but the system assured that initially they would get mud on their boots as they learned the nitty-gritty of soldiering. But, alas, ladies were not permitted to join the Infantry, Armor, or Field Artillery. They would opt for other branches. It was decided—presumably after much pulling of beards and searching of souls—that men would likewise be permitted to opt for duties other than "combat arms." Call the damned ripples equity: after two hundred years of marching the long gray line into harm's way, the fit young men of 1980 could choose to care for the gear in the rear with their lady classmates.

These were some of the sugar plums dancing in my head in the millisecond after I feebly ducked my star student's question.

She was bright, confident, and inquisitive. I still don't know whether she pressed the issue out of curiosity or out of amusement at putting one of her tormentors on the defensive. Marx would advise that she had history on her side. It didn't please me to know that rednecks, Cro-Magnon men, and the old and obtuse were my allies. And she was certainly more intimately absorbed in the issue, better armed and informed than I was. She would not permit me to fob off her question.

"C'mon, sir! What do you think of women at West Point?"

No ducking.

What the hell does a professor do if he doesn't profess? In a classroom, no less!

"You won't like it, Mary. Sooner or later women simply being at West Point will put women in harm's way, in the name of equity. I didn't like stuffing nineteen-year-old boys in body bags. I don't know how I'd react to stuffing a nineteen-year-old girl in a body bag."

The business at hand, learning about the good old days when white men were in charge, intervened, ending the student-professor exchange that made teaching at West Point so special to kids and old war horses, even dull old war horses.

I had the impression that I saw less of Mary in the weeks that followed and assumed that my response to her question had offended her. She was probably avoiding me.

Five or six years later in an officers' club in Kaiserslautern, Germany, on a Friday afternoon, there was Mary, now a Captain about to take command of a company. I'm pleased to report that she saw me, gave me a hug in greeting, smiling in a friendly way that was natural, and we sat down to sip beer as we chatted, catching up on her classmates and the faculty from our shared West Point years.

At some point I told her that I had expected a chilly greeting. My recollection was that she had rather boycotted me in her last years at school, a reaction, I thought to my response to a question she once asked. Mary looked at me in an open and honest way as she assured me that she never bore me animosity.

"Do you remember the incident, the question you asked?"

She repeated verbatim what I had said at that time:

" 'I don't know how I would respond to stuffing a nineteen-year-old girl in a body bag,' " adding, "neither do I. I hope I never find out how it is to do that, regardless of gender."

"Amen."

That behind us, we continued our amicable stroll down memory lane. The young lady probably enjoyed the moment. The old soldier certainly did. He felt as though he had been given absolution.

Almost twenty years after that happy meeting in Germany, in another academic setting, a male Army colonel student of mine married to a lady colonel, both graduates of West Point, asked for my views on gender issues. I told my story about Mary. Then I added honest commentary I know to be politically incorrect in the twenty-first century. Born in 1933, socialized by the standards of the time, I open doors for women, surrender my seat to women standing in public transportation, and have a personal problem with putting women in harm's way. Realizing that I had relegated myself to the dustbin of history, I offered my personal solution to how I intend to reconcile my personal view with the official position: I intend to die.

Don't You Speak English?

etween 30 June 1950 and 30 June 1953, the Lodge Act (PL 597, 30 June 1950) provided qualified unmarried male aliens from 18 to 35 years of age with the opportunity to enlist in the Regular Army of the United States for a period of five years. Honorable service would earn American citizenship. This was a good deal for those qualified. It became a very good deal for the United States.

Among the large numbers of "Displaced Persons" in Europe after World War II were Nazi slave laborers, released and escaped prisoners of war, refugees who had fled battlefields, former soldiers, those fleeing Communist regimes in eastern Europe, and only God knows what others washed up on the shore of some place not home. Among the cold, hungry, lonely, and rootless young men totally without prospects in a world turned upside-down, "three hots and a cot" in a warm barracks in a clean uniform satisfied basic short-term needs. Purposeful employment provided dignity. Becoming a citizen of the greatest nation on earth was to many a dream come true.

Over the years Uncle Sam has nurtured two core impulses (and this is not the place to apportion them). One is idealism, altruism, concern for the world's "huddled masses," or more specific concern for Uncle Willi in the old country—call it what one will. It was certainly an ingredient in the CARE packages, Berlin Airlift, and Marshall Plan. The other impulse is Realpolitik: concern that the Red Army, to paraphrase Winston Churchill, was the most potent force between the white cliffs of Dover and the white snows of the Urals. In any event, after getting "our boys" back home from Europe as soon as possible after World War II, and turning to passionate consumerism after fifteen years of denial caused by depression and war, the ugly realities of the Cold War crashed the party. Uncle Sam needed soldiers; Americans chose consumerism over service. Displaced Persons represented an available manpower pool.

Enter Wenzel. His German name. He might be embarrassed if I used his full Czech name.

Lack of enthusiasm for Communism and complicity in assisting people to escape from Czechoslovakia to Germany resulted in a whispered warning, suggesting that it was time for him to get out. He made it through a wooded and swampy chunk of real estate, crossing into Bavaria with two other men, one of whom was shot in the process. This began a period of wandering penniless with little more than the clothes on his back in a strange place at the age of eighteen. There is more than one way to get a liberal arts education, most of them better than being young, hungry, and alone. He wound up in a DP (Displaced Persons) camp near Nuremberg that served as his base camp as he followed hope rumors, attempting to get to America, Canada, or Australia. Thousands sought those solutions to statelessness. Competition was keen, and the best and worst qualities of the species emerged as generosity and baseness competed, testing the veneer of civilization. Rumors of interviews at distant places meant preparation: fresh newspapers in shoes long worn out and hitch-hiking to places to learn that the quota had been filled or that he was too scrawny for the Canadian Army. Every day was a struggle for survival. Then he got lucky.

The undermanned U.S. Army in Europe established so-called Labor Service units whose chief function was to guard installations and U.S. Government properties. The units were organized along national lines, and Wenzel found himself, after rudimentary military training in the Czech Labor Service, armed with a rifle or carbine, pulling guard duty. He did not know then that he had taken the first step leading to a military career as an officer who would serve in war and peace in a variety of assignments in Europe, Asia, North America, and the Middle East.

He was one of the first Lodge Act recruits. The first hurdle to be overcome was a written test given in English, French, German, and Russian. Since he had almost no French or English, survival German, and some schoolboy Russian, to the best of his recollection he took the test in Russian. Fifty years after the event, he doesn't remember which of the languages he didn't know took him to fame and fortune, but it was the one he didn't know least. Taking a test in Russian to serve in the U.S. Army in the Cold War just has to tickle the funny bone.

Success put him on a boat out of Bremerhaven. A short course at Fort Devens, Massachusetts, taught him to say spoon, fork, and knife, skills acquired as one in a mob of multinational babble repeating or mispronouncing the words said by someone in front of the class who waved said objects in the air. That prepared Wenzel for basic training and life in America. The brief stay in New England was followed by training in the American south. One of his lasting memories is of the kindness shown to him by the simple Americans he met casually on the streets of Ayer, Massachusetts, as he tried to understand the language and ways of strangers. He is particularly fond of one of his yarns concerning the locals in a bar who refused to allow the funny-talking strangers in American uniforms to buy a drink and then delivered the tipsy soldiers back to the Army post.

Upon first entering the barracks that would be home for the duration of basic training in North Carolina, the four Czech Lodge Act soldiers clung together in their new universe, taking the first two bunks left and right of the entrance. Among them they might be able to decipher the instructions and orders bellowed in language best described as a kind of English. Their experience in the Labor Service told them to empty their duffel bags, display field gear on the shelf over the bed, hang clothing in a military manner, store underwear and socks in their foot lockers, make the beds tight and ready for inspection, and stand by. European conformity coincided with military good order and discipline, proving once again that the road to hell is paved with good intentions.

In due course their platoon sergeant entered the barracks, took in all at a glance, noting an island of order in the chaos of confused and frightened recruits. He strode into the center aisle of the barracks between the beds, pointed to the four neat bunks framed by the displayed personal items, and roared, "First squad leader, second squad leader, third squad leader, fourth squad leader!" Alas, the uncomprehending quartet had been ordained leaders of men, men whose language, except for important nouns like "spoon," remained a mystery to the newly ordained squad leaders.

Surviving basic training, Wenzel watched his mates vanish to the four winds to their first assignments as soldiers. Puzzled to be separated from the others, he waited. Then he was transported to an airplane. After not very long, as the aircraft prepared to land he recognized the 250-foot towers used to train paratroopers and terror struck! One of his enthusiastic "Yes, sergeant!" responses to a query had volunteered him for jump school.

In basic training he had broken the code to survival in the Army. He responded, "Yes, sergeant" to NCOs, "Yes, sir" to officers, whom he also saluted. When anyone in authority singled him out for personal attention, he promptly dove to the front-leaning-rest position and pumped out 20 push-ups, assuming that he had somehow violated good order and discipline. These skills, combined with taking his cue from what the others did, had worked thus far. Then came 34-foot tower week, a means of practicing actions to be taken in the aircraft, while exiting in fright and during initial descent in a parachute. An important aspect of the drills was to avoid fouling the suspension line connecting the parachute to the aircraft. Best that jumpers not hang themselves.

The trainees wore simulated main parachutes on their backs and reserve parachutes on their stomachs. They climbed stairs to the inside of a make-believe aircraft to the door at the 34-foot point. There they were met by a sergeant who asked, "Which door?" The trainee responded, placing the suspension line on the correct shoulder. The sergeant then slapped the jumper on his behind, shouting, "Go!"

The jumper fell toward Mother Earth until the suspension line was arrested by a cable, simulating the opening shock of the parachute on the jumper. Instructions were shouted from the ground, requiring the jumper to react to said instructions.

Wenzel's mastery of English words like "fork" and "spoon" was very useful in the mess hall. But the instructors' shouts in a southern drawl alleged to be English, as the Czech who had "volunteered" for Jump School found himself in life-threatening circumstances, were, alas, incomprehensible. Moreover, in his previous military training he had learned to carefully observe and scrupulously imitate the actions of other trainees. That had gotten him through basic training. On this day, that was precisely the wrong thing to do, since jumpers were alternating exits from the left and right doors of the make-believe airplane that was really a wooden tower. By imitating the man in front of him he succeeded in being wrong every time. Because push-ups could not be done while in the parachutes, his punishment required him to do squat-jumpers again and again. The training cadre was very attentive to the stupid trainee who was finally permitted to exit the aircraft.

Wenzel heard some reference to the number on his helmet as he fell from the 250-foot tower, but that was the last thing he registered clearly. The instructions were lost in the rush of shouts, falling, opening shock, and the realization that the earth was nearing at an alarming rate of speed. He did not follow instructions, he crashed in a heap of arms and legs, helmet askew, breathing hard from fright and grateful that he was still alive.

A sergeant purple of complexion pounced on him, exploding much verbal abuse and a little spittle. Wenzel executed Plan A, his only plan. He said "Yes, sergeant" and pumped out 40 squat-jumpers. Astounded, the sergeant screamed, "Goddamit, don't you understand English?"

Wenzel, perhaps for the first time in his short military career, understood every word and responded with a combination of relief and frustration, "No, sergeant! I dunt spik English! No! No English!"

Thank heaven, boys and girls, for the American melting pot. The sergeant, noting the trainee's nametag, tried his Polish on the sorry lump of humanity in front of him. For the first time in his dealing with officialdom, Wenzel communicated with it in languages he knew, Polish and Czech. He survived the sergeant's wrath and amusement. He also survived jump school.

In due course he also survived leadership school, OCS, the Infantry Career Course, Command and General Staff College, two combat tours in Vietnam, command of several Special Forces units, service as a division G-2, staff duty at an Army Headquarters, advising the Iranian Gendarmerie, and being the senior adviser with Pennsylvania's 28th Division before retiring as an infantry lieutenant colonel. He then earned bachelor's and master's degrees and taught as a civilian. Two of his four children served as officers in the U.S. Army, one a graduate of the United States Military Academy and an artillery officer, the other as a nurse captain. Another is a Ph.D. scientist, and another is a social worker.

Seems we got our money's worth from that Lodge Act American.

62

How To Be a Lieutenant General

To the old sweat and hopeless romantic, the pay-off of military service is not the King's shilling. It is trust and confidence, up and down. It has other names: loyalty, mateship, bonding, camaraderie, brotherhood. In good outfits, those in which men willingly die for one another, it exists up-and-down and laterally. In outfits that have not come together, it is and remains a foreign concept, a poetic conceit, a fiction, a lie to be mentioned in pep talks. Perhaps trust and confidence, like morale, exist where unmentioned and do not exist where talked about. These are "doing" things, not the subject of motivation talks recognized by even the dullest soldiers as wishes of commanders rather than something in evidence.

Outside of elite outfits, the up-and-down kind has gone the way of the carrier pigeon and the concept of shame, even in the crunch of pressure and high risk, where they count most. Lateral fellow-feeling, by whatever name, seems to persist at the squad, team, and crew level, defying the tendency in the chain of command to see loyalty as a one-way street. At its best, trust and confidence can be projected even in a paper-shuffling operation. It looks like this Lieutenant General.

Diane, a major who served as Lieutenant General George Forsythe's executive officer in 1971, gave the first clue to the kind of man our boss was. Most generals in the top jobs in the Pentagon designated their biggest, ugliest, and dumbest colonels as XOs, keepers of the gate. Or they went to the local zoo to find fearsome creatures whose mere presence said, "Do not enter; do not disturb His Eminence." The presence of the pleasant lady major signaled, "Welcome. Nothing in this world would please the general more than seeing you." The general did the rest.

She called me, another major, on the phone one morning in 1971 or 1972.

"Henry, the boss would like to see you at your convenience."

"Right." Pause. "When is it convenient for me?"

"Well, nobody's in with him now."

"Rog. On the way."

Diane showed me to his door, and the general rose from behind his air-craft-carrier-sized desk, beaming a welcome and inviting me to join him on the government-issue leather couch that was new in 1943.

General Forsythe had been brought to the Pentagon by Army Chief of Staff General William Westmoreland to plan and implement the transition from conscript to all-volunteer Army, as directed by President Richard M. Nixon. His title in the ad hoc position was Special Assistant for the Modern Volunteer Army, SAMVA in Pentagonese. He selected a small cell of talented people to help him in uncharted waters. Then turned them loose. I was a new guy who sneaked in the back door when no one was looking.

"Henry, I'm about to have a cup of coffee. Will you join me?"

He then spun a yarn whose purpose was to relax me with small talk as we sipped, before he got to the business for which I had been summoned. That was his style, and it was a marvelous means of establishing a "just us guys shooting the breeze" atmosphere of casual openness. We were smart enough to remember who was the general and who was not, who had the monkey on his back and who was daddy's little helper, but he had a knack for winning the loyalty and affection of his guys and gals.

He then asked, in a tone suggesting the reason I had been summoned to The Presence, "If I told you such-and-such, what is your gut reaction?" I forget the pressing issue of thirty years ago, but I gave him my views in three or four crisp points in the staff officer manner: be right, be brief, be gone. "Good, good," he said. "Could you write that up?"

I could and did. I asked my office mate to give it a sanity check for substance. Then I edited, rewrote and re-read with pride. That would do it. I called Diane and found myself at the general's door again. Same routine: to the couch, a cup of coffee (*that* Army ran on coffee during the week and happy hour on Friday after work), small talk, and finally, "Oh, Henry, did you write up those points you made this morning?" "Yessir. They are on the corner of your desk." Without interrupting the tale he was spinning, he signed the papers without reading them and called the sergeant from the outer office, saying, "Please take this to General Westmoreland." Off went the sergeant.

That impressed me mightily. Most of the little old ladies posing as senior officers and running the Army would have played copyeditor and school-marm. George Forsythe did not speak of trust and confidence. He gave it, and he got it. He treated subordinates with respect, as junior colleagues seeking the same excellence he pursued. We responded with our best efforts for a man who gave and deserved loyalty. The papers I wrote would go out as I wrote them. That told me to do it right. I experienced some fine leaders over the years, but he was the best of the senior leaders, an exemplar, the helpful uncle to the willing younger colleague. But, alas, he was an exception. Many regarded by the system as leaders were, in fact, journeymen shouters who endorsed the "when in doubt, yell and shout" principle.

63

How Not To Be a Lieutenant General

My penultimate assignment, as a Colonel in the mid-1980s, was made miserable by a martinet lieutenant general who revived all of the bad lessons of leadership experienced in my career. His interminable staff meetings and apoplectic behavior took their cues from Hitler's regaling of his staff and dinner companions. It was painful to decent people. The Cretins imitated the boss.

The general prided himself in being "a details man," and ruled by fear. As a consequence, there was an inclination by subordinates to conceal problems and avoid giving bad news. For example, a sergeant in a warehouse somewhere in the command designed a clever, practical, and inexpensive means of addressing a repetitive function with a contraption of his design. The general saw it and never tired of telling the world about the great innovation by a junior guy, even long after the practice had been discontinued due to some bad unintended consequence. One suspects that the general will go to his grave in a state of euphoria, blissfully unaware that the neat idea simply went away. Trust and confidence were to him, just words. He didn't give them. He didn't get them.

The general boasted of his triumphs, most of which had a down side that simply eluded him. Among his favorites: He fixed a problem in the Pentagon by removing the upper portion of solid walls and putting in glass, thereby creating a large bay area so that he could watch his minions, mostly lieutenant colonel action officers. Issued oars, they might have propelled the Pentagon on the Potomac River. One wonders how the handpicked officers making Army policy enjoyed playing scribes at writing tables in their reenactment of *A Christmas Carol*. He didn't say if he allowed them to go home for a Christmas goose.

As a two-star general he ran a complex worldwide shipping operation from a perch on the New Jersey side of the Hudson River. Of the many logistics or leadership lessons he might have passed on to his staff from his long experience and great responsibility, he particularly relished his recounting of the case of the fired coffee shop female employee. Since I heard it several times, he must have liked the story a lot. Her sin, as I recall the yarn, was that she was not properly deferential in responding to the general's complaint about service, elevating it from venial to mortal sin by indicating how difficult it would for her to be fired. Poor thing! She knew not the meaning of petty. That he would win in going *mano a mano* with a little old lady from Joisey was not surprising. That he was right to can a surly and defiant employee is not at issue. That he told the story to his captive audience as a morality tale, or as a victory in the coliseum, strikes me as being odd.

Another favorite heard more than once at marathon staff calls that lasted hours was The Briefing Story. He was in Thailand. A lieutenant colonel someplace up-country needed help with a briefing. Our hero, then a major, was dispatched to help the half-colonel. The punch line was that the responsible person finally asked the general, then a major, to brief. Without a roll of drums or the clash of symbols, the point was made. I think. Our general was not only one helluva guy now. He was one helluva guy when he was a major.

I worked for this petty man and hated it. The irony is that Army truism of long standing: pay-off for the service and the officer is serving as a colonel. Experience and challenge result in good things for the United States and a sense of a job well done in the old warhorse's heart before he heads to pasture. That's the way it was supposed to be. Alas, 'twas not to be.

There were ironies, as usual. The work was inherently interesting. It was to get maximum support of the U.S. Army from our Continental allies. The locale was Germany, a second home to me. My people were very good. The only problem was that the general and I were oil and water. I wanted latitude. He wanted the kind of control I hadn't experienced since I was a private, maybe since dog training courses. After a few weeks in his command, I found him alone on a Saturday morning and told him I didn't think it would work. He took it surprisingly well. I expected the usual apoplexy, but he assured me I was just what he wanted. At that point a professional soldier salutes and gets in the last words: "Yes, sir."

An ugly incident was prevented much later by an excellent chief of staff, who was sensitive and bright, even wise. I was seething with anger and insisted upon seeing the boss who had just behaved arbitrarily in his patented petty and mean-spirited style. The chief of staff was the only one in the headquarters other than I with all the facts of the situation. As a matter of fact, he had been informed of and approved what had become the issue at hand. To his great credit, he behaved like Solomon. I think he clearly saw that the general was wrong and I was right, angry, and about to use some very intemperate words. A long-simmering pot was about to boil over.

The chief of staff determined the need to prevent a face-to-face confrontation between his boss and an enraged colonel, a meeting almost certain to have serious consequences, mostly for me. Because I trusted and respected the chief, and because he assured me that he would produce an outcome satisfactory to me, I allowed him to take the matter into his own hands, one of my better decisions. Association with that general remains the nadir of my long if not distinguished military career, but at least I didn't end it with a court-martial for reverting to a solution from my blue-collar roots.

64

Many Armies

The difference between my two lieutenant generals triggered a reflection on the possibly unique perspective I brought to the Army after being away from it between 1954 and 1961. I determined that there are several U.S. Armies. Among them are the muddy Fighting Army; the spit and polish Show Army; the Businessman's Army, Inc., that manages wholesale and retail assets other than collateral damage (that belongs to the Fighting Army until it is passed to the Image & Slogan Army); the Thinkers' Army; the Pentagon Army (not necessarily the same as the Thinkers' Army—in fact, they may be mutually exclusive); and the Image & Slogan Army that talks to journalists, the U.S. Congress, advertising agencies, and other members of the Image & Slogan Army. There may be others. Since I retired in 1988 we discovered information warfare; there may be a Bullshit Army lurking in the basement of the Pentagon, where steam pipes and study groups co-exist and heat The Building.

After adventures in Korea I resumed my studies from 1954 to 1958 before teaching in Baldwin Senior High School, out on Long Island some twenty-five miles from midtown Manhattan. In 1961 President Kennedy asked me to do something for my country.

The Army had changed. I had more latitude as a leader when I was a sergeant in 1954 than a lieutenant in 1961. I'm not certain, but I think the reduction in forces—RIF in Army jargon—after the Korean War is the probable cause. The survivors learned from the turtle to be very cautious about sticking out their neck. It seemed to me at the time that to be a major, one needed to be fat and stupid. Of course, I was wrong. It was enough to be stupid. And many of the super-careful types didn't remain majors forever. The tendency to centralize all decisions continues to rob junior and middle-grade leaders of initiative and creativity at the beginning of the 21st century. In 1961 the most evident change was that officers did what soldiers used to do, such as supervising the maintenance of vehicles and giving bayonet training. Taking authority from sergeants and inordinately emphasizing appearance struck me as very bad ideas with serious consequences for the spirit of my Army.

Between the wars in Korea and Vietnam, my Army became a hyper-conservative organization attempting to regulate all activities by checklists imposed from on high. Fear of failure, even in training, caused a zero-defects ethos to pervade the system. Individual initiative at the lower end of the chain of command and risk taking by sergeants and company grade officers surrendered to appearance, resulting in white rocks in peace and body count in war. Leaders lied about readiness and deaths. One sees the hand of Robert S. MacNamara in the systems approach and quantification that sucked the heart and soul out of the Army. Perfect realization of MacNamara's intended outcome would have made puppets of soldiers whose controlling strings were in the hands of the SECDEF. That end was almost achieved as romantics nurtured by legends of courage and sacrifice were replaced by accountants, whose God was cost-effectiveness. The Army no longer closed with and destroyed the enemy. We serviced targets. We lacked the complex and beautiful ships and impressive aircraft of the other services, and we made do with mostly conscripts, but that didn't prevent that Army from using business models stressing nonhuman (if not inhuman) efficiencies and cost-effectiveness. Cheap labor from conscription combined with an engineering approach—another step toward the industrialization of war that deemphasizes the human dimension of soldiering.

As I entered the barracks of the rifle company to which I had been assigned in 1961 in Bamberg, Germany, after that seven-year break in service, the halls glistened, symbolic of the overwhelming emphasis on appearance that dominated the pre-Vietnam Army. I passed a soldier, a member of my new company, on my way to the orderly room to report in. He slapped himself, back to the wall, with a brisk, "Good morning, sir." That's what prisoners do in military jails! My reaction was basic. Oh shit! What's going on? I found out.

I reported to my company commander in the prescribed military manner, saluting smartly, orders in left hand. My already bad impression was reinforced as the captain made a feeble effort at wit: "Three things I can't stand, lieutenant: cold coffee, wet toilet paper, and second lieutenants." No good morning, no welcome, and clearly no wit. It was downhill from there as leaders lived in accordance with a senior general's mantra that said, "Troops only do what the boss checks." This message was somehow garbled so that troops were oversupervised and undertrained. Subordinates were not to be trusted. Officers saw everything. NCOs were brushed aside. Appearances and clichés were substituted for substance and brains. I had serious doubts about my response to President Kennedy's call to service. Jerks and cretins were in charge of the mainstream Army.

But God was on my side. I escaped to happy Special Forces tours in Germany and Vietnam, satisfaction and excitement in war, fascinating and constructive work with good people in Washington, challenging and gratifying duty in Bonn, and a chance to jump into teaching, thinking, and writing at West Point and the Army War College. Except for my first assignment in Bamberg and the one with the martinet, my career was gratifying. The suspicion difficult to prove is that what I missed, the years from 1954 to 1961, saw fundamental changes affecting the very ethos of military service. My opinion is that MacNamara's band destroyed the band of brothers. My two generals personify the extremes of the romantic, charismatic, beloved uncle and the bloodless manager of systems. My preferences are evident.

65

Contemplating Retirement

I n 1979 I was eligible to retire as a lieutenant colonel. I thought about retiring in 1980, upon completion of my tour teaching history at West Point.

Fourteen years overseas; three years in two wars; separations in peacetime due to field exercises, command post exercises, guard duty, "courtesy patrols" (a euphemism for keeping troops from the clutches of the military police), and temporary duty absences too numerous to count. A reminder from the bride that she had twenty-five kitchens in our years of connubial bliss; realization that my boy had experienced nine schools before arriving at the high school from which he would graduate; and a mirror telling me that I had literally grown gray in Service. The time had come to consider retirement from the Army.

William Shakespeare begins one of his sonnets with the lines:

> When forty winters shall besiege thy brow,
> And dig deep trenches in thy beauty's field . . .

Hell, I was well past that without having heard any reference to how time affected my beauty. It was thirty-six winters from basic training to when I did my swan song in 1988. The sonnet is about the little girls of my youth who had become wrinkled, not about me. But:

> Devouring Time, blunt thou the lion's paws . . .

That's more like it! Let the young guys show sharp paws. Soldiering is a young man's game. Other armies use the experience of graybeards into their 60s, but a youth cult drives the American system, chasing all but a few of us away early in our 40s or 50s. Then Alexander Pope spoke to me, not for the first time:

> Behold the child, by Nature's kindly law,
> Pleased with a rattle, tickled with a straw:

Some livelier plaything gives his youth delight,
A little louder, but as empty quite:
Scarfs, garters, gold amuse his riper stage;
And beads and pray'r-books are the toys of age:
Pleased with this bauble still, as that before;
Till tired he sleeps, and life's poor play is o'er!

Yes, there I am! Right between garters and beads. Youth is gone, but life's poor play is not o'er. Not yet.

There are practical considerations as one considers hanging up the uniform for the last time, but the wolf is not at my door. An empty nest, an almost-paid-off mortgage, and a working wife means that I can do what I want to do. And what, pray tell, is that? I'll finish my doctorate, write, and perhaps teach. The practical aspect of retirement is not an issue. What happens in my guts as I reflect on an end to soldiering is far more powerful. Positive images and feelings emerge unsolicited. And some angry thoughts.

Good vibes echo foreign sounds and smells; fear; a sense of purpose; loneliness; pompous asses; the company of strangers; a familiar face in the new assignment; skiing in Austria; relief felt upon return to a safe place; dead friends; red ants; pull-push-tap-aim-fire; my name on a promotion list; sore hips rubbed by the belt carrying ammo, grenades, flares, water, the kitchen sink; Bahnhof bustle; coffee in the mess hall; a son who has grown while I was away; spongy feet in Mickey Mouse boots; dirty looks directed at me in American uniform in an American airport; pride in standing reveille and retreat with good men; slipping and sliding coming out of the stream and up the steep slope; the morning sun; piss tubes; mermite can; homecoming after a short tour; sweating from exertion and shivering at the same time on a cold and windy hill; rice paddies; Kumwa, Chorwon, Seoul, Bamberg, Frankfurt, Bad Toelz, Garmisch, Bonn, K-town, Nha Trang, Pleiku, Dong Ba Thin, Kontum, Plei Trap, Dak H'drai; Gasthaus; incoming; engineer stakes; barbed wire; commo wire; rotation; new quarters; break's over; IG Inspection; the bunker in Korea; the German forest like a garden; unit party; a banged shin in an armored personnel carrier; the hammock in Vietnam; *Fremdenverkehrsburo*; clean sheets; honey buckets; Asahi, Nippon, 33, Kulmbacher, San Miguel, Becks, Heineken; gnats; stand in the door; malaria pills; the Red Book; dog tags; shot record; push-ups; PLF, EE8, PRC-6, PRC-10, PRC-25, ETH, APC, BAR, PT, SOS, P38, TS, SOG, CCC, SOP, SNAFU, MG, E5, O6, KP, VC, T-10, DZ, LZ, ASAP, KIA, MIA, LD, 37, 57, TOT, 105, 120, 155, 106, 8 inch, 60, 8I, 82, 4.2, XO, S4, ETA, AM, FM, 11B, 1745, 1666, 201, 1049, C-4, KATUSA, MAAG, SF, CIDG, ARVN, NVA, AGCT, OG, MP, OP, LP, DP; numbah one; numbah ten; Saigon tea; Cheap Charlie; Mr. Charles; *ba; ong; co*; Yard; Nung; five-by; Kim; Fritz; Heinz; Fat Albert; Montana, Delaware, California, Arizona; hills;

dust; rain; fog; snow; mud; steel pot; pile cap; boonie hat, beret; rats; mice; snakes; lice; ants; monkeys; leeches; triple canopy; he says, "I'll go," when common sense says, "Don't go"; and the bachelors volunteering for the duties on Christmas Eve so the married guys could be home with their families.

Angry thoughts creep into my happy reverie as a profession characterized by personal courage, scrupulous honesty, affection for comrades, and a spirit of self-sacrifice is poisoned by those who make it antiseptically impersonal and efficient, indistinguishable from a soulless commercial operation focused on the bottom line. Aping industry, Army leadership carves heart and soul out of the Army. Religious orders are better models for professional soldiers. Neither the monks, who are about eternal salvation of souls, nor the Army, which is about winning wars, have a profit line. Both depend upon acolytes, true believers more concerned with preserving simple values in pursuit of their ends—salvation or victory—than techniques whose purpose is personal advancement and profit.

It should not be a revelation that the U.S. Marine Corps is successful in recruiting American youth by directly appealing to a spirit of sacrifice to be invested in a proud band of brothers deserving unreserved loyalty, a willingness to fight, and the depiction of an American fighter as a knight combating evil. More of that and less slavish imitation of the Fortune 500 is the ticket. Profit, advancement, and efficiency are almost certainly not on the mind of the rifleman who stays in a very dangerous place with a wounded buddy when safety is in flight to the rear. The Army needs to tap into the idealism of American youth in recruiting and to cultivate it in training. Why don't we know that?

Bonding in small teams is the *sine qua non* of fighting formations. It is built through any number of inefficiencies, such as hard and dangerous training (that will kill and injure some young tigers and cue the Greek choir of military critics); unit mess halls—the "family room" of a company, battery, or troop (that we will not have because they are not as cost-effective as large, cafeteria-like dining facilities; civilians have no idea of the value of unit mess halls; an Army that calls a mess hall a "dining facility" is an Army looking for ways to give every soldier a purse and pantyhose); trusting soldiers and building trust and skills by allowing troops and leaders to make mistakes (can't you hear it: "You allowed an eighteen-year-old to do what?!"?).

Mixing lots of initiative with lots of hard discipline is a very complex task. The Army goes "peacetime," inventing new criteria for the next promotion board to measure the worth of officers. "Sensitivity to others" training displaces time on the rifle range. The obvious is overlooked. The Armed Forces are armed to be at war. If we kept that in mind we wouldn't return the wartime officer to his permanent NCO grade after the last war. We need the nose-picking Centurions to command the rifle companies we intend to send to the next war first.

Do our political leaders really believe that a rifle company of Marines or airborne troops would respect and follow a known gay company commander into harm's way without hesitation? Out of touch, it is time to retire. The sanctimonious SOBs and managers of sensitivity have taken over.

Old soldiers meditate on how good they were and how the new Army can't hold a candle to the old Army. That's the way God designed old soldiers. But in the company of 10th Special Forces Group soldiers at Fort Carson, Colorado, in December of 2003, this old soldier asked in a fit of honesty, "Was I ever that good?" Probably not, I concluded. They were the best soldiers I've ever seen. The Republic is in skilled hands.

66

Ripples: Tailwind

A pebble tossed in a Vietnamese pond in 1970 caused a ripple felt in the United States in 1998, a decade after I retired from active duty. Journalist April Oliver called me about a story she was working on as a producer for CNN and writer for *Time*. During a telephone conversation that lasted over an hour she alleged that she had information indicating that CCC (Command and Control Center), a ground element of SOG (Studies and Observation Group), in September 1970 conducted a mission called Tailwind, in which the Special Operations Forces out of Kontum used lethal gas, attempted to assassinate American POW/defectors, and killed innocents in Laos. She named people on the operation, cited dates and times, and generally established that she and colleagues at CNN and *Time* had done a lot of homework. She said that they had conducted numerous interviews, including some with distinguished generals and admirals, the entire chain of command, and men who had been on the mission, intimating that she had it all wrapped up. My name had come up in the course of her interviews. Could she ask me some questions?

If you have it all wrapped up, what can you get from me? Detail, nuance, corroboration.

Knowing that she didn't have it right and hoping to influence her in at least approximating the truth, I said, OK, ask away.

After establishing that I became the intelligence officer for CCC immediately after Operation Tailwind and was later Director of Operations and Intelligence, we understood that I had knowledge of the operational details of CCC operations. She seemed convinced that we used nerve gas, intended to kill Caucasians (possibly American defectors), and killed noncombatants in the area of operations.

I cautioned April Oliver regarding her version of the story by taking the allegations one by one.

Regarding the use of gas: Nonlethal incapacitating agents had been used by some reconnaissance teams to break contact when in danger of being overrun by enemy hunter-killer teams. The gas used was tear gas and vomiting agents to temporarily disable enemy troops, the stuff used in crowd control. It was unpleasant for sure. American soldiers will recall being subjected to a gas chamber in basic training to practice the use of gas masks. It wasn't fun, but neither was it lethal. After making it clear that there was no way nerve agents could have been used without my knowledge and asserting that they were not used, I explained that the nerve gas used as alleged would have been suicide for the user. A speck of it inescapably led to a spasm of sheer agony and sure death, not the kind of stuff one tosses around like horseshoes. Certainly not the kind of stuff one places on an objective one plans to assault and occupy.

Regarding the assassination of Caucasians: Pure fantasy. It didn't happen. Moreover, the capture of *any* Caucasian would have been a great coup for any SOG operating element. A European would have been either a Warsaw Pact advisor to the enemy or an American POW, either of which would have been a prize of great interest to any intelligence officer, commander, or anyone else in our line of work.

The lady had no idea how outrageous it was to charge SOG men with intent to kill our POWs. Many of our men extended their tours or returned to SOG repeatedly for one reason: to be on the mission that liberated our POWs. In fact, the veterans of the Son Thay Raid in North Vietnam were given a choice of assignment, and several asked to come back to SOG, specifically saying they did so because it was their best chance to free American POWs.

Regarding the killing of innocents: The target of Tailwind was a *binh tram*, a place on the Ho Chi Minh Trail that was a vehicle transfer point, a relatively safe place to park vehicles, a rest area for both local logistics troops and troops in transit to the South, and a maintenance facility. Enemy transportation normally operated over a segment of the trail, usually a segment that could be traveled in a day, and one with which the transporter was very familiar. The segments had these *binh trams*, logistical support sites, at the start and end points. (The U.S. Army ran its lines of communication from Bremerhaven to the south of Germany in a similar way for the entire Cold War. Drivers typically drove on a segment of the route to a trailer transfer point and back. They did not travel the entire route.) The people staffing such places were enemy soldiers. They were soldiers like the American cooks, clerks, and bakers who grabbed rifles to fight Germans at Bastogne in the Battle of the Bulge. Presumably the North Vietnamese at Tailwind were no happier in their infantry role than the logistics guys at Bastogne, but they were soldiers and combatants, not innocent civilians.

I also pointed out that all of the Americans on the mission were wounded and continued the mission. It wasn't a walk in the park for anyone. The American commander on the ground pressed on in the midst of chaos, fatigue, fear, wounds, and the unknown that pervaded the battlefield. He and his men were heroes.

My conversation with April Oliver was civil, both of us doing our best imitation of rational human beings, but I knew that I had failed to change her mind. Toward the end of our conversation, I pointed out that we Americans aren't very good at keeping secrets. Had we done the terrible deeds she attributed to us, the secret would have been out in days, not years. Finally, in almost these words, I said: You have a fascinating story with one major fault. It is absolutely false. No lethal gas was used or planned; no Caucasians were targeted or killed; no noncombatants were targeted. She would be embarrassed if she ran with the story. It was not true.

She ran it. "Valley of Death" was part of the inaugural broadcast of *NewsStand: CNN* and *Time* on 7 June 1998, and Ms. Oliver, sharing a byline with Peter Arnett, made the big time with the false story in *Time*, 15 June 1998. "A CNN investigation charges that the U.S. used gas [sarin, GB, nerve gas] in 1970 to save troops sent into Laos to kill defectors," a lead in the *Time* piece screamed.

Alarums and excursions followed. Responsible journalists smelled a rat, and there was a flurry of Tailwind pieces and media introspection. The story didn't ring true to professional reporters. I received a couple of calls from print and TV reporters, the national media joined the fray, and in due course CNN and *Time* retracted the false story.

A wag has said that the first casualty of war is the truth. Anyone who has ever debriefed participants in a recent firefight knows how difficult it is to get the whole story. Deception is the least of the problems. Participants in a violent action normally see only a piece of the action and indulge in a lot of speculation about "what must have" happened. Even among very tough and experienced combat soldiers, fear, responsibility, confusion, pumping adrenaline, and relief to have survived scramble fact and fiction to produce a more or less reasonable account of what is usually brief, violent, shocking craziness.

Plausibility can become the enemy of truth. Experienced soldiers have pictures in their heads of what should have happened, what usually happens. These pictures affect what the senses are saying about what in fact did happen. The pictures may explain what happened if the objective facts don't. If two soldiers compare notes to piece together what happened, it is entirely likely that 10% plus 10% will add up to 100% as gaps between facts are filled with "what must have happened." Try as we might, it is very difficult to get it right and almost impossible to tell it right. CNN and *Time* wanted a man-bites-dog story to kick off their new TV feature. The lie was an inherently sensational story. The truth was not good enough.

I confess to being angry as the lie unfolded. The craving for a big scandalous story won. In my teaching at the Army War College, I have demanded that my students be objective about journalists, pointing out that among soldiers the ratio of scoundrels to good guys is probably about the same as the ratio of lying SOBs to honest reporters, doing their best in pursuit of the always-elusive truth. We had our Calley, they have their April Oliver. She chose to press on with her false thesis and to disregard what I—and, as I learned later—others had told her: the truth.

I hope that one day she will be able to place this experience in perspective. I'm reminded of Lady Macbeth's assessment of her husband early in the play: "His ambition doth o'erleap itself." As an intelligent person, a graduate of a premier university, and a privileged citizen in a privileged society, she seems oblivious to having provided her nation's enemies with a story that will be used against the United States. Our enemies will edit out the retractions the way April Oliver edited out the truth provided her as she fabricated her story. They will tell the phony story, and there's an audience out there prepared to believe the worst about us. It is ironic that the kind of people prepared to lay down their lives to protect her person and her right to free speech come from a segment of American society with which she seems to have little contact and less empathy. That is a pity. Blue-collar Americans have much to teach her about honor.

There were some personally gratifying moments in this brouhaha. Ms. Oliver and some fellow conspirators were fired, and I reestablished contact after thirty years with some of the finest men I have ever known. I called Pete Landon and John Kinstry, junior officers then when I was a major, and Gene McCarley, the ground commander of Tailwind, called me. Later I met with Bernie Bright and Pete. One of the several men who sued the liars gave me happy news when he said that he didn't have to worry about his grandchildren's college educations, the implication being that some of the old sweats made a buck in court on their moment of infamy or in out-of-court settlements.

I like most ripples from the pebbles tossed into the pond over the last fifty years. I particularly like the idea of some children of brave Special Forces soldiers going to school on a free ride paid for by CNN and *Time*. The warm and fuzzy knowledge that some lying journalists seek other work also pleases this vindictive old sweat.

67

Postscript

Since I passed the biblical three score and ten while spinning these yarns, it seemed appropriate to ask if it was right to spend the bulk of my adult life soldiering, an activity most adults get out of their systems as they get serious about life, right after they leave the boy scouts. In fact, soldiers say that the difference between the Army and the Boy Scouts is that the Boy Scouts have adult supervision. We pass through this vale of tears but once. Did I please God? Did I spend my allotted time wisely?

My first reaction is to ask: What would I have done instead? The world of business, industry, and commerce never attracted me. I began high school teaching in 1958, after completing my military service, a degree in English, and a graduate degree in History and Politics. I did so because I needed a job, because I thought I could do it, and because it seemed important and noble. The demand for teachers to educate the so-called baby boomers was enormous, and it was accelerated after the fright caused by the launching of Sputnik by the Soviets. The Russians, scorned then and now for being clumsy and backward, had beaten the United States in the race to space. America decided that emphasis on education—particularly emphasis on math, science, and foreign languages—was the ticket to success in the struggle. I would kill a Communist for Christ via American youth.

Teaching English and history for three years in a fine high school was fun, but I didn't want that for the long haul. While teaching, I mulled over alternative careers in university teaching and writing, the CIA or State Department, and military service, also considering my wife's preference for me, law. That's when John F. Kennedy pushed me over the brink with his inaugural address. I took my lance and charged. (Or did I begin to push a stone up the hill, only to watch it roll down each time I neared the top?) Upon my departure from the teaching game, a group of school psychologists—no joke intended—gave me a party. All had served in the military. They wondered how the most anarchistic of our group could willingly subject himself to the arbitrary authority of the Army. Good point—and one raised by more than one of my military seniors over the years. My response is that willing subordination was the price of a noble career.

I enjoyed all of my military assignments in my new incarnation as an officer, except the first and the penultimate. The first was an infantry assignment characterized by unimaginative leaders and an arrogant style that belittled junior leaders and the troops. I believe that the lock-step mentality I experienced as a junior officer in the early 1960s set us up for defeat in Vietnam. Political muddling may have been the chief cause of our national disgrace in Vietnam, but the military leadership did not distinguish itself at the tactical or operational level. The next-to-last assignment was in a kind of U.S. Army, Inc., a logistics outfit in which there was a total lack of trust by the commander, a highly intelligent senior general who behaved like a dimwit corporal mesmerized by his personal power over others.

The other assignments were either intellectually gratifying or the gathering of brothers that made me proud to be in the company of good men, loyal to one another unto death.

The Pentagon job, an unhappy experience for so many officers, was pure fun for me. With a splendid general, gifted colleagues, and a free hand, I explored the implications of the transition from a conscript to an all-volunteer Army and the ways to make the Army better. The tour in Bonn in the American Embassy was an opportunity to work closely with German military leadership, men I liked personally and admired professionally. Studying at Stanford and teaching the fine young people at the U.S. Military Academy at West Point was no less than an honor. The research, writing, and teaching at the U.S. Army War College in Carlisle, Pennsylvania, gave me access to information and to a faculty and student body that would lead the Army in the following ten to fifteen years. The brainy jobs absorbed me, but reflecting on the years from 1952, when asked to do so by a friend as I retired from the Army, I see the men.

The best thing about the Army to the nineteen-year-old in Korea was the company of men; the best thing about the Army to the fifty-five-year-old colonel was the men. Standing reveille and retreat with the men of the 10th Special Forces Group in Prince Heinrich Kaserne in the mid-1960s was a thrill each time I did it. So was living with Franklin Miller, Bob Howard, Ruff, Mike Shepherd, Joe Walker, Robbie, John Kinstry, Pete Landon, Heinz Roesch, Fritz Krupa, Chuck Behler, little Bemis, Sergeant Rose, Jim Storter, and First Sergeant Billy Greenwood. Thinking about it is an emotional experience. An unresolved issue arises when I think these thoughts. The most agnostic group of men I've ever met were the recon men who lived on the edge and died bravely. Memorial services in Vietnam from 1966 to 1971 for dead friends was potent stuff then. Taps at night, at Arlington—hell, anytime—now rip my guts.

Was it worth it? Yeah.

Why? The men. It was always the men.

Glossary

AO	area of operations
APC	Armored Personnel Carrier
BAR	Browning Automatic Rifle
EE-8	"double-E-Eight," a field telephone in a form-fitting canvas bag with a carrying strap
"go-go"	full automatic
KIA	killed in action
lister bag	water bag
MIA	missing in action
MLR	the Main Line of Resistance
MOS	military occupational specialty
oh-dark-hundred	early a.m., the middle of the night
OP	outpost
SOP	standard operating procedure
TLs	kit consisting of pliers for cutting wire and a folding knife used to strip the black rubbery-plastic protective covering from the wire underneath; it attached to one's belt.
WD-1	black commo wire designed for communications; GIs used it for dozens of purposes.
XO	executive officer

Index

251

About the Author

HENRY G. GOLE, Col., USA (Ret.), Ph.D., fought in Korea as an enlisted rifleman and served two tours in Vietnam as a Special Forces officer. He also served four tours in Germany and worked as a research analyst for the U.S. Army's War College's Strategic Studies Institute and as a staff officer at the Pentagon. Colonel Gole earned a doctorate in history at Temple University and has taught at West Point, the U.S. Army War College, the University of Maryland, and Dickinson College. He is the author of *The Road to Rainbow: Army Planning for Global War, 1934–1940* as well as over thirty articles. He lives in Mechanicsburg, Pennsylvania.